THE 49TH ANNUAL
BRIGHAM YOUNG UNIVERSITY
SIDNEY B. SPERRY SYMPOSIUM

HOW AND WHAT YOU WORSHIP

CHRISTOLOGY AND PRAXIS IN THE REVELATIONS OF JOSEPH SMITH

Edited by Rachel Cope,
Carter Charles, and Jordan T. Watkins

RSC
BYU

DESERET
BOOK

Published by the Religious Studies Center, Brigham Young University, Provo, Utah, in cooperation with Deseret Book Company, Salt Lake City, Utah.

Printed in the United States of America by Sheridan Books, Inc.

DESERET BOOK is a registered trademark of Deseret Book Company. Visit us at DeseretBook.com.

Cover and interior design by Emily V. Strong
Cover image courtesy of Del Parson
ISBN 978-1-9443-9499-8

Library of Congress Cataloging-in-Publication Data

Names: Cope, Rachel, editor. | Charles, Carter, editor. | Watkins, Jordan T., editor.
Title: How and what you worship : Christology and praxis in the revelations of
    Joseph Smith / edited by Rachel Cope, Carter Charles, and Jordan T. Watkins.
Description: Provo, Utah : Religious Studies Center, Brigham Young University,
    [2020] | Includes index. | Summary: "Section 93 of the Doctrine and Covenants
    deals with concepts that scholars term Christology and praxis. Christology has to
    do with the study of Christ's nature, while praxis involves religious practice. That
    this revelation should insist on the both the "how" and the "what" of worship indi-
    cates that knowledge and practice are inseparable. As this volume demonstrates,
    Joseph Smith's revelations and teachings constitute a unique textual setting to
    analyze this relationship"-- Provided by publisher.
Identifiers: LCCN 2020018630 | ISBN 9781944394998 (hardcover)
Subjects: LCSH: Jesus Christ--Person and offices. | Smith, Joseph, Jr.,
    1805-1844--Teachings. | Church of Jesus Christ of Latter-day Saints--Liturgy.
    | Church of Jesus Christ of Latter-day Saints--Doctrines. | Mormon Church--
    Liturgy. | Kingdom of God (Mormon theology) | Mormon Church--Doctrines.
Classification: LCC BX8643.J4 H68 2020 | DDC 232.0882893--dc23
LC record available at https://lccn.loc.gov/2020018630

Contents

Introduction

In 1820 Joseph Smith experienced a glorious theophany that opened an era of restoration. This singular event occurred because one young man acted upon his knowledge of Christ. As a result of such efforts, Joseph received what he had been seeking: forgiveness of his sins. He also received divine instruction, the import of which he only came to understand during the subsequent two decades. While the Father and the Son had appeared to the teenage Joseph and revealed significant truths to him, it took learning, experience, and reflection for him to fully comprehend the profound nature of what he had seen and heard. His efforts to translate the Book of Mormon, organize the Church of Christ, revise the Bible, and restore other sacred scriptures, structures, truths, and practices shed light on his initial encounter with deity. Over time, he achieved a mature understanding of his youthful experience. In his later accounts of what became known as the First Vision, Joseph emphasized the Lord's command to not join other churches and the promise that the truth would be made known to him in due time. His successive experiences and ongoing revelations helped him recognize the salience of these early directions. They also gifted him an understanding of what he had heard, as well as what he had seen; they provided him with insight into the nature of God and of Jesus Christ, the beings whom he worshipped and to whom he would consecrate the remainder of his life.

On 6 May 1833, about thirteen years after his First Vision, Joseph received a revelation that expanded his knowledge of Christ and his understanding of how to act upon that knowledge. In drawing upon and clarifying Johannine teachings about the Lord, the latter-day revelation shared truths meant to help early Church members "understand and know how to worship and know what [they] worship" (Doctrine and Covenants 93:19). This revelatory reworking of the Prologue of John (John 1:1–18) sheds light not only on the subject of our worship, Christ, but also on the process of how to worship him. Although the immediate context of the revelation remains obscure— and perhaps tellingly so—it uncovered truths about the nature of Christ, who, according to the account, "continued from a grace to grace, until he received a fulness" (Doctrine and Covenants 93:13). The revelation went further in linking those truths to the process of worship by instructing its audience to obey Christ's commandments, which would allow *them* to "receive grace for grace" (93:20). It also clarified that the revealed understanding of the nature of Christ had power to unveil the erstwhile obscured nature of those who worship him.

In addressing both the *who* and the *how* of worship, the revelation now known as section 93 of the Doctrine and Covenants deals with concepts that scholars term *Christology* and *praxis*. Christology has to do with the study of Christ's nature and mission, while praxis involves religious practice and worship. In light of Smith's experiences and revelations, the study of Christ demands attention to the spiritual and intellectual quest (Doctrine and Covenants 88:118) to "know" the Savior (John 17:3). That section 93 should insist on the "how" of worship indicates that *praxis* is inseparable from knowledge of Christ: as King Benjamin taught, it is a mark of discipleship, the outward manifestation of knowledge (Mosiah 5:15). But it is also more encompassing; it is more wholistic. In a revelation dictated by Joseph Smith in 1829, the Lord enjoined those who "embark in the service of God" to "serve him with all your heart, might, mind and strength" (Doctrine and Covenants 4:2). *Praxis*, in other words, also comprises the imperceptible workings of both heart and mind. When knowledge and practice combine, the outward manifestation may be insufficient to convey the intensity and beauty of inner devotion (1 Samuel 1:9–13).

Although something essential about the interaction between knowledge and practice remains hidden from view, the revelations and teachings of Joseph Smith open up vistas on this relationship and constitute a unique textual setting to analyze its meaning and power. Joseph's latter-day scriptural productions and instructions on Christ and discipleship in particular prize learning as both a form of worship and a central component in the process of salvation. In one such revelation, the Lord taught the members, "seek ye out of the best books words of wisdom; seek learning, even by study and also by faith" (Doctrine and Covenants 88:118).

Latter-day Saint commentary on this passage has a long and illustrious history. After citing it in the introduction to the final volume of his *Seventy's Course in Theology*, early twentieth-century historian and writer B. H. Roberts illustrated the connection between study and faith by referencing another revelatory passage, the one in which the Lord explained to Oliver Cowdery that he had failed to translate the Book of Mormon because he had not studied "it out in [his] mind" (Doctrine and Covenants 9:8).[1] Roberts, a President of the Seventy, found in Joseph's revelations an imperative to apply the intellect to sacred truths. "Men seem to think that because inspiration and revelation are factors in connection with the things of God," he wrote, "the pain and stress of mental effort are not required." Observing in his time what seems to be a perennial problem, he noted that "it is much in fashion to laud 'the simple faith,' which is content to believe without understanding, or even without much effort to understand. And doubtless many good people regard this course as indicative of reverence," he continued, before suggesting that "this sort of 'reverence' is easily simulated . . . and falls into the same category as the simulated humility couched in 'I don't know,' which so often really means 'I don't care, and do not intend to trouble myself to find out.'"[2] In response to such intellectual complacency, Roberts called on "the mighty exhortations and rebukes of the New Dispensations of the Gospel of the Christ," which included numerous quotations from Joseph's revelations and teachings.[3]

Near the end of the twentieth century, a member of the Quorum of the Twelve Apostles also addressed the scriptural view of "faith and learning as mutually facilitating."[4] After quoting the very revelation—section 88—that Roberts had used to begin his commentary on faith and intellect, Elder Neal A. Maxwell described the disciple-scholar as one who worships through scholarship.[5] "For a disciple of Jesus Christ," he said, "academic scholarship is a form of worship. It is actually another dimension of consecration."[6] The application of one's mind—a gift of God—constitutes a form of consecration. "Hence," Elder Maxwell continued, "one who seeks to be a disciple-scholar will take both scholarship and discipleship seriously; and, likewise, gospel covenants. For the disciple-scholar, the first and second great commandments frame and prioritize life. How else," he asked, "could one worship God with all of one's heart, might, mind, and strength?" Elder Maxwell taught that the two great commandments should train our attention on God and Christ and on the those who seek to worship them.

In light of the insistence that the life of the mind is bound up with the life of faith and that the things of God require critical thinking, the 2020 Sidney B. Sperry Symposium explores Christology and praxis in the revelations and teachings of Joseph Smith.[7] This focus gives shape to the scope of this volume and its corresponding symposium. We think readers will find confirmation that Joseph's revelations and teachings on the topics of Christ and religious practice encourage the cultivation of a number of fruitful topics. These subjects include the First Vision, the nature of God, Christ, and humankind, the process of becoming like Christ and God, the nature of the light of Christ and the location of his Atonement, the various critical roles the Lord desires and expects for women in the Church as indicated in the revelation to Emma Smith, and worship as a call to learn, promote peace, tolerate difference, and obtain exaltation. Joseph's revelatory productions on these topics and the records of his efforts to explain them lend themselves to a wide variety of disciplinary approaches and interpretations. In addressing questions related to Christology and praxis, the authors provide historical, exegetical, theological, and comparative readings of the revelations. In combination, these essays—these works of discipleship—shed light on fundamental gospel topics, though admittedly, they only begin to approach the grandeur of what the Lord revealed through the Prophet of the Restoration.

The creation of this volume has not only allowed us to consider the themes of Christology and praxis; it has encouraged us to reflect on how the theme of the symposium relates to our daily lives—the process of writing, revising, and editing have all fostered and encouraged a more worshipful way of living and being. Such a way of being demands the cultivation of relationships among those who worship God and Christ. Working on this volume has been a community effort, a work of collaboration that has strengthened friendships and fostered a deeper sense of respect for colleagues around the globe. Because scholarship is a form of discipleship, we understood that our editorial mission and the resulting volume had to be a mark of our devotion; what we present to God and to the Saints should reflect our best efforts. Despite these efforts, it will quickly become obvious to readers that the volume is far from perfect. We do hope, however, that readers will see the spirit of a disciple-scholar reflected in each chapter. We also hope that this volume will spur readers to consider their own heartfelt and mindful worship of God and of his Son, Jesus Christ.

We are grateful for those who submitted proposals and papers for the symposium and for those who sacrificed their time to peer review papers for potential publication. Our thanks go also to those who presented and to those who worked tirelessly to prepare their essays for inclusion in this volume. We are positively impressed by their generosity and are grateful to count all of them as fellow disciples in the kingdom and colleagues in the profession. Each deserves to be applauded for their commitment to this symposium and this volume.

We would like to thank all others who have been involved in this year's symposium and associated volume. We express our thanks to the deans who invited us to steer this project; it has proven to be a wonderful opportunity and an enriching experience. We are also grateful to the personnel in the Religious Studies Center at Brigham Young University and at Deseret Book in helping this volume reach its published form. We would like to thank in particular Scott Esplin and his staff, including Brent Nordgren, Shirley Ricks, Sarah Johnson, and Emily Strong. Most importantly, Beverly Yellowhorse, a committee member and the director of our Faculty Support Center in Religious Education, cannot be thanked enough for the time she has invested, both in front and behind the scenes, to bring this volume and symposium to fruition. She has been involved in the process from the call for proposals to the closing prayer of the symposium, and to the publication of the actual book in between. Her work has been so much more than clerical. We cherish the great professionalism and devotion she displayed even through hardships, and we are grateful for her patience with us.

Rachel Cope
Carter Charles
Jordan T. Watkins

Notes

1. B. H. Roberts, *The Seventy's Course in Theology* (Salt Lake City: Salt Lake City, The Deseret News, 1907–1912), 5:iv.

2. Roberts, *Seventy's Course in Theology*, 5:v.

3. Roberts, *Seventy's Course in Theology*, 5:vi, vi–vii.

4. Neal A. Maxwell, "The Disciple-Scholar," in *On Becoming a Disciple-Scholar*, ed. Henry B. Eyring (Salt Lake City: Bookcraft, 1995), 1–23.

5. Maxwell, "The Disciple-Scholar," 7.

6. Maxwell, "The Disciple-Scholar," 7.

7. For examples of existing scholarship on Christology in Joseph Smith's revelations, see Blake T. Ostler, *Exploring Mormon Thought: The Attributes of God* (Salt Lake City: Greg Kofford Books, 2001), 409–85; Blake T. Ostler, *Exploring Mormon Thought: Of God and Gods* (Salt Lake City: Greg Kofford Books, 2008); Douglas J. Davies, *Joseph Smith, Jesus, and Satanic Opposition* (Burlington, VT: Ashgate, 2010), 221–35; Terryl L. Givens, *Wrestling the Angel: The Foundations of Mormon Thought; Cosmos, God, Humanity* (New York: Oxford University Press, 2015), 117–24; and John G. Turner, *The Mormon Jesus: A Biography* (Cambridge, MA: Belknap Press of Harvard University Press, 2016), 153–83.

1

First Vision–Based Christology and Praxis for Anxious Teens

Steven C. Harper

There is a sacred grove about fifty feet from my office. It is in the atrium of the Joseph Smith Building on the campus of Brigham Young University. The trees are blossoming as I write. A bronze figure of Joseph Smith is kneeling among them. He is about fourteen years old. He is looking up.

When Henry B. Eyring unveiled and dedicated this sculpture in 1997, he praised the artist, Avard Fairbanks, for what Joseph's heavenward gaze invites us to imagine. President Eyring said, "From studying the various accounts of the First Vision, we learn that young Joseph went into the grove not only to learn which church he should join but also to obtain forgiveness for his sins, something he seems not to have understood how to do."

President Eyring hopes that every young person who sees the statue will relate to Joseph in the moment depicted, "that moment when Joseph Smith learned there was a way for the power of the

Avard T. Fairbanks's sculpture The Vision *is located in the courtyard of the Joseph Smith Building at Brigham Young University. When Elder Henry B. Eyring unveiled the sculpture in 1997, he paid tribute to the sculpture "for what he didn't show," referring to the implied presence of the Father and the Son.* Photo courtesy of Brent R. Nordgren.

Atonement of Jesus Christ to be unlocked fully." According to President Eyring, "in more than one account the Lord addressed the young truth seeker and said, 'Joseph, my son, thy sins are forgiven thee.'"[1]

Joseph's parents "spared no pains" in teaching him "the Christian religion." They taught him that the scriptures "contained the word of God." Joseph wrote that he was about twelve when he began to worry about the welfare of his immortal soul. His "all important concerns" led him to exercise faith in his parents' teachings. He began searching the scriptures for himself and doing what he called "applying myself to them." That is how he discovered that various Christian churches professed things the Bible did not.

Joseph grieved over that. He could see that contention characterized Christianity. He became deeply distressed because he believed the Christian teachings about his sinful and fallen state. He knew he needed to be redeemed by Jesus Christ, but "there was no society or denomination," as far as he could tell, "that built upon the gospel of Jesus Christ as recorded in the New Testament." He wrote, "I felt to mourn for my own sins and for the sins of the world."[2]

Joseph took the welfare of his soul seriously. For a few years he thought about his problem and what he should do. He considered the option of giving up his faith in God, but he could not. To him, the sun, moon, and stars testified that God lived—and lived by divine laws—and should be worshipped. "Therefore," Joseph wrote, "I cried unto the Lord for mercy, for there was none else to whom I could go."[3]

My focus is on Joseph's actions as described in that last sentence and why he acted as he did. He chose a powerful verb in *cried*. Joseph cried to the Lord for mercy because he was losing hope. There was no one else to extend him mercy. So he cried because he believed, or at least hoped, that the Lord would be merciful to him. Scholars call it *praxis* when a person does something to worship the Lord, something like hoping in Christ or crying unto the Lord.

Scholars use the word *Christology* to describe what people believe about Jesus Christ. Who is he? What is he like? Joseph believed, or at least hoped, that Christ is merciful. Joseph's Christology and his praxis were connected. He did what he did because of what he thought about Jesus. He cried unto the Lord for mercy because he believed the Lord alone could give him the mercy he needed.

In his revelations to Joseph, Jesus Christ tells who he is and shows what he is like. He revealed lots of beautiful Christology. He also instructed us to do (and not do) specific things. In other words, he revealed much praxis. The focus here, however, is only on Joseph's first revelation. It is about how the teenage Joseph worshipped Jesus Christ and what he learned about him.

As President Eyring demonstrated, there is value in learning Christology and praxis from Joseph's various accounts of his vision. They tell us what Joseph did. He believed his parents' teachings about Jesus Christ. He searched the scriptures and believed that they contained the word of God. He applied himself to them. He worked hard to understand them and to discover what he should do because of them. He became intimately acquainted with people who believed different things about Christ and worshipped him in various ways. He paid attention to what they believed and what they did. For a few years he read, observed, and pondered. He thought about what he was becoming. He mourned when there was conflict between what he believed he should be and what he was. He became "exceedingly distressed" when he realized he was at an impasse. He was guilty of sin, and he could find no church built on the gospel of Jesus Christ who redeemed people from their sins. So he cried out to the Lord for mercy.[4]

One of the best things Joseph did was to balance urgency and caution. That is good praxis. He recognized that he needed knowledge and power from God. Learning how to get it became his priority. "Information was what I most desired," he said, and he formed a "fixed determination to obtain it." He said it was "of the first importance that I should be right in matters that involve eternal consequences."[5] Joseph put first things first. He relentlessly sought the most important truths.[6] Because his "immortal soul" was at stake, he acted both urgently and deliberately.[7]

He did not make rash decisions or jump to conclusions. "I made it an object of much study and reflection," he related.[8] "I kept myself aloof from all these parties," he said, "though I attended their several meetings as often as occasion would permit." By exercising faith in God, studying much, observing closely, yet remaining aloof, Joseph positioned himself to make informed decisions. He could see that "contradictory opinions and principles laid the foundation for the rise of such different sects and denominations." Being deliberate helped Joseph remain above the partisan prejudices "too often poisoned by hate, contention, resentment and anger."[9]

Joseph tested Methodism. "In process of time my mind became somewhat partial to the Methodist sect," he said, "and I felt some desire to be united with them." If the Methodist teachings were right, Joseph would be able to seek and receive God's prevenient grace. That is, despite his fallen nature, Joseph would receive a gift of God's power that would enable him to come to Christ and be saved by him. He would know if it worked because it would be joyful, overwhelmingly joyful. Joseph watched as people experienced that joy. He tried it himself. He wanted his own Methodist conversion experience. "He wanted to get Religion too wanted to feel & shout like the Rest but could feel nothing."[10] So despite his desire to follow Methodist Christology, Joseph kept seeking.

He sought more evidence before concluding whether Methodism or one of the other versions of Christianity had the right doctrine of Christ. He realized that he was not able to discern by himself whether Methodists were right, or Presbyterians, or Baptists. Each made compelling, Bible-based arguments. That confused, distressed, and perplexed Joseph.[11]

What did he do in those circumstances? What was his religious praxis or practice when experts offered conflicting, consequential choices? He kept his faith. He worked hard. He turned to the scriptures. He received a revelation. Then he acted on it. "While I was laboring under the extreme difficulties caused by the contests of these parties of religionists," he said, "I was one day reading the Epistle of James, First Chapter and fifth verse." The scripture taught him to ask God directly and with faith. That was a revelation to Joseph, "like a light shining forth in a dark place."[12] Before he read and reflected on it, he felt paralyzed; after, he knew what to do.

"I must do as James directs," he said, "that is, Ask of God." Joseph chose the word *determination* to describe his resolve to act on the scripture.[13] He used it twice in his history. Another time he called it "a fixed determination."[14] Joseph's was no passive praxis. He was going to act on the revelation he had received. He said, "I just determined I'd ask him." Joseph unwaveringly resolved to act in faith and do something he had never tried before. He went to the woods to take the next step in his quest for God's redeeming love.[15]

Joseph knelt and "began to offer up the desires of my heart to God." He had never prayed aloud before.[16] It was good praxis to pray, to ask God to grant the sincere desires of one's heart. Joseph barely got started, however, before he stopped. He called it "a fruitless attempt to pray."[17] It felt like his tongue swelled. He could not speak. It sounded like someone was walking up behind him. He tried to pray again but failed. The noise seemed to come closer. He sprang up and turned toward it. There was nothing making the noise, nothing he could see anyway.

He knelt again and "called on the Lord in mighty prayer."[18] Something seized him, "some power which entirely overcame me," he said. It was an enemy, "an actual being from the unseen world." Joseph was shocked at its power.[19] Doubts filled his mind.[20] Thick darkness enveloped him. He felt doomed. He was ready to give up, "to sink into despair and abandon myself to destruction," he said. He chose not to do so, however. He chose instead, at that moment, to exert all his "powers to call upon God to deliver me out of the power of this enemy."

Just then Joseph saw a brilliant light descending from above. He called it a "pillar of flame." As soon as it appeared the darkness left. The spirit of God filled Joseph, replacing the feeling of despair. Unspeakable joy replaced doom. Joseph heard his name. He looked into the light and saw God, who introduced Joseph to his Beloved Son. Joseph saw Jesus Christ, standing in the air with his Father. "Joseph," the Savior said, "thy sins are forgiven." He continued, "I am the Lord of glory. I was crucified for the sins of the world that all those who believe on my name may have eternal life."[21]

Once he could speak, Joseph asked if he should join the Methodists. "No," came the answer.[22] None of the current Christian churches had their Christology right. They relied too much on con-fusing creeds. The person and work of Jesus Christ was simpler than they taught. "Jesus Christ is the son of God," Joseph learned. He was crucified for sinners. He forgives the repentant and gives them eter-nal life. He can stand next to his Father, and not just in heaven. They can visit in person. They answer the prayers of anxious teenagers who ask in faith.

Joseph learned well. He put his faith in the crucified and resurrected Savior who had atoned for his sins, and he repented. Joseph knew what to do later when he realized "that I had not kept the commandments." Every time he "fell into transgressions and sinned in many things," he went back to his knees, chose hope over despair, and acted on the christological knowledge he had successfully tried before. He trusted the Savior who was crucified for him and "repented heartily for all my sins."[23] That praxis worked every time.[24]

Primary General President Joy D. Jones taught, "we can draw principles of truth from the Prophet Joseph's experiences that provide insights for receiving our own revelation." She noted these examples of good practice: "We labor under difficulties. We turn to the scriptures to receive wisdom to act. We demonstrate our faith and trust in God. We exert our power to plead with God to help us thwart the adversary's influence. We offer up the desires of our hearts to God. We focus on His light guiding our life choices and resting upon us when we turn to Him. We realize He knows each of us by name and has individual roles for us to fulfill."[25] That praxis works every time.

When he unveiled the sculpture of Joseph in the grove near my office, President Eyring similarly linked Christology and praxis. Like President Jones, he based the connection on what Joseph learned in the grove. President Eyring testified, "Jesus is the Christ. He lives. I know He lives. I know Joseph Smith saw Him, and I know that because He lives and because Joseph Smith looked up and saw Him and because He sent other messengers, you and I may have the thing that the Prophet Joseph wanted as he went to the grove: to know, not just to hope, that our sins can be washed away."[26]

Notes

1. Henry B. Eyring, "Remarks Given at the Unveiling Ceremony of 'The Vision,'" *Religious Education History*, Brigham Young University, 66–68.
2. "History, circa Summer 1832," pp. 1–2, The Joseph Smith Papers, https://josephsmithpapers.org/paper-summary/history-circa-summer-1832.

3. "History, circa Summer 1832," pp. 2–3.

4. "History, circa Summer 1832," pp. 2–3.

5. "Journal, 1835–1836," p. 23, The Joseph Smith Papers, https://josephsmith papers.org/paper-summary/journal-1835-1836/24.

6. "Journal, 1835–1836," p. 23.

7. "History, circa Summer 1832," p. 2.

8. "History, circa 1841, fair copy," p. 2, The Joseph Smith Papers, https:// josephsmithpapers.org/paper-summary/history-circa-1841-fair-copy/2. "History, circa 1841, draft [Draft 3]," p. 2, The Joseph Smith Papers, https://josephsmithpapers.org/paper-summary/history-circa-1841-draft -draft-3/2.

9. "Orson Hyde, Ein Ruf aus der Wüste (A Cry out of the Wilderness), 1842, extract, English translation," The Joseph Smith Papers, https:// josephsmithpapers.org/paper-summary/orson-hyde-ein-ruf-aus-der -wste-a-cry-out-of-the-wilderness-1842-extract-english-translation/1.

10. "Alexander Neibaur, Journal, 24 May 1844, extract," p. [23], The Joseph Smith Papers, https://josephsmithpapers.org/paper-summary/alexander -neibaur-journal-24-may-1844-extract/1.

11. "History, circa Summer 1832," p. 2. "History, circa June 1839–circa 1841 [Draft 2]," p. 3, The Joseph Smith Papers, https://josephsmithpapers.org /paper-summary/history-circa-june-1839-circa-1841-draft-2/3. "Journal, 1835–1836," p. 23, The Joseph Smith Papers, https://josephsmithpapers .org/paper-summary/journal-1835-1836/24.

12. "Appendix: Orson Pratt, A[n] Interesting Account of Several Remarkable Visions, 1840," p. 4, The Joseph Smith Papers, https://josephsmithpapers .org/paper-summary/appendix-orson-pratt-an-interesting-account-of -several-remarkable-visions-1840/4.

13. "History, circa June 1839–circa 1841 [Draft 2]," p. 3.

14. "Journal, 1835–1836," p. 23.

15. "History, circa June 1839–circa 1841 [Draft 2]," p. 3.

16. "History, circa June 1839–circa 1841 [Draft 2]," p. 3.

17. "Journal, 1835–1836," p. 23.

18. "Journal, 1835–1836," p. 24.

19. "History, circa June 1839–circa 1841 [Draft 2]," p. 3. "History, circa 1841, draft [Draft 3]," p. 3.

20. "Orson Hyde, Ein Ruf aus der Wüste (A Cry out of the Wilderness), 1842, extract, English translation."

21. "History, circa Summer 1832," pp. 2–3.

22. "Alexander Neibaur, Journal, 24 May 1844, extract," p. [23].

23. "Journal, 1835–1836," p. 24; spelling corrected.

24. "Journal, 1835–1836," p. 24. "Revelation, July 1828 [D&C 3]," p. 1, The Joseph Smith Papers, https://josephsmithpapers.org/paper-summary/revelation-july-1828-dc-3/1. "Letter to Emma Smith, 6 June 1832," p. [1], The Joseph Smith Papers, https://josephsmithpapers.org/paper-summary/letter-to-emma-smith-6-june-1832/1. "Visions, 3 April 1836 [D&C 110]," p. 192, The Joseph Smith Papers, https://josephsmithpapers.org/paper-summary/visions-3-april-1836-dc-110/1.

25. President Joy D. Jones, "An Especially Noble Calling," *Ensign*, May 2020, https://churchofjesuschrist.org/study/general-conference/2020/04/14jones.

26. Eyring, "Remarks Given at the Unveiling Ceremony," 66–68.

2

Incarnation, Exaltation, and Christological Tension in Doctrine and Covenants 93:1–20

Nicholas J. Frederick

It goes without saying that Christianity's central figure—the person so important to the gospel message that he is literally the namesake for all of global Christianity—is Jesus Christ. Within the Christian tradition, however, there exists a wide variety of perspectives on who Jesus is and how we are to understand the significance of his life, death, and Resurrection. This is a topic that has consumed Christian writers and scholars for nearly two thousand years and given rise to the theological discipline of Christology.[1] Christology, at its core, is a branch of theology devoted to understanding how a given text portrays Jesus Christ, particularly how his *divinity* relates to his *humanity*. For instance, what does it mean that Jesus is the "Son of God"? Did he exist premortally as a divine being who then took on the appearance of a mortal man, or was he a mortal man who was elevated to divinity? Furthermore, if he is somehow both divine and human, how do those two natures interact? Does his divinity succumb to his humanity, or does his humanity get swallowed up in his divinity? These questions are further complicated by the many different descriptions of Jesus contained in the scriptures. In Matthew 5–7, for instance, Jesus is the new Moses; in John 1:1 he is the immortal Word; in Hebrews 2:17–18 he is the Great High Priest who atones for the sins of Israel.[2] The Book of Mormon also presents a diverse witness when it comes to the nature of Jesus. Nephi's Jesus is "the son of the most high God" (1 Nephi 11:6), while Abinadi describes Jesus as being both "Father" and "Son," titles that Jesus uses in presenting himself to the brother of Jared (Mosiah 15:1–4; Ether 3:14). In the Nephites' grand Christophany in 3 Nephi, Jesus describes himself as being, among other things, "in" the Father (3 Nephi 19:23).[3] While so many different titles could be taken to mean that their various authors lacked a full understanding of who Jesus is, it is more likely that each simply chose to emphasize different elements of Jesus's nature and mission.

For Latter-day Saints, however, the New Testament and the Book of Mormon are not the only books of scripture containing an impressive witness of Christ. Section 93 of the Doctrine and Covenants is also critical to understanding the Latter-day Saint conception of Jesus and his nature. Section 93, in fact, is one of the most theologically rich and provocative revelations Joseph Smith received. Beginning with a short discussion on the nature of the Savior and his relationship with the Father, the revelation quickly transitions into what seems to be an excerpt of a record written by John that describes several key events relating to Jesus, such as his baptism and his reception of power. The revelation then transitions again, this time into a discussion of the origins of humanity and an elaboration of the principles of truth and intelligence. Then, perhaps most surprisingly of all, beginning in verse 40 the revelation abruptly transitions from these theologically complex topics toward more practical, mundane affairs as the Lord mentions several members of the Church by name and chastens them for, among other things, their lack of attention to their families. Because of the consideration paid in section 93 to

Jesus's relationship with the Father and his own progression through mortality, this revelation is particularly important for understanding the development of christological ideas in Joseph Smith's revelations.[4]

With these introductory thoughts in mind, I explore more fully the Christology presented in Doctrine and Covenants 93 with an eye toward how it fits within the classic theological spectrum between *exaltation* Christology (the notion that Jesus was a man elevated to divinity) and *incarnation* Christology (the notion that Jesus was always God). The thesis of this paper is that Doctrine and Covenants 93:1–20 intentionally introduces a tension between exaltation and incarnation Christologies as a means of highlighting (and perhaps even attempting to solve) the paradox of Jesus Christ's dual nature, which was a topic of much debate in the late eighteenth and early nineteenth centuries. In this paper I will proceed as follows: I will first attempt to frame the christological controversy that was brewing in New England during the early decades of the nineteenth century. I will then briefly introduce what is meant by exaltation and incarnation models of Christology and quickly discuss the reception of section 93 in its earliest context. I will then turn to the primary focus of this paper, looking specifically at how the section, and the record of John in particular, presents its twofold christological depiction of Jesus.

Christology and the Nineteenth-Century Christological Context of Doctrine and Covenants 93

Exaltation Christology

Exaltation Christology[5] expresses the belief that "God raised Jesus from the dead—not in order to give him a longer life here on earth, but in order to exalt him as his own Son up to the heavenly realms, where he could sit beside God at his right hand, ruling together with the Lord God Almighty himself."[6] A crucial element to this

Christology is the idea that Jesus began life as a regular human being. As scholar Bart Ehrman describes, Jesus "may have been more righteous than others; he may have earned God's special favor more than others. But he started out as a human and nothing more."[7] The key component of exaltation Christology is the belief that at some point in his life, either at the Resurrection or at an earlier point such as his baptism,[8] Jesus was lifted up or exalted by God the Father, elevating Jesus to a level of divinity such that he eventually shares God's reign after his ascension. Importantly, exaltation Christology holds that this exaltation is a gift bestowed upon a mortal Jesus, not a reinstitution of a divine position held prior to coming to earth. In Romans, Paul presented what may be the earliest form of this Christology: "Concerning his Son Jesus Christ our Lord, which was made of the seed of David according to the flesh; and declared to be the Son of God with power, according to the spirit of holiness, by the resurrection from the dead" (Romans 1:3–4). Paul's words could be read to suggest that Jesus was "declared" to be something (that is, the Son of God) that he was not already because his origins were in "the flesh."

Incarnation Christology

While exaltation Christology suggests that Jesus was a man who was lifted up by God to a state of divinity as God's son, incarnation Christology argues for the opposite: Jesus was always the divine Son of God. He was "a superhuman divine being who existed before his birth and became human for the salvation of the human race."[9] According to this view, Jesus's divinity persisted in some fashion across every stage of his existence: he was divine prior to his incarnation, he retained some element of divinity during his mortal life, and he remains divine following his Resurrection and ascension to the Father's right hand. Paul seems to have had this idea in mind when he wrote to the Philippians that Jesus, prior to coming to earth, was "in the form of God" (Philippians 2:6). However, as the passage goes on, Paul declares that Jesus enacts the plan of salvation by making himself "of no reputation," exchanging the explicit form of divinity for "the form of a servant" instead (Philippians 2:7). The Greek word rendered by King James translators as "of no reputation" is the verb ἐκένωσεν (*ekenosen*), which simply means "to empty." Jesus, now finding himself "as a man," humbles himself and demonstrates obedience, finally dying "even the death of the cross" (Philippians 2:8). Although Philippians goes on to mention that following the Crucifixion "God also hath highly exalted him, and given him a name which is above every name" (Philippians 2:9), incarnationist interpreters understand this exaltation to be simply a return to a more explicit form of Jesus's innate and constant divinity. The Crucifixion and Resurrection may entitle Jesus Christ to exaltation, in their view, but that exaltation was never a question of his nature being changed from that of a human being into a god; rather, Jesus's divinity was always constant. Readers of John's Gospel experience a similar sentiment from the very opening verse: "In the beginning was the Word, and the Word was with God, and the Word was God." John's introduction informs its readers that Jesus Christ is somehow divine from "the beginning." Jesus is, in some fashion, one with the Father, but he is also a separate entity described by John as "the Word," a title that perhaps hints at Jesus's role as mediator between the divine realm and the mortal world. Of Jesus's birth John said only, "And the Word was made flesh, and dwelt among us" (John 1:14).

Debates such as these over the relationship between the Father and Son have deep roots, dating back to the fourth century CE. A similar controversy, which became quite heated and for a time divided the Roman Empire, centered around the question of whether Jesus Christ was *homoousia* (of the same substance) or simply *homoiousia* (of a similar substance) with the Father. The latter position was termed Arianism after one of its most prominent proponents, a fourth-century bishop named Arius. Although debates such as these can seem tedious and arcane to many Christians today, it's important to recognize how high these theological stakes really were. The dispute had to do, in large part, with nothing less than the divinity of Jesus, and by extension his ability to reconcile humanity to God. This

Arian position thus opened up an insurmountable chasm between God and humanity, while leaving Jesus to occupy a middle position in which he is neither God nor human. The Council of Nicaea ruled against Arianism in favor of those who advocated Jesus's *homoousia* with the Father, and thus Trinitarianism, with its emphasis upon the shared essence of substance of the Father, Son, and Spirit, became the accepted theological viewpoint of the emerging Catholic Church. For the next fifteen hundred years, theologians attempting to critique Trinitarianism often resorted to an Arian position. However, many found it hard to balance the Arian theology of the Father's superiority to Christ who is in turn superior to humanity (Father > Christ > Humanity) without eventually asserting a Trinitarian theology that the Father is like Christ who is superior to humanity (Father = Christ > Humanity) or the Socinian Christology that the Father is superior to Christ who is human (Father > Christ = Humanity).[10]

This theological positioning of Jesus becomes crucial when we recognize that, as Latter-day Saints, we rely upon him completely for our salvation. The deity of Jesus Christ is, in the words of Roger E. Olson, "the linchpin of the gospel. If it were removed in any way then the hope for eternal participation in God's own life and for forgiveness and restoration to the image of God would fall apart. The gospel itself would be wrecked."[11]

The early years of the nineteenth century were tense when it came to the subject of Christology. One prominent example of these tensions was the election of the liberal Calvinist Henry Ware as Professor of Divinity at Harvard in 1805, which only widened a developing rift between strict, conservative Calvinists and liberals such as Ware.[12] The debate revolved around whether or not liberal Calvinists were attempting to phase out some of Calvinism's more severe doctrines, such as predestination and total depravity. The thought that Calvinism might be weakened by such liberalizing concessions angered conservative Calvinists, who worried that the election of Ware to such a prominent position might signal a theological changing of the guard. In 1815 Jedidiah Morse, a conservative, published a harsh critique of what he perceived to be the theological views of his liberal opponents.[13] Prominent among his criticisms was his feeling that the teachings of American liberal Calvinists aligned with those of English Unitarians. Morse's identification was problematic because English Unitarians advocated a Socinian Christology, meaning they viewed Jesus not as a divine figure but as a human man, born of Mary by purely natural means.[14] According to the Socinian christological position, (1) Jesus had no existence prior to his birth and (2) by way of consequence, what had been understood as "atonement" demanded reevaluation. Though liberal Calvinists denied Morse's claim that their theology bordered on Socinianism, Morse was unconvinced. He vehemently denounced them as hypocrites and further argued that the liberals ought not to be termed Christians since they obviously did not believe in the divinity of Jesus Christ.

It was this christological debate that occupied so much of the attention of Joseph Priestley. Priestly had emerged in the late eighteenth century as the leader of the Unitarians in Britain and had espoused both Trinitarian and Arian views before eventually being swayed by the Socinian position, as had many others.[15] Priestley and the Socinians attempted to answer the question of the relation between God, Christ, and man by bringing Jesus down to man's level. In Priestley's opinion, Christ was a man in whom the Jews found their Messiah: "Jesus Christ . . . [was] a man approved of God, by wonders and signs which God did by him."[16] For Priestly, Jesus was actually just a human being whom history and tradition elevated to a deified state. Jesus's death was not intended in itself to be salvific but to grant hope to humanity that God would look upon them with similar favor and raise them from the dead as well. Priestly reasoned that "the death and resurrection of a man, in all respects like themselves, . . . [was] better calculated to give other men an assurance of their own resurrection, than that of any super-angelic being, the laws of whose nature they might think to be very different from those of their own."[17] Priestly believed that the influence of Oriental or the Greek philosophy led later Christian thinkers "to raise the dignity of the *person* of Christ, that it might appear less disgraceful to be ranked amongst his disciples."[18] However, while Priestley's view offered a partial solution to the problems of Arianism by asserting that there exists a common nature linking humanity and Christ, it failed to provide a solution to the thorny ontological question of how the nature of humanity relates to the nature of God.

William Ellery Channing advocated a similar christological position but advanced a somewhat different ontological view. Channing was a Harvard graduate who held the pastorate at Boston's Federal Street Church. In 1819 he delivered a sermon in Baltimore entitled "Unitarian Christianity" in which he laid out the framework and theology for American Unitarians while also consolidating the liberal position and answering the critique of conservative Calvinists.[19] One of the primary purposes of this sermon was to better define the Unitarian christological position, one that reflected elements of Arianism in its explanation of Jesus's mediation between God and humanity, although, as with Priestly, Jesus himself is not necessarily seen as divine:[20] "If we examine the passages in which Jesus is distinguished from God, we shall see, that they not only speak of him as another being, but seem to labor to express his inferiority. He is continually spoken of as the Son of God, sent of God, receiving all his power from God, working miracles because God was with him, judging justly because God taught him, having claims on our belief, because he was anointed and sealed by God, and was able of himself to do nothing."[21] The value of Jesus in Channing's mind was that in fully subsuming his will to that of the Father and in living a sinless life, he became the perfect role model to humanity—Jesus communicated the will of God to those around him and as such provided a path of righteous living.

Channing, who had been grappling with the relationship between God and humanity for some time, made another major theological move in 1828 with a sermon entitled "Likeness to God." For Channing, humanity's potential to become like God was a primary crux of the Christian faith: "In truth, the very essence of Christian faith is, that we trust in God's mercy, as revealed in Jesus Christ, for a state of celestial purity, in which we shall grow forever in the likeness, and knowledge, and enjoyment of the Infinite Father."[22] Channing saw this "likeness" as a teleological goal that symbolized the ultimate accomplishment of humanity: "I affirm, and would maintain, that true religion consists in proposing, as our great end, a growing likeness to the Supreme Being. Its noblest influence consists in making us more and more partakers of the Divinity."[23] Statements such as these represented an explicit disavowal of total depravity (the idea that men and women are, by their very nature, inclined to indulge their own desires) and suggested that rather than equip humanity with the overwhelming urge to sin, God had instead prepared them to be partakers of the Divine: "Likeness to God is the supreme gift. He can communicate nothing so precious, glorious, blessed, as himself. To hold intellectual and moral affinity with the Supreme Being, to partake of his spirit, to be his children by derivations of kindred excellence, to bear a growing conformity to the perfection which we adore, this is a felicity which obscures and annihilates all other good."[24] E. Brooks Holifield has written that Channing's concept of humanity's likeness to God referred "not to its inherent or achieved goodness but to its capacity for transcendence, its ability to yield to the new, to push in thought, imagination, and moral harmony beyond its current limits."[25] Without resorting to messy theological language such as "uncreated" or "ex nihilo," Channing constructed a paradigm in which God, Jesus Christ, and humanity all share *something* in common, and there is clearly an affinity between God and humanity throughout Channing's writings. As Holifield notes, "If a growing likeness to God was the goal, it was unwise to posit a God whose perfection could have nothing in common with human perfection."[26]

The preceding paragraphs have presented only a small portion of the many debates that occupied Western Europe and North America during the seventeenth, eighteenth, and early nineteenth centuries, where reason, revelation, and religion found an uneasy coexistence. Due to the emerging confidence in humanity's ability to discern the will of God through reason, the need for a divine, atoning Jesus gave way to a Jesus who provided the model of a perfect Christian life. Likewise, humanity's capacity to grasp and understand the revealed will of God through their own intellect suggested that a Calvinist theology centered upon the fall of Adam and subsequent original sin was flawed. Men like Priestly and Channing mined the Bible for evidence that the Trinitarian position, with its triune God, was unsustainable, and by the early 1830s the question of Jesus's relationship to God and the need for a divine atonement had been called into serious question. Most agreed that Jesus provided a crucial bridge between humanity and the Father. However, the nature and purpose of that bridge was in doubt.

Against this theological backdrop, Doctrine and Covenants 93, in my opinion, can best be understood. Currents of christological controversies had been sweeping through the eastern states during the early decades of the nineteenth century, and this revelation provided the Lord's response to the debate—one that proved particularly timely due to subsequent trends in biblical scholarship.[27] Section 93 directly addresses the relationship between God and humanity, identifies when that relationship originated, and relates how Jesus Christ figures in that relationship. The revelation carefully and concisely traces Jesus's trajectory as both divine and human, directly linked to both God the Father and humanity, and in the process settles from a Latter-day Saint perspective the christological controversies to which Priestly, Channing, and others had contributed.

Christology and Doctrine and Covenants 93:1–20

With this framework in mind, attention can now be directed specifically toward Doctrine and Covenants 93, a revelation with opaque origins. Our earliest historical sources for the reception of Doctrine and Covenants 93 amount to just two short statements. The first, written in Joseph Smith's history, states only that "on the 6th I received the following."[28] The second, written by Newel K. Whitney, gives some additional details: "Revelation to Joseph, Sidny Frederick & Newell by chastisement & also relative to the Father & Son 6 May 1833."[29] Whitney's statement raises an intriguing question about the catalyst for the May 1833 revelation. By placing the primary emphasis upon *chastisement*, Whitney introduced the possibility that the more theologically oriented content (things "relative to the Father & Son") found in the first two-thirds of the revelation needs to be read in light of the final third of the revelation in which individuals are called out by name and encouraged to be more effective parents. Just as the revelation begins with a discussion of the relationship between Heavenly Father and his Son, it concludes with a reflection on human parental relationships. And since the revelation reminds readers that human beings can, like Christ, receive "grace for grace" and be "partakers of the glory" (Doctrine and Covenants 93:20, 22), parents are encouraged to reflect on the eternal nature of their children's spirits.

Reminding the recipients of the trajectory of Jesus Christ's own development and growth places attention both on the relationship between him and his Father as well as on the lengthy measures Jesus went through to ensure that salvation would be made available for all of God's spirit children. Parents in mortality have an important charge that they must not forget as they raise their children—all children are ultimately God's children, and Jesus has demonstrated, through his own journey, the model for how all of God's children can return safely to him as they learn to properly exercise their God-given agency. As Steven Harper has noted, "Section 93 is a masterpiece of parenting from a most concerned Father and a commandment to go and do likewise."[30]

Seen in this light, readers can better appreciate why a revelation on parenthood might open with a christological discussion. Note, for instance, how the revelation begins:[31]

> Verily, thus saith the Lord: . . . I am the true light that lighteth every man that cometh into the world; . . . I am in the Father,

> and the Father in me, and the Father and I are one—the
> Father because he gave me of his fulness, and the Son because
> I was in the world and made flesh my tabernacle, and dwelt
> among the sons of men. I was in the world and received of my
> Father, and the works of him were plainly manifest. (Doctrine
> and Covenants 93:1–5)

The first two verses strongly hint at an incarnation Christology. Verse 1 repeats the "I Am" formula found so prominently in the Gospel of John, reinforcing that the speaker of this revelation, the divine Lord, is simultaneously Jesus and Jehovah.[32] The "I Am" carries over into verse 2, in which the Lord declares, "I am the true light that lighteth every man that cometh into the world." The reference to "true light" again returns readers to John 1, in which the "word" is also described as "the true Light, which lighteth every man that cometh into the world" (John 1:9). Verse 3 introduces another element of incarnation Christology, namely the extremely close connection between Jesus and the Father. They are, in fact, so closely linked that Jesus can say that he is "in the Father, and the Father in me" (compare John 14:10). This connection between the Father and Jesus is made even more explicit through the phrase "the Father and I are one" (compare John 10:30). Whether this sameness in the Johannine text amounts to something ontological (a shared nature) or something teleological (a shared purpose) is not made clear at this point. What is clear, however, is that these two figures are so closely linked that they are practically indistinguishable. What Doctrine and Covenants 93 has presented thus far is not so much a picture of Jesus *and* God but Jesus *as* God.

However, in light of the christological questions summarized above, readers might well wonder *when* in time this divine unity occurs. Because the revelation was received in May 1833, we can safely assert that the postresurrected Jesus is God, but we might still wonder whether that divinity was assumed prior to mortality, during mortality, or after mortality.

Some clarification is received in the next two verses. Rather abruptly, verse 4 moves readers from two personages (Lord and Father) to two titles ("Father" and "Son"), both of which apply to Jesus. In a statement that echoes Abinadi's language in Mosiah 15:1–4, Jesus explains that he can be called "Father" because Heavenly Father "gave [him] of his fulness." The nature of this fulness remains unspecified at this point in the revelation, but the implication is that the moment when Jesus was granted or given fulness was when he became fully divine.[33] Related passages in the Gospel of John and Doctrine and Covenants 76 add further complications to the question. In the Gospel of John, the "fulness" (Greek *pleroma*) is something that "we all have received," but here it is applied specifically to Jesus. Based on Doctrine and Covenants 76:56 and 76, fulness must be different from grace or glory, but it is difficult to know what else to call it. A few verses later in 93:6, fulness will specifically become the fulness "of my glory," but that does not line up very closely with the use of the word in Doctrine and Covenants 76, in which fullness and glory are two separate things.[34] Does the fulness somehow emanate from the Father, and those who are permanently brought into his presence are able to absorb or receive it? Further complicating matters is that Joseph Smith in section 76 says that he and Sidney Rigdon "beheld the glory of the Son, on the right hand of the Father, and *received of his fulness*" (76:20; emphasis added). But perhaps the difference here is the Son's fulness as opposed to that of the Father.

The remainder of verse 4 and verse 5 clarify why Jesus is called the Son. First, Jesus is the Son because he was "in the world" and because he "made flesh [his] tabernacle." In other words, he willingly condescended to a telestial world and lived in an incarnate form. It is unclear, however, from a christological perspective how to position this statement. Is Jesus saying that he was divine but then came to earth and became flesh, a course that allowed him to live "among the sons of men"? Or is he speaking of his experience as a mortal—he lived on earth in a physical body and lived among other men and women? Because Doctrine and Covenants 93:4 alludes to John 1 (in particular 1:12, 14) with its explicit incarnation Christology and because 1 Nephi 11 discusses God's condescension, it is natural for Latter-day Saints to read this as a statement supporting incarnation Christology; but actually the verse can be read either way. This ambiguity is especially pronounced when we keep in mind the reference to Jesus having "received [the fulness] of my Father" (Doctrine and Covenants 93:5), while "in the world." This phrase could be taken to mean that his status was elevated during his mortality, placing this within the spectrum of exaltation Christology. The statement that "the works of [the Father] were plainly manifest" seems to return the reader to verse 3 and the idea that "the Father and I are one." But again, there is ambiguity. Does Doctrine and Covenants 93:5 mean that what Jesus did in mortality (his healings, his miracles, and his sacrifice) mirrors the will and desire of the Father? Or does it mean that the works of the Father prepared Jesus (through elevating him and bestowing power upon him during his mortal ministry) to be able to reflect the Father's will? In short, these first five verses leave readers with a clear sense of tension between Jesus's mortality and divinity. He is simultaneously divine and is one with the Father, but how he arrived at that state remains, at least to this point in the revelation, unclear.

The next section of Doctrine and Covenants 93 introduces what readers are meant to assume is an excerpt from an ancient text, the "record of John" (Doctrine and Covenants 93:18). According to verse 6, an individual named John both witnessed the fullness of Jesus's glory and, more importantly, wrote that account down in a text that has not yet been revealed. The identity of this John is never stated outright, but several overlapping words and phrases show a clear connection between the record of John that appears in section 93 and the Gospel of John, particularly John 1.[35] However, the prominence of John the Baptist in John 1 leaves open the possibility that the referenced record was written by John the Baptist and was subsequently redacted in the Gospel of John.[36] These questions only illustrate yet again the complexity of section 93's christological message.

The record of John in Doctrine and Covenants 93 begins, "I saw his glory, that he was in the beginning, before the world was; therefore, in the beginning the Word was, for he was the Word, even the messenger of salvation" (Doctrine and Covenants 93:7–8). There is much here that suggests an incarnation Christology, primarily the application of the title "Word" to Jesus. In the Gospel of John, the Word was "in the beginning" and also "with God," and the "Word" was, notably, also "God."[37] One senses a similar portrayal of Jesus in the record of John mentioned in section 93. Here the revelation relays that Jesus was "in the beginning," probably meaning that Jesus existed prior to the creation of the world since John goes on to clarify that "beginning" has reference to a time "before the world was." The implication of verses 7 and 8 is not simply that Jesus *existed* prior to the creation of the earth but that he existed as the *Word*. In other words, "In the beginning *he* was the Word." The revelation also goes on to clarify what Jesus's status as Word amounted to: specifically, Jesus functioned as the "messenger of salvation" (93:8). This could simply mean that Jesus spoke for the Father, vocalizing the Father's will and commands. Or more likely, the verse implies a sense of Jesus as God's divine agent—he is the one who will bring to pass salvation through creating the earth and participating in the Atonement. It is Jesus, the Word, who will bring to pass the Father's will.

Unlike the ambiguous Christology of verses 1–5, the information about Jesus presented in verses 7 and 8 fully suggests an incarnation Christology. Jesus is divine not because he was resurrected or because the fullness of the Father came upon him at his baptism or at his birth but because of his nearness with God and the divine status he held long before the creation of the world. This information was apparently relayed to John the Baptist in some way through witnessing Jesus's glory (Doctrine and Covenants 93:7)—and this too, it should be noted, is again suggestive of an incarnation Christology. The real oddity of verses 7 and 8, though, is not what is present in these verses but what is conspicuously absent. Although these verses share much in common with John 1:1 (the use of the title "Word," the phrase "in the beginning"), they also omit the crucial phrase in John 1:1 that the Word "was God."[38] Section 93 elevates Jesus to a divine, premortal status but stops just short of referring to him directly as "God."

The same pattern holds true in the next two verses: Jesus is "the light and the Redeemer of the world; the Spirit of truth, who came into the world, because the world was made by him, and in him was the life of men and the light of men. The worlds were made by him; men were made by him; all things were made by him, and through him, and of him" (Doctrine and Covenants 93:9–10). Here Jesus is again (but now explicitly) attributed the role of creator of the world, but the scope has been expanded to include many worlds. Jesus's relationship with humanity is made more explicit since he is described as both the *creator* of humanity and the *sustainer* of individuals. It is in Jesus that the life and the light of humanity find their origin or source. In a rather striking statement, we learn that Jesus's creative power extends to all things that owe their existence to having been brought into existence "by," "through," and even "of" Jesus. The last phrase ("of [Jesus]") teases an ontological connection between Jesus and humanity that challenges a hard and fast division between creator and created.

In these verses as well, the revelation continues to disclose titles for Jesus. In addition to "Word" and "messenger of salvation," readers encounter "redeemer of the world" and "Spirit of truth," titles that continue to reinforce the salvific nature of Jesus's mission: he will redeem humanity, and through him humanity will find truth. However, verses 9 and 10 also continue to develop the christological tension introduced in verses 7 and 8. Jesus is, on the one hand, so important that the creation and sustaining of life not only on this world but on many worlds are attributed to him, yet on the other hand John's record stops short of referring to him the way John 1:1 does, as "God." This omission could simply be attributed to John believing that Jesus's divinity is already implied in his description of Jesus in these first four verses and so does not require explicit statement. However, for the record of John to so closely align with the text of John 1:1–18 but then omit the most theologically striking phrase feels measured, as if section 93 is intended to deconstruct, in the minds of its readers, Jesus's true christological nature. The revelation seems to say, "You thought you knew where this revelation was going based upon your familiarity with John's Gospel, but now watch this," as it tells its readers to look one way and then, in verses 11–14, takes them in the exact opposite direction.

Indeed, from this point on in the revelation, readers encounter a key christological shift.

> And I, John, bear record that I beheld his glory, as the glory of the Only Begotten of the Father, full of grace and truth, even the Spirit of truth, which came and dwelt in the flesh, and dwelt among us. And I, John, saw that he received not of the fulness at the first, but received grace for grace; and he received not of the fulness at first, but continued from grace to grace, until he received a fulness; and thus he was called the Son of God, because he received not of the fulness at the first. (Doctrine and Covenants 93:11–14)

Here in these crucial verses the incarnation Christology of section 93 confronts its most explicit exaltation Christology. The shift is subtle, as verse 11 continues to expand on the incarnation Christology of verses 7–10. The scene shifts from premortality to mortality as Jesus's incarnation becomes a reality—the divine Word "dwelt in the flesh, and dwelt among us." John again mentions Jesus's glory, as he did in verse 7, but the source of glory appears to have shifted as well—now Jesus's glory is linked not to his premortal status, "before the world was," but to his being "the Only Begotten of the Father." This title, which in the Bible is distinctly Johannine (Greek *monogenes*), is perhaps better rendered God's "one and only" or "most precious" Son.[39] Jesus is unique in the Father's eyes, and in this sense the phrase "Only Begotten of the Father" echoes the Father's words to Jesus at the baptism: "This is my beloved son" (Matthew 3:17). This title becomes critical in section 93 as the focus shifts to Jesus's subordinate role as

Son as opposed to his codivinity with the Father. Jesus retains all his titles and descriptors from verses 7–10, but at this point in John's story, he is distinctly a son.

The nature of this sonship becomes clear in the next three verses. First, readers learn that Jesus has not always possessed fullness. According to verse 12, Jesus didn't have the fullness "at the first," and this lack of fullness is mentioned again in verse 13. It is unclear if "first" refers to the premortal Jesus, the creator and sustainer of the universe, or the mortal Jesus, who "came and dwelt in the flesh." Based upon the placement of these verses, it seems more likely that John intends the latter: When Jesus came into mortality, he lacked fullness.[40] It seems likely, based upon the duplication of "at [the] first," that John wants to emphasize that this ante-fullness was merely temporary—only at the beginning of his time on earth did Jesus lack fullness.

The process between Jesus lacking and securing fullness can be seen in two key phrases from verses 12 and 13: "grace *for* grace" and "grace *to* grace." The first, "grace for grace," is also present in the Gospel of John, where its meaning is debated. Is John saying that (some) grace is given in addition to (other) grace—that is, blessings follow one after the other—or is he saying that grace is given (by God) as a reward for the grace shown (by his children)?[41] Some modern translations (NIV, NRSV) follow the former, interpreting the expression as a demonstration of how God compounds his blessings. But this makes little sense in the context of Doctrine and Covenants 93, which is about the process by which Jesus receives fullness. If we look at how the Book of Mormon uses this particular phrase—and others like it—we see that the latter interpretation has precedent for restored scripture: "And may God grant, in his great fulness, that men might be brought unto repentance and good works, that they might be restored unto grace for grace, according to their works" (Helaman 12:24).

This language suggests something of an exchange of grace. As we repent and perform good works, we receive grace in exchange for our acts of grace. The use of *restored* links this verse with Alma's discourse to Corianton, in which he teaches a similar idea: "O, my son, this is not the case; but the meaning of the word restoration is to bring back again evil for evil, or carnal for carnal, or devilish for devilish—good for that which is good; righteous for that which is righteous; just for that which is just; merciful for that which is merciful" (Alma 41:13).

If this idea of restoration is used as a lens, Doctrine and Covenants 93:12 seems to state that Jesus attained a fullness by receiving blessings from the Father as he himself did what the Father asked—grace was granted to him in exchange for his grace. While this notion of exchange is foreign to the Gospel of John, it fits nicely with the overall trajectory of Doctrine and Covenants 93.[42]

The second phrase, "grace *to* grace," is a little more complicated. This phrase appears nowhere in the Bible or in Restoration scripture outside of Doctrine and Covenants 93:13.[43] The similarity between "grace *for* grace" and "grace *to* grace" suggests that John views them both as acting somehow in tandem, with the shift in prepositions from *for* to *to* being the key in how they act differently. Rather than an exchange, as suggested by *for*, *to* may suggest a progression of sorts—that is, the idea that Jesus advanced from one stage to another while in mortality. This is the view taken by Stephen E. Robinson, who argues that "the key to this verse is the word *to*, indicating that there are levels of grace, or degrees to which one may enjoy the grace of God and act graciously toward others. Thus, from birth on, we move forward in a process of learning and responding to God's grace."[44] Both verse 12 and verse 13 thus portray Jesus as progressing. In verse 12, this progress is shown by way of individual moments of exchange between Jesus's righteous actions and the Father's subsequent blessings. In verse 13, however, this progress is narrated with wider scope, emphasizing the resulting movement as each divine exchange advanced Jesus to a new level of grace. Thus, taken together, verses 12 and 13 narrate Jesus's development to the point where he was ready to receive the fullness of the Father. Indeed, according to the revelation, Jesus's sonship is a direct result of this developmental process: *"and thus he was called* the Son of God, *because* he received not of the fulness at first" (Doctrine and Covenants 93:14; emphasis added). In the process, section 93 has shifted subtly from an incarnation Christology to an exaltation Christology.[45]

From here, the revelation (and with it, the record of John from which the revelation takes its account) now turns to focus specifically on one point in Jesus's life: his baptism.

> And I, John, bear record, and lo, the heavens were opened, and the Holy Ghost descended upon him in the form of a dove, and sat upon him, and there came a voice out of heaven saying: This is my beloved Son. And I, John, bear record that he received a fulness of the glory of the Father; and he received all power, both in heaven and on earth, and the glory of the Father was with him, for he dwelt in him. (Doctrine and Covenants 93:15–17)

It is perhaps not surprising, then, that readers learn that Jesus finally received of the fullness at the baptism.[46] This, too, is in perfect keeping with the revelation's shift to an exaltation Christology. As I mentioned earlier, exaltation Christology attempts to locate a point within the ministry of Jesus at which he is raised up or exalted by the Father and endued with some measure of divinity. In some texts, such as the book of Romans, this exaltation takes place at the Resurrection. For others, such as the Gospel of Mark, this exaltation happens at the baptism (see Mark 1:10–11). Doctrine and Covenants 93 presents a scene very much in this latter vein. Jesus, having spent the first three decades of his life learning how to exchange grace for grace and to progress from grace to grace, now finds himself ready to receive the "fulness of the glory of the Father." While the text of section 93 does not explicitly link verses 15 and 16 as contemporaneous, their quick succession is suggestive. It is hard not to hear an implication that Jesus's reception of fullness in verses 16 and 17 follows directly on the heels of the events of verse 15. Although Jesus's baptism seems to root this portion of the revelation firmly in exaltation

Christology, the concepts and phrases return to themes of incarnation Christology from earlier in section 93, reminding readers that the two Christologies continue to exist in tension with one another.

The reason for this sudden summary becomes clear in the next three verses: the Lord hopes to turn now from the content of the record of John to its primary lesson for readers:

> And it shall come to pass, that if you are faithful you shall receive the fulness of the record of John. I give unto you these sayings that you may understand and know how to worship, and know what you worship, that you may come unto the Father in my name, and in due time receive of his fulness. For if you keep my commandments you shall receive of his fulness, and be glorified in me as I am in the Father; therefore, I say unto you, you shall receive grace for grace. (Doctrine and Covenants 93:18–20)

In quite an amazing statement, readers are informed that Jesus's trajectory is not unique but is in fact the model for all of God's children. The Father desires that we *all* receive his fullness. We do this, we are told, by keeping the commandments, and in the process we, like Jesus, will "receive grace for grace." Presumably, all of us must also progress grace to grace, with the promise that those who complete this journey will "be glorified in me as I am in the Father." The importance of these verses is summarized by Latter-day Saint scholar Terryl L. Givens, who writes that "[Doctrine and Covenants 93] promises to the obedient the same inheritance of the Father's 'fulness' that Christ obtained, and an eventual 'glorifi[cation] in' Christ, as he is glorified 'in the Father.' It draws a linguistic parallel, in other words, between Christ receiving a fulness, but not 'at the first,' and humans receiving an eventual fulness."[47]

It is here in these three verses that *praxis* intersects with *Christology* and that we begin to understand the tension that exists between the section's two seemingly disparate christological paths. Because Jesus is our ultimate exemplar for how to progress and receive a fullness, section 93 portrays Jesus as an amalgamation of mortality and immortality, humanity and divinity, Son and Father. By combining incarnation Christology with exaltation Christology, the revelation allows us to find commonalities with Christ's mortal sonship while at the same time aspiring to Jesus's divinity and glory. In the tension between the two Christologies, Doctrine and Covenants 93 helps us locate ourselves at the crux between mortality and godhood. As Blake Ostler has written, "Christ became what we are that we might become what Christ is."[48] Deification is, in actuality, Christification.[49]

Conclusion

The nineteenth century was a time when the divine nature of Jesus Christ was called into question. Was he divine or was he human? Was he ontologically nearest to God or to humanity? The brilliance of the Christology in Doctrine and Covenants 93 is evident in how carefully it combines two different Christologies.[50] Through the elements of exaltation Christology that emerge in section 93, readers see how Jesus's path can be their own. Jesus, like each of us, came to mortality without the fullness of the Father's glory. Each of us, like Jesus, progresses grace for grace and from grace to grace. Yet, lest readers get too carried away by the human element of Jesus's nature, the verses on exaltation Christology also include reminders that Jesus held creative power and authority prior to coming to earth. Likewise, section 93 uses elements of incarnation Christology to help readers understand how Jesus possesses the capacity to bring us to the Father. He must be able to perform an atonement, die on the cross, and be raised again—experiences that are far removed from our capacity. Readers of Doctrine and Covenants 93 come away with the understanding that Jesus's divinity is just as real as his humanity—and just as important. But again, lest readers begin to tilt too heavily toward incarnation Christology, the record of John reminds us that Jesus's acquisition of the fullness happened not at birth but at baptism.

Over the last two thousand years, hundreds of writers have written thousands of pages in an attempt to define just who Jesus is.[51] However, because of both the importance and complexity of the topic, confusion naturally remains. In many ways, Doctrine and Covenants 93 represents what Joseph Smith accomplished with the Restoration. It is not only that Joseph created new ideas or brought back old ideas that had been lost; rather, as in section 93, he often took confusing, opaque, and misconstrued concepts and applied a practical, commonsense approach, providing meaning to what had been mystifying. The tension created by this revelation's skillful weaving of two Christologies is a healthy one because it forces readers to abandon a false binary and instead to embrace the Jesus who is, in some fashion, fully God and, in another fashion, fully human, one who can successfully lift us up to the Father both because he has been where we are now and because he fully understands what is waiting for us when we get to where he is.

Notes

1. For a good introduction to the study of Christology, see Thomas P. Rauch, *Who Is Jesus? An Introduction to Christology* (Collegeville, MN: Liturgical Press, 2003); for a more academic approach that surveys more recent issues, see Francesca Aran Murphy, ed., *The Oxford Handbook of Christology* (Oxford: Oxford University Press, 2015).

2. For more on how the different ways the New Testament authors present Jesus, see Larry W. Hurtado, *Lord Jesus Christ: Devotion to Jesus in Earliest Christianity* (Grand Rapids, MI: Eerdmans, 2003); and Eric D. Huntsman, Lincoln H. Blumell, and Tyler J. Griffin, eds., *Thou Art the Christ: The Person and Work of Jesus in the New Testament* (Provo, UT: Religious Studies Center, Brigham Young University; Salt Lake City: Deseret Book, 2018).

3. For more on how Book of Mormon Christology is developed in 3 Nephi, see David L. Paulsen and Ari D. Bruening, "The Social Model of the Trinity in 3 Nephi," in *Third Nephi: An Incomparable Scripture*, ed. Andrew C.

Skinner and Gaye Strathearn (Provo, UT: The Neal A Maxwell Institute for Religious Scholarship; Salt Lake City: Deseret Book, 2012), 191–234.

4. For how Doctrine and Covenants 93 fits into Joseph Smith's larger christological project beyond the Doctrine and Covenants, see John G. Turner, *The Mormon Jesus: A Biography* (Cambridge, MA: Harvard University Press, 2016), 157–58.

5. It is important to note that christological categories can be very fluid, and the limits of a given category are often left up to the author's interpretation. For ease of interpretation and to avoid getting bogged down in minute theological debates, I'm adopting the two categories Bart D. Ehrman focuses on in his study of early Christian theology, *How Jesus Became God: The Exaltation of a Jewish Preacher from Galilee* (New York: HarperOne, 2014), 211–82. I do recognize that other authors may present these categories differently and even adopt further categories. I highly recommend one such study, James L. Papandrea, *The Earliest Christologies: Five Images of Christ in the Postapostolic Age* (Downers Grove, IL: IVP Academic, 2016). For a response and critique of Ehrman's book, see Michael F. Bird et al., eds., *How God Became Jesus: The Real Origins of Belief in Jesus' Divine Nature—A Response to Bart D. Ehrman* (Grand Rapids, MI: Zondervan, 2014).

6. Ehrman, *How Jesus Became God*, 230.

7. Ehrman, *How Jesus Became God*, 230.

8. One variation of this idea, termed spirit adoptionism, argues that "after Jesus was baptized, the Christ spirit descended on him in the form of a dove and entered into him. . . . After his baptism Jesus was given power from God through the Holy Spirit and was therefore able to perform miracles." Papandrea, *Earliest Christologies*, 34–35.

9. Ehrman, *How Jesus Became God*, 251.

10. For more on the intricacies of the Arian debate, see Rowan Williams, *Arius: Heresy and Tradition* (Grand Rapids, MI: Eerdmans, 2001). For a Latter-day Saint perspective, see Lincoln H. Blumell, "Rereading the Council of Nicaea and Its Creed," in *Standing Apart: Mormon Historical Consciousness and the Concept of Apostasy*, ed. Miranda Wilcox and John D. Young (Oxford: Oxford University Press, 2015), 196–217.

11. Roger E. Olson, *The Story of Christian Theology: Twenty Centuries of Tradition and Reform* (Downers Grove, IL: InterVarsity Press, 1999), 150.

12. For more detail on this pivotal moment in both Harvard and Unitarian history, see Conrad Wright, *The Unitarian Controversy: Essays on American Unitarian History* (Boston: Skinner House Books, 2016), 1–16.

13. See Jedidiah Morse, *Review of American Unitarianism* (Boston: Samuel T. Armstrong, 1815).

14. Priestly's use of the label *Socinian* to impugn the liberals was not an uncommon move, as "the sling of Socinian was a common one in the seventeenth and eighteenth centuries." Lydia Willsky-Ciollo, *American Unitarianism and the Protestant Dilemma: The Conundrum of Biblical Authority* (Lanham, MD: Lexington Books, 2015), 13. Willsky-Ciollo further explains that "Socinians, so named for their founder Faustus Socinus, employed a rational exegesis of scripture grounded in a belief in the literal sense of the Bible, one that led to a radically Unitarian understanding of God. Socinian theology disputes the pre-existence of Christ and views him not as a 'reconciler' of humanity to God, but as the revealer of a particular and perfect morality, which if emulated, could lead to eternal life."

15. Priestley described his conversion process as moving "from Trinitariansim to high Arianism; from high Arianism to low Arianism; and from this to Socinianism even of the lowest sort." Maurice Wiles, *Archetypal Heresy: Arianism through the Centuries* (Oxford: Clarendon, 1996), 148.

16. Joseph Priestley, *A History of the Corruption of Christianity* (London: The British and Foreign Unitarian Association, 1871), 1.

17. Priestley, *History*, 8.

18. Priestley, *History*, 8.

19. Mark A. Noll describes the impact and import of Channing's 1819 sermon: "[It], which provided an unambiguous answer to questions about what the Boston liberals actually believed, was a masterpiece of rhetorical adaptation as well as religious exposition. In it Channing did set forth clearly what the Unitarians believed. . . . But he did so through a masterful deployment of the intellectual warrants that virtually all the more orthodox religious thinkers of his day were also scrambling to enlist for their

versions of Christian faith." Mark A. Noll, *America's God: From Jonathan Edwards to Abraham Lincoln* (Oxford: Oxford University Press, 2002), 235.

20. Channing's biographer and nephew, William Henry Channing, would later write of Channing that "in a word, he was then an Arian." William Henry Channing, *William Ellery Channing, with Extracts from His Correspondence and Manuscripts* (London: George Routledge, Soho Square, 1850), 397.

21. Channing, *Works*, 373.

22. Channing, *Works*, 293.

23. Channing, *Works*, 291.

24. Channing, *Works*, 291. It is important to note that Channing is not advocating for the deification of humanity in the sense that men and women become gods and goddesses themselves. Rather, "To Channing, it was appropriate to speak of life-giving, love-inspiring spiritual experience as revelatory, but not as the realization of supernatural empowerment. He affirmed that human beings possess the God-given capacity to experience divinity, and he insisted that revelation is knowable only as personal experience, but he pointedly admonished that human beings do not become gods or infallible interpreters of Divinity by virtue of the experience of revelatory feeling." Gary Dorrien, *The Making of American Liberal Theology: Imagining Progressive Religion 1805–1900* (Louisville: Westminster John Knox Press, 2001), 57.

25. E. Brooks Holifield, *Theology in America* (New Haven: Yale University Press, 2003), 204.

26. Holifield, *Theology*, 206. It is not hard to see why transcendentalists such as Ralph Waldo Emerson saw Channing as a predecessor, although they would differ on the very important point of how to understand the nature of Jesus Christ.

27. In 1835, two years after the reception of the revelation now contained in Doctrine and Covenants 93, David Strauss published his highly influential *Life of Jesus Critically Examined*, which argued that many of the divine events and circumstances surrounding the life and death of Jesus were simply the product of the social imagination of the ancient world. Subsequent trends in biblical scholarship throughout the nineteenth and

into the twentieth century would only widen this divide. Viewed from the perspective of faith, it is hard not to see section 93 as given specifically to address these growing concerns.

28. Joseph Smith, History, 1838–1856, vol. A-1, p. 291, Church History Library.

29. Gerrit J. Dirkmaat, Brent M. Rogers, Grant Underwood, Robert J. Woodford, and William G. Hartley, eds., *Documents, Volume 3: February 1833–March 1834*, vol. 3 of the Documents series of *The Joseph Smith Papers*, ed. Ronald K. Esplin and Matthew J. Grow (Salt Lake City: Church Historian's Press, 2014), 83.

30. Steven C. Harper, *Making Sense of the Doctrine and Covenants: A Guided Tour through Modern Revelation* (Salt Lake City: Deseret Book, 2008), 347.

31. For a deeper analysis of Doctrine and Covenants 93, including its intertextual connections with the Bible and possible theological implications, see Nicholas J. Frederick, *The Bible, Mormon Scripture, and the Rhetoric of Allusivity* (Madison, NJ: Fairleigh Dickinson University Press, 2016), 95–129.

32. One of the elements of John's Gospel is that Jesus consistently speaks in an "I Am" (*ego eimi*) formula (compare 4:26; 6:35; 8:58). This alludes back to Exodus 3:14, where Jehovah identifies himself to Moses as "I Am that I Am" (*ego eimi ho on*). The idea is that Jesus is using this language to intentionally allude to his position as Jehovah. See the discussion in Raymond E. Brown, *The Gospel according to John I–XII* (New Haven: Yale University Press, 2008), 533–38. For more on how the Gospel of John interacts with the Doctrine and Covenants, including Doctrine and Covenants 93, see Nicholas J. Frederick, "Using the Gospel of John to Understand the Text of the Revelations," in *You Shall Have My Word: Exploring the Text of the Doctrine and Covenants*, ed. Scott C. Esplin, Richard O. Cowan, and Rachel Cope (Salt Lake Citiy: Desert Book, 2012), 205–19; and Nicholas J. Frederick, "Of Life Eternal and Eternal Lives: Joseph Smith's Engagement with the Gospel of John," in *Approaching Antiquity: Joseph Smith and the Ancient World*, ed. Lincoln H. Blumell, Matthew J. Grey, and Andrew H. Hedges (Provo, UT: Religious Studies Center, Brigham Young University; Salt Lake City: Deseret Book, 2015), 194–228.

33. Blake T. Ostler offers this definition of *fulness*: "The concept of 'a fulness' is intimately connected with the divine glory that characterizes the divine life. 'A fulness' in Joseph Smith's revelations refers to the fulness of life and glory that is given by the Father to the Son and which is received by grace from one glory to another in a process of growth and progression." Blake T. Ostler, *Exploring Mormon Thought: Of God and Gods* (Salt Lake City: Greg Kofford Books, 2008), 366.

34. "These are they who receive of his glory, but not of his fulness" (Doctrine and Covenants 76:76).

35. I deal with the rhetorical and theological implications of the presence of the record of John in Doctrine and Covenants 93 in "Translation, Revelation, and the Hermeneutics of Theological Innovation: Joseph Smith and the Record of John," in *Producing Ancient Scripture: Joseph Smith's Translation Projects in the Development of Mormon Christianity*, ed. Michael Hubbard MacKay, Mark Ashurst-McGee, and Brian M. Hauglid (Salt Lake City: University of Utah Press, 2020), 304–27.

36. That Doctrine and Covenants 93 preserves a record originating with John the Baptist has been argued by some Latter-day Saint writers. In his *Mediation and Atonement*, John Taylor quotes Doctrine and Covenants 93 and lists it under the title "Record of John the Baptist." Taylor, *Mediation and Atonement* (Salt Lake City: Deseret Book, 1975), 55. Orson Pratt described the record of John as being penned by "him who baptized the Lamb of God." Orson Pratt, in *Journal of Discourses* (London: Latter Day Saints' Book Depot, 1854–86), 16:58. Writing much later, Bruce R. McConkie wrote that "there is little doubt but that the Beloved Disciple had before him the Baptist's account when he wrote his gospel. The latter John either copied or paraphrased what the earlier prophet of the same name had written." Bruce R. McConkie, *Doctrinal New Testament Commentary* (Salt Lake City: Bookcraft, 1966), 1:70–71. However, the issue is not necessarily without a counterargument. Historian Steven C. Harper noted that "all editions of the Doctrine and Covenants since 1921 imply that these were the writings of John the Apostle." Harper, *Making Sense of the Doctrine and Covenants*, 560. Perhaps the safest approach has been that of historian John G. Turner, who wrote simply that the record

of John was attributed to "either John the Baptist or John the Evangelist."
Turner, *Mormon Jesus*, 158.

37. The Gospel of John's usage of the title "Word" (Greek *logos*) was probably
intended to communicate a mediating figure between the transcendent,
divine realm and the immanent, mortal realm. God the Father, being fully
divine, does not come to the corrupt mortal world but instead sends a messenger, the Word, to act as his spokesman or divine agent. In some fashion,
the Word was associated with God the Father but was also himself God—
"While the Word is God, God is more than just the Word." See discussion in Craig S. Keener, *The Gospel of John: A Commentary* (Peabody, MA:
Hendrickson, 2003), 298–320; and J. Ramsey Michaels, *The Gospel of John*
(Grand Rapids, MI: Eerdmans, 2010), 47.

38. The theological significance of these four words is hinted at by D. A.
Carson, who wrote, "Here then are some of the crucial constituents of a
full-blown doctrine of the Trinity." Carson, *The Gospel according to John*
(Grand Rapids, MI: Eerdmans, 1991), 117. As such, its omission from
Doctrine and Covenants 93 is striking.

39. As Raymond Brown points out, "Although *genos* is distantly related to
gennan, 'to beget,' there is little Greek justification for the translation
of *monogenēs* as 'only begotten.'" It was the influence of Jerome's Latin
Vulgate on the translators of the King James Bible that led to *only begotten* becoming the standard reading. Isaac is likewise called Abraham's
monogenēs son in Hebrews 11:17, but that was to signify Isaac's status as
Abraham's favorite son, as Isaac was not Abraham's only son. See Brown,
Gospel according to John, 13.

40. It is unclear why verse 12 of Doctrine and Covenants 93 would not just
repeat the phrase "in the world" from verse 4 if John meant to refer to
Jesus's mortal sojourn.

41. See discussion in Carson, *Gospel according to John*, 131–34.

42. "The idea of grace being given 'in return for' something else, a kind of *quid
pro quo*, is alien to the New Testament in general and to John in particular." Carson, *Gospel according to John*, 131.

43. *Grace to grace* does appear in the writings of Methodist founder John
Wesley in the context of sanctification: "From the time of our being *born*

again, the gradual work of sanctification takes place. . . . We go on from grace to grace." *The Works of the Rev. John Wesley* (London: John Mason, 1829), 6:46.

44. Stephen E. Robinson and H. Dean Garrett, *A Commentary on the Doctrine and Covenants* (Salt Lake City: Deseret Book, 2004), 3:183.

45. Some have seen in these verses in Doctrine and Covenants 93 evidence that Latter-day Saints embrace Arian ideas when it comes to the person and nature of Jesus Christ. For a response, see Brian D. Birch, "Mormonism and the Heresies," in *Let Us Reason Together: Essays in Honor of the Life's Work of Robert L. Millet*, ed. J. Spencer Fluhman and Brent L. Top (Provo, UT: Religious Studies Center, Brigham Young University; Salt Lake City: Deseret Book, 2016), 249–63.

46. What is surprising from a biblical perspective is that the record of John includes the baptism scene at all. The Gospel of John, which apparently relied upon this lost record of John, contains John's testimony of Jesus's divinity but completely omits the baptism scene itself. The recounting of the baptism in Doctrine and Covenants 93:15 seems to draw upon the description of the baptism preserved in Matthew 3:16–17.

47. Terryl L. Givens, *Wrestling the Angel: The Foundations of Mormon Thought; Cosmos, God, Humanity* (New York: Oxford University Press, 2015), 120. Speaking to the tension present in the Christology of Doctrine and Covenants 93, Givens continues, "The phrasing, therefore, might be construed as indicating—in contradistinction to the council of Chalcedon's pronouncement that Jesus was fully human and fully divine at birth, and 'perfect in his divinity'—a process of total divinization, or Christ's receipt of the Father's fullness, finally achieved through the experience of mortality. . . . At the same time, Mormons believe there is no diminishment to Christ's divinity in asserting the precedence of God the Father. Mormons worship the Father, in the name of the Son, while holding both to be God." Givens, *Wrestling the Angel*, 121.

48. Ostler, *Of God and Gods*, 369.

49. As Ostler writes, "We are Christified to the extent we receive the glory of God or light and truth. We are deified to the extent that we keep the commandments of God because, to the same extent, we express the love

that is definitive of participating in the divine nature." Ostler, *Of God and Gods*, 369.

50. The fact that this new christological and anthropological vision of Jesus Christ and his relationship with humanity originated from an ancient text, the record of John, is a perfect encapsulation of how Joseph Smith pushed back against the canonical restraints of his day by turning back, in a fashion, to the Bible, an irony David Holland highlights in his *Sacred Borders: Continuing Revelation and Canonical Restraint in Early America* (New York: Oxford University Press, 2011), 143–57.

51. See, for example, R. P. C. Hanson, *The Search for the Christian Doctrine of God: The Arian Controversy, 318–381*, 2nd ed. (Ada, MI: Baker Academic, 2006), which comes in at a hefty 954 pages.

3

Choosing Divinity, Choosing Christ

Jennifer C. Lane

Joseph Smith's revelations provide a radically different starting point for thinking about Christ's nature and our relationship to him than the traditional Christian belief in the ontological divide between Creator and creation. After the loss of apostolic authority in the early Christian era, Christians were seeking to understand God and scriptures. This led to many different forms of Christianity and Christian doctrine, much like Joseph Smith encountered as a young man. The efforts of the different councils were usually in response to this variety, and the creedal decisions indicate the councils' efforts to avoid what they saw as heretical options.[1]

The classical Christian teaching of Christ being in two natures, both human and divine—known as the Definition of Chalcedon—emerged to solve a doctrinal problem about how we are saved that arose in the fifth century.[2] This belief of Christ being in two natures addressed the pressing question of how God acts for human salvation and, while not adopted by all, became the orthodox doctrine of Catholics, Eastern Orthodoxy, and many Protestants.[3] The general Christian understanding in the fifth century affirmed both that Christ was divine and that he had suffered for our sins, but holding both of these beliefs was problematized by the contemporary belief of a radical break between God—seen as the Trinity or the triune God which had always existed—and all other things that were created by God, including humanity. This struggle to define how Christ could be both human and divine, the Creator but also part of the created world, was resolved for many Christians in the Definition of Chalcedon articulated by the Council of Chalcedon.

Even as Joseph's theophany in the Sacred Grove gave a divine voice above the varied interpretations offered by different Christian groups, the subsequent revelations given to Joseph Smith about both Christ and our relationship to God provide a radically different starting point for thinking about Christ's nature and our relationship to him and to the Father. The perspective of modern-day revelation offers a dramatic change from the assumptions of an ontological divide between Creator and creation that is foundational in traditional Christian theology. At the same time, these latter-day revelations also push back at casual perceptions of a low Christology—that humans and Christ are comparable—as critics charge we believe and Church members sometimes unwittingly accept. This low Christology emphasizes our brotherhood to Christ in ways that might diminish our understanding and faith in his role as our Savior, Redeemer, and Lord.[4]

What we find in the revelations given to Joseph Smith is both a rejection of a fundamental ontological difference between God, including Christ, and all humanity and also a reaffirmation of Christ's divinity. As Latter-day Saints we believe that we, along with Christ, are spirit children of the Father, but these revelations also give additional witness to Christ's role and nature as divine, emphasizing that he was the Jehovah of the Old Testament and is our Redeeming Lord. Throughout this paper I will explore this tension between how we are similar to and different from Christ. I will explore implications from understanding that we were also in the beginning with God and were also spirit children of God, while simultaneously examining ways in which we are not like Christ by considering what it might mean to say that Christ is divine.

Development of Classical Christology

Greek thought was deeply influential in developing the early Christian ontological framework or worldview. From the assumptions of this worldview, the divine was seen as impassible—meaning that weakness, suffering, and change were not the properties of the divine.[5] Within the world of early Christianity and in the theological traditions that it generated, Christ had to be God in order to be our Savior, but he also had to be human in order to suffer. Since humanity and the divine were seen as so radically different, this created a dilemma. Thus in AD 451 the fourth ecumenical council met at Chalcedon in Asia Minor (the area we know today as Turkey) and articulated a solution known as the Definition of Chalcedon—Jesus Christ was one person "in two natures, without confusion, without change, without division, without separation."[6] This creedal solution was part of a continuing effort by the councils to clarify the way in which God should be understood. The Definition of Chalcedon remains an important part of creedal Christianity for most Christians today, including Catholics, Orthodox, and most Protestants.

Rather than approaching latter-day revelations about Christ's nature chronologically as the concepts developed, I will approach the insights from a descriptive, comparative theological point of view. With this approach, I seek to explain the implications and differences from historical Christianity that arise from these revelations about the nature of Christ that have a different premise about what it means to be divine and what it means to be human. Some of these insights derive from the scriptures we have through Joseph Smith, and other insights arise from biblical texts that we understand differently as Latter-day Saints because of Restoration scripture and teachings.

Starting Premises

To understand the Christology of The Church of Jesus Christ of Latter-day Saints as developed from the revelations given to Joseph, it is essential to keep in mind that this Christology is based on a different ontological framework than that of early Christianity. As members of the Church of Jesus Christ, we believe that Christ is divine. We also believe that Christ suffered for the sins of the world. This combination is not, however, a theological problem because there is no doctrine of divine impassibility in the revelations given to Joseph Smith. On the contrary, the revelations he received show us a God who weeps (see Moses 7:28).

Joseph Smith's revelations establish an ontological framework that does not divide Creator and created but lays out instead what might be termed stages of progression between humanity, the Son, and the Father. Unlike the doctrine of traditional Christianity, in the revelations given to Joseph Smith there is not a distinct *ousia* or "essence" or "being" that belongs to divinity and one that belongs to humanity.[7] All, both divine and human, share in the same substance or essence or being. I argue that the essential point to understand is that in the ontological framework of the revelations of Joseph Smith, this essence or being is not deterministic—in other words, God does not act as God simply as a function of his being God. It would be better to describe this ousia as agency, or the capacity to choose. God has a godly nature through choice rather than as an inevitable result of what his nature or being/ousia requires him to be.

In traditional Christianity, God's nature or being is seen as determining what he is and what he does. God the Father and the Son are good because God is good, rather than saying that because God is good he is God.[8] Understanding this can help us appreciate the confusion and even astonishment that those from other Christian traditions experience when they learn that Latter-day Saints view both Jesus and Satan as sons of God, as brothers. For those who see one's essence or ousia as deterministic, this kind of relationship is incomprehensible.

A way to think about our understanding of both God's nature and our natures is to say that for Latter-day Saints, our ousia is not deterministic. Our being or nature does not require us to act in a certain way—instead, one could say that our choices and our desires are our being. This way of understanding agency means that at the deepest level, we do what we want. The choices one makes lead to different kinds of beings or different ways of being. The choices of different agents can and will differ and so, as a result, each individual's way of being is different in respect to their degree of godliness, light, life, and love. Latter-day Saints also distinguish between states such as being premortal spirits, having a mortal embodied existence and a postmortal disembodied state, and finally receiving a resurrected state. The restored doctrine of the resurrection into degrees of glory illustrates the effect of choices on different ways of being (see Doctrine and Covenants 88:27–32). As I will demonstrate throughout this paper, the doctrine of agency allows us to see Christ's nature as God through his use of agency rather than as an ontologically given state.

The ontological framework grounded in the revelations given to Joseph Smith articulates foundational beliefs about human beings and their relationship to God the Father and God the Son. While the classical theological contrast maintains that there is a human kind of ousia that is distinct from the divine ousia, we Latter-day Saints understand both Christ and humanity (all other children of God born into mortality) to be spirit children of God the Father. Just as classical Christology speaks of Christ as being generated rather than created, Latter-day Saints understand human beings' relationship to God the Father as child to parent—he is literally the father of our spirits just as he is the father of Christ's spirit. In addition, we believe that we did not come into being with spiritual creation. Both Christ and humanity are understood to be coeternal with God the Father as "intelligence" (or the light of truth), which is not created or made (see Doctrine and Covenants 93:29).[9] We understand this intelligence to be foundational to our existence.[10] We do not believe in creation ex nihilo and thus maintain that the essence of who we are is "independent" (see Doctrine and Covenants 93:30), even though we do recognize that God places us in a sphere in which we use our agency. This helps us understand how God can create us spiritually and physically without determining how we will use our agency.[11]

These fundamental premises that both Christ and human beings are spiritually begotten by God the Father and that both Christ and human beings are coeternal with God the Father as intelligences set up an ontological framework in which the classical dichotomy of divine and human, Creator and created, does not apply.[12] In addition to confusing those not of our faith, this understanding of both Christ and human beings as offspring of God—while at different places along a continuum of spiritual development—can sometimes cause a problem for Latter-day Saints. What is it that we mean when we say that Christ is God when we do not see him on the other side of the gulf between the Creator and all that is created? We leave behind the idea of a divine ousia that is radically different from our own as created beings, but do we simultaneously risk leaving behind the understanding of Christ as divine? One will, in fact, sometimes hear Christ referred to as "our elder brother." This term is doctrinally true for Latter-day Saints, but it can be emphasized in ways so as to distort the fundamental doctrine of the Church.[13]

Just as for the early Christians, the ontological framework of the doctrine of The Church of Jesus Christ of Latter-day Saints has serious implications for soteriology, or the study of salvation. While we do not assert that Christ is different from us as a function of his distinctively divine nature, we do assert that Christ is and was perfect and that he is and was part of the Godhead. Although we are also spirit children of the Father, we are not perfect and are not God. Christ is. We are saved by faith in him that leads to repentance, baptism, the gift of the Holy Ghost, and enduring to the end.[14] We are saved *through* Christ.

This is where the interesting question arises for Latter-day Saints. If Christ is also a spirit child of the Father, how is he different from humanity in such a way that allows him to be the Savior? The traditional Christian answer is found in the Nicene Creed that defined the Trinity: Christ and the Father are one because they are *homoousios*, "of the same essence or being." The Restoration answer to this question goes directly to the issue of what it means to be divine for Latter-day Saints. Based on the revelations given to Joseph Smith, Christ's unity with the Father comes not from their shared ontological essence of being "God" but from unity of will or purpose. This unity that we understand to comprise the relationship of the Godhead can be understood to come from agency, not a divine ousia.

As Latter-day Saints, we can explain that being divine is a choice, not a given. Being divine is a way of being that is chosen, not a way of being that that happens to you without your participation. It is not an unchosen characteristic, something that you are or are not, or something that is a given or compulsory. This perspective not only is key to clarifying the Christology of the Church of Jesus Christ but also has serious implications for its soteriology. The inviolate principle of our doctrine, based on the foundational revelations given to Joseph Smith, is one of agency, that we receive what we are willing to receive (see Doctrine and Covenants 88:32). Christ is God because he chooses light, life, and truth and thus participates in the kind of life that God the Father experiences, not because he is part of an absolute principle or essence of light, life, and truth.[15]

Christ as Human and Divine

Based on these premises, I will explore what we as Latter-day Saints mean when we say that Christ is God and what we mean when we say that Christ is human. As we have seen, these are not radically distinct categories for Latter-day Saints as they are in the classical christological formula of the creeds. The problem for us is not how to combine God and man in the person of Christ but how to separate God and man. For traditional Christians, there is such a tremendous gap between Christ as God and humans as God's creation that the Definition of Chalcedon was needed to articulate how Christ could be both God and human. Building from the revelations given to Joseph Smith that some part of us has always existed as intelligence and that we were also premortally existent children of God, as was Christ, we face the challenge of explaining how we as humans are *distinct* from Christ. We need to consider what it means for Christ to be divine in a way that is distinct from other spirit children of Heavenly Parents.

To clarify how it is that Christ is both divine and human, the distinctive Latter-day Saint understanding of God as an actor or agent rather than an absolute principle will be essential. I will now review the scriptural points that inform our teaching of Christ as God and Savior, starting with the issues grappled with in the early creeds, then returning to a discussion of Christ's premortal state to more fully explore what might separate Christ from all other children of Heavenly Parents. With that I will further consider Christ's conception and birth and his mortal condition, along with what we know about his premortal existence. My intention is to explain what it means for him to be God, the only one capable of offering his expiatory suffering, death, and Resurrection to allow us to receive his nature and become as he is.

Christ's mortal ministry

In the Definition of Chalcedon, the biblical account of Christ's perfect life is attributed to his divine nature, just as the biblical account of Christ's weakness is attributed to his human nature.[16] The formula of the two natures is a meaningful solution given the premise that the divine and human have a different ontological status. Within this ontological framework, the doctrine of the two natures explains for many Christians how Christ could be God to save us, but man to suffer for us. The doctrine of the Church of Jesus Christ, however, does not have this dichotomy. Instead, our soteriology insists that Christ had to be mortal rather than immortal so that he could have weakness and the capacity to die. But, while mortal, he had to suffer as God, that is to say, he had to suffer beyond the capacity of mortal suffering: "He shall suffer temptations, and pain of body, hunger, thirst, and fatigue, even more than man can suffer, except it be unto death; for behold, blood cometh from every pore, so great shall be his anguish for the wickedness and the abominations of his people" (Mosiah 3:7).

One of the classic examples of this kind of divine suffering is the Lord's statement to Joseph Smith that is recorded in Doctrine and Covenants 19: "For behold, I, God, have suffered these things for all, that they might not suffer if they would repent; But if they would not repent they must suffer even as I; Which suffering caused myself, even God, the greatest of all, to tremble because of pain, and to bleed at every pore, and to suffer both body and spirit—and would that I might not drink the bitter cup, and shrink—Nevertheless, glory be to the Father, and I partook and finished my preparations unto the children of men" (19:16–19). Here the Savior emphasizes that he suffered as God. Unlike the traditional understanding from Chalcedon in which only the humanity of Christ could suffer because his divinity was impassible, the direct revelation of the Savior to Joseph Smith emphasizes his integrated suffering on our behalf.

Book of Mormon passages emphasize how Christ's suffering had to be unique and underscore that it is Jehovah, the premortal Christ, a member of the Godhead, who comes down to suffer in a way that transcends human capacity to suffer in order to redeem us: "For it is expedient that there should be a great and last sacrifice; yea, not a sacrifice of man, neither of beast, neither of any manner of fowl; for it shall not be a human sacrifice; but it must be an infinite and eternal sacrifice," and "this is the whole meaning of the law, every whit pointing to that great and last sacrifice; and that great and last sacrifice will be the Son of God, yea, infinite and eternal" (Alma 34:10, 14). Christ was mortal in that he could suffer and die, but he was also God so his suffering could be an infinite and eternal offering on our behalf to ransom us from the consequences of our sin.

The biblical account of Christ's life recounts his limits in ability and knowledge. As the centuries continued and Christianity spread throughout the Greco-Roman world, these biblical texts became difficult for Christians to reconcile with their understanding of God, which had been influenced by Greek philosophical thought. The ideas of Plato were widely accepted in this broader world and, based on these assumptions that undergirded the ontological framework of early Christianity, weakness could not be attributed to an omnipotent divine being.[17] In line with these basic shared assumptions of Platonic dualism in the early Christian world were assumptions that the body was a prison to the spirit, something that was less than divine. The creedal solution was that the human Jesus could be weak or suffer, but not the divine Christ. The solution of the Council of Chalcedon, as we saw in the Definition of Chalcedon, was to describe Jesus Christ as one person in two natures. Weakness is part of his human nature, but not his divine nature, which was understood as impassible, not moved by the passions.[18] Because the ontological position of the restored Church of Jesus Christ does not follow this characterization of the divine and the accompanying dichotomy between the human and the divine, it is not a problem for Latter-day Saints to talk about Jesus Christ, as God, suffering or experiencing pain or temptations. In our understanding, the unified experience of Jesus Christ makes our salvation possible.[19]

From the scriptural record, it would seem as though Jesus Christ was imperfect or weak with regard to his knowledge. Latter-day Saints believe that human beings have what is known as a veil drawn over their understanding that makes it impossible to remember their premortal existence. Even though Jesus Christ's spirit or soul was that of premortal Jehovah, the Creator of the world, there seems to have been a process in which he gained knowledge of his identity. He "increased in wisdom and stature, and in favour with God and man" (Luke 2:52) and "learned . . . obedience by the things which he suffered" (Hebrews 5:8). This process of increasing, learning, and being made perfect is not read by Latter-day Saints to mean that Christ had moral flaws or sinned. In Doctrine and Covenants 93, we learn that "that he received not of the fulness at the first, but received grace for grace, until he received a fulness; he received not of the fullness at first, but continued from grace to grace, . . . until he received a fulness; and thus he was called the Son of God, because he received not of the fulness at the first" (93:12–14). This might be described as a progression in perfection.

Even though Latter-day Saints understand the mortal Christ to have been subject to weakness and suffering, we do not believe that he ceased to be God in his character and agency. Because Christ is seen as an agent with genuine choices, Latter-day Saints maintain that Christ could have sinned but did not. In the Book of Mormon we read that he "suffereth temptation, and yieldeth not to the temptation" (Mosiah 15:5). Because of this experience of temptation, Jesus Christ is in a position to intercede and assist all others. As is written in Hebrews, "Ours is not a high priest unable to sympathize with our weaknesses, but one who, because of his likeness to us, has been tested every way, only without sin" (Hebrews 4:15 New English Bible).

Jesus Christ's full participation in the mortal experience, while remaining without sin, is key to understanding the doctrine of salvation in the Church of Jesus Christ. One of the most important restoration passages on the passibility of God and its role in the economy of salvation is found in the Book of Mormon: "And he shall go forth, suffering pains and afflictions and temptations of every kind; and this that the word might be fulfilled which saith that he will take upon him the pains and the sicknesses of his people" (Alma 7:11).

Through his mortal choices to obey, Christ continued the unity of purpose that existed with the Father in his premortal existence.[20] This submission to the Father can be seen in Christ's statement in John 6: "I came down from heaven, not to do mine own will, but the will of him that sent me" (John 6:38). For Latter-day Saints the passage in John 8 expresses the eternal relationship of the Father and the Son: "I do always those things that please him" (John 8:29). The soteriological framework of this statement is matched by the key passage in the Book of Mormon in which Christ explains his gospel, saying, "I came into the world to do the will of my Father, because my Father sent me" (3 Nephi 27:13). This willingness that "not my will, but thine, be done" is seen by Latter-day Saints as the continuation of an obedience of Son to Father that existed from the beginning.[21]

The premortal Christ

In traditional Christianity, the persons of the Trinity are seen as separate persons, but they are also believed to share a divine nature that, as God, is radically different from all creation, including all created human beings. In addition to the concept of *homoousios* established at the Council of Nicaea, the Council of Chalcedon emphasized that there is a distinction between the human Jesus and the Son of God, the Second Person of the Trinity.

Latter-day Saints understand the Father and the Son as distinct perfect spirits, both part of the Godhead even before Christ's incarnation. There is a unity within the Godhead, but the nature of God, the Godhead, is not seen as radically different from all creation or as the source of all creation, the existence of everything else. Likewise, these separate persons of the Godhead are also understood as separate personages. In addition, we believe that God the Father has a perfect, glorified body of flesh and bones (see Doctrine and Covenants 130:22). After his Resurrection Christ also received a separate, glorified, and immortal body, but before his incarnation and Resurrection he did not have the same kind of embodied existence as the Father. This is a clear sense in which we understand Christ to be like the Father, but not the same as the Father.

Human beings also existed as spirit children of God the Father before mortality; this spiritual kinship establishes a sense of potential and capacity to become like God that transcends any sense of theosis or deification found in traditional Christianity. In the traditional understanding of the Trinity, only Christ is understood as spiritually begotten of the Father.[22] These latter-day revelations about all human beings existing premortally are extraordinary in the potential they suggest is inherent in each child of God while also singling out the premortal Christ as the only one being "like unto God" (Abraham 3:24). It seems that Christ's choice to obey the Father and thereby live in complete unity with his light and love allowed him to receive the Father's glory and power in a unique way in the premortal world. This unique premortal status of Christ can be seen in the descriptions of him as the Firstborn, the Word of God, the Creator, Jehovah, and the Savior.

The first of these terms, *the Firstborn*, is at the same time perhaps the most enigmatic and the most significant. Christ revealed in Doctrine and Covenants 93:21 that "I was in the beginning with the Father, and am the Firstborn" (Doctrine and Covenants 93:21). It is not clear exactly what this means. We are told in verse 23 that we "were also in the beginning with the Father," and so Christ being the Firstborn is usually taken to include temporal precedence as a spirit, following the Latter-day Saint understanding of Hebrews 1:6, describing Christ as "the firstbegotten." In addition to emphasizing temporal precedence, the title may also suggest his distinctive nature as a Spirit who was so identical to the Father in purpose and will that Christ could say, "he that hath seen me hath seen the Father" (John 14:9). This similarity is suggested by the passage in Colossians describing Christ as "the image of the invisible God, the firstborn of every creature" (Colossians 1:15).

This sense of Christ as the Firstborn might mean that he was the first to fully receive the fullness of the Father. For Latter-day Saints, this is a particularly important title because all those who inherit the celestial kingdom as joint-heirs with Christ are referred to as the Church of the Firstborn.[23] The passage in section 93 verse 21 in which Christ declares, "I was in the beginning with the Father, and am the Firstborn," directly explains our potential to receive the celestial glory through our receiving him, being born again through faith in him and the covenants and ordinances of the gospel: "And all those who are begotten through me are partakers of the glory of the same, and are the church of the Firstborn" (Doctrine and Covenants 93:22). A critical part of Joseph Smith's teachings of Christ's role in the Father's plan is that through him we can be born again, begotten sons and daughters unto God in the fullest sense in which he is the Son of God: "we heard the voice bearing record that he is the Only Begotten of the Father—That by him, and through him, and of him, the worlds are and were created, and the inhabitants thereof are begotten sons and daughters unto God" (Doctrine and Covenants 76:23–24).

The description of Christ as the Word of God in John 1 is accepted and used by Latter-day Saints, but it does not have the same resonance or meaning that it would have had in the thought world of Middle Platonism or that it would to other Christians today. Christ is not seen as an emanation of God that is distinct from humanity. Instead, we can see his connection with the Father and his acting as an agent of the Father as a product of his agency, his choice to accept and act upon the Father's will, rather than his essence. In the Book of Moses, God the Father refers to Christ as his word. "And by the word of my power, have I created them, which is mine Only Begotten Son, who is full of grace and truth" (Moses 1:32). This directly ties in to our doctrine that Christ is the Creator, under the direction of the Father.[24] In the creation accounts found in the Books of Abraham and Moses, Christ as the Creator is portrayed as an agent of the Father and is described as being "like unto God" and the "Only Begotten."[25]

So, while Latter-day Saints do maintain that all human beings are literally spirit children of God the Father, the premortal Christ had a divine quality giving him the relationship of a God to all of his spirit brothers and sisters. Jesus Christ is understood by Latter-day Saints as the premortal Jehovah. The passage in John 8:58, "Before Abraham was, I am," is understood by Latter-day Saints as Jesus Christ's self-identification with Yahweh, the God of the Old Testament. Additionally, Christ identifies himself in a post-Resurrection visit recorded in the Book of Mormon, saying, "I am he that gave the law, and I am he who covenanted with my people Israel" (3 Nephi 15:5).

Latter-day Saints not only understand the premortal Christ as Creator and Revealer but also describe him as Savior since he was the "Lamb . . . slain from the foundation of the world" (Moses 7:47).[26] Here again it is important to note that Christ was the divine Savior through the exercise of his agency. In the Book of Moses the Father describes his choice of Christ as our Savior: "my Beloved Son, which was my Beloved and Chosen from the beginning, said unto me—Father, thy will be done, and the glory be thine forever" (Moses 4:2). While having Christ be our Savior was the Father's plan, in the council in heaven Christ used his agency to accept the Father's will that he was to make salvation possible for all others, saying, "Here I am, send me" (Abraham 3:27). Christ was willing to be "the Lamb slain from the foundation of the world" (Revelation 13:8).

To summarize my articulation of our belief regarding the difference between the premortal Jesus Christ and all human beings who also existed premortally, all others did not make the same choices and thereby do not have the same character, glory, and power as Jesus Christ.[27] We learn in Doctrine and Covenants section 93 that "man was also in the beginning with God" (Doctrine and Covenants 93:29). But being premortal offspring of God or even coeternal with God does not make one a God. Agency implies choice, and what scripture we do have about the premortal world indicates that Christ's choices were distinctive. In section 93, after clarifying that intelligence, or the light of truth, was not created, the role of agency is emphasized: "All truth is independent in that sphere in which God has placed it, to act for itself, as all intelligence also; otherwise there is no existence. Behold, here is the agency of man, and here is the condemnation of man; because that which was from the beginning is plainly manifest unto them, and they receive not the light. And every man whose spirit receiveth not the light is under condemnation" (Doctrine and Covenants 93:30–32).

In Doctrine and Covenants 93 we read, "That which was from the beginning was plainly manifest unto them, and they receive not the light." We usually read this passage in relation to the concepts in the Prologue of the Gospel of John, which refers to how people responded to Christ in his mortal ministry.[28] However, the phrase about those whose spirits "receiveth not the light" being under condemnation is set in a discussion of the premortal world. It might seem that this would just refer to those sons of perdition who rebelled and followed Satan, but I would suggest that we use this passage as a way to think about ourselves in relation to Christ. This interpretation might give us a way to understand what makes us different from Christ in how we used our agency premortally. "Behold, here is the agency of man, and here is the condemnation of man" (93:31). We should not have to see our limited light and truth, our lesser intelligence, in the premortal world as something that was done to us or the way we were made. We had our agency and we chose the light and truth that we wanted to receive. Those who come into mortality did choose to accept the Father's plan to give his children a chance to repent and grow and receive more light, but that acceptance necessitated a plan of redemption—a plan that enabled us to move from the limited condition of light and truth in which we existed and to overcome through the intercession of Christ and our choice to have faith in and accept him. Herein lies the difference between Christ, who is the light of the world, and those that received not the fullness of the light as did Christ.[29]

Much of this view of Christ and human beings as agents that choose is different than the Christology of historical Christianity. To connect it with traditional christological and soteriological discussion, one could say that, like the Arians, members of the Church of Jesus Christ see the unity of God the Father and the Son as coming from the perfection of Christ's will rather than from divine essence or substance. While we would use the Arian term *homoiousios*, being *like* God rather than being "of one substance with the Father" (*homoousios*), for us this does not result in Christ being a creature (that is, not divine) because we do not believe in an ontologically distinct divine substance or essence.[30] This is the core difference between the formulations of classical Christology and the doctrine that follows from the revelations given to Joseph Smith.

The classical Christian theological premise that God's nature is infinite and human nature is finite means that explaining how Christ became human is the great mystery and wonder that the creeds try to articulate. As Latter-day Saints, we can affirm, with the Council of Nicaea, both that Christ eternally coexisted with the Father and that he was generated but not created and did not have a beginning; however, this alone cannot make Christ God for members of The Church of Jesus Christ of Latter-day Saints because it does not distinguish Christ from the rest of Heavenly Father's children who likewise are understood to have been "also in the beginning with God. Intelligence, or the light of truth, was not created or made, neither indeed can be" (Doctrine and Covenants 93:29). I believe that for us divinity lies in agency, not essence. Our potential as the children of God is to become even as he is, but that potential in itself does not make us divine. Understanding Christ as the premortal Jehovah, the one "like unto God," while we are all children of God, points us to unique choices on his part.

The incarnation

Much as they do regarding the premortal existence of Christ, the revelations of Joseph Smith present a view of the incarnation that is different from that of traditional Christianity. We do not say that the divine assumed humanity because this implies a dichotomy between the human and the divine. We do, however, maintain that the spirit (or soul, in traditional terminology) that entered into Christ's body was the premortal Word of God (see Moses 1:32).[31]

Based on the revelations given to Joseph Smith, the framework in which Latter-day Saints talk about the incarnation, as with the premortal existence of Christ, parallels the experience of other children of God. Thus, again, the challenge is to articulate in what way

Christ is distinctive and divine for Latter-day Saints. Christ's spirit was joined with a physical body just as Latter-day Saints believe all spirit offspring of God are in their earth life. The difference between the incarnation and the experience of all other spirit children of God entering mortality is that Latter-day Saints believe that Christ was literally the Son of God. When Latter-day Saints talk about Jesus Christ being the Only Begotten Son of God, they are not speaking metaphorically; he is understood as having the properties and powers of both a mortal mother and an immortal, perfect, and embodied Father. He was conceived by the Virgin Mary and begotten by God the Father in a process that the Bible and the Book of Mormon describe as being overshadowed by the Holy Ghost.[32] The language of *The Living Christ* emphasizes that Christ was "the Only Begotten Son in the flesh."[33]

Having a divine, immortal father and a mortal mother, Jesus Christ had a distinctive mortal existence. For Latter-day Saints this distinctiveness is not a soteriological problem as it would be in a traditional model. "That which is not assumed is not healed" is the classic statement of this need for Christ to be fully human as well as fully divine—thus the Council of Chalcedon's formula of one person in two natures. Because God was not understood to have any physical quality, the physical dimension of Christ's incarnation was understood to have come from Mary. This doctrine that Christ's body, his humanity and physical nature, is entirely from Mary is more fully developed later in the Middle Ages.[34]

Instead, in the doctrine of the Church of Jesus Christ, the blending of Mary's mortality and Heavenly Father's immortality is understood to provide Christ's capacity to accomplish the Atonement and the Resurrection. He needed to have a capacity to suffer and die for others and then to live again, but other than these extraordinary and essential capacities, we do not consider his mortal condition to have been different from other mortals. He knew the experience of pain, sickness, weakness, and temptation. Our understanding of what it means for Christ to have been divine preserves his ability to choose how to respond to choices and temptation rather than believing that he had to be good by definition because of his divinity, his divine being, or ousia. Christ's being the offspring of Deity is not understood to have required him to have made perfect choices or to have prevented him from physical weakness and suffering.

Christology and atonement

For Latter-day Saints, Christ, being sinless and the Son of God, literally suffered for the sins of all humanity. Since for us there is no distinction between the divine and human in him, we say that *he* suffered, not that his human nature suffered. He took upon himself, with a capacity that no one else had, "the iniquity of us all" (Isaiah 53:6).[35]

Latter-day Saints believe that Christ at some level knew all human sin, pain, and sorrow as a premortal God, but at the same time assert that only as the incarnate Son of God could he experience it fully. An important passage in the Book of Mormon notes that "the Spirit knoweth all things; nevertheless the Son of God suffereth according to the flesh that he might take upon him the sins of his people" (Alma 7:13). While Christ as a premortal God knew all things, there seems to have been an abstraction to this knowledge. His embodiment completed his knowledge. His experiential acquaintance with mortal weakness, suffering, and sin became part of the intercession of redemption.[36]

No other being could suffer for the sins of another. As God incarnate, infinite and eternal, the perfect Son of God, Christ could take upon himself the sins of all of Heavenly Father's spirit children.[37] He took our place. In the Book of Mormon we are told that "God himself should come down among the children of men (Mosiah 13:34) "and shall redeem his people" (Mosiah 15:1). This identification of the one who suffered with God is consistent with the revelation in the Doctrine and Covenants in which Christ reveals that "I, God, have suffered these things for all. . . . Which suffering caused myself, even God, the greatest of all, to tremble because of pain, and to bleed at every pore, and to suffer both body and spirit" (Doctrine and Covenants 19:16, 18).[38] For Latter-day Saints, this Christological understanding of God made flesh does not imply a separation of divine and human natures because *in* Christ's unity lies the means of salvation.

The view of the incarnation found in The Church of Jesus Christ of Latter-day Saints might be compared with the *Logos-sarx* (Word-flesh) Christology of Apollinarianism, a fourth-century form of one-nature Christology in which the Logos took the place of the soul of the man Jesus. It was problematic from a soteriological standpoint because there was no assumption of a human mind and in the classical christological model that which is not assumed is not healed or saved.[39] The model of soteriology based on the revelations of Joseph Smith, however, is different because we do not see redemption coming from the assumption of something "human" that is radically other, but rather from *all* of Christ "taking upon himself" the sins, weaknesses, and sicknesses of humanity.

Parallel to the process of his taking upon himself our sins, the Book of Mormon describes Christ as taking "upon him death, that he may loose the bands of death which bind his people" (Alma 7:12). To do this he needed to be able to suffer and die, but he also needed to be able to suffer vicariously beyond mortal ability and to give up his life, not have it taken from him.[40] This required a being who was both mortal and divine, without having to separate these paradoxes as is done in traditional Christianity. Jesus Christ was a mortal, the son of Mary, and therefore he was able to suffer and die. Simultaneously, we understand him to have a physical inheritance from a glorified, immortal, and embodied Father that allowed him, as a God, to suffer and die so as to take the suffering and death of all others upon himself.[41] Latter-day Saints believe that only the Son of God in the flesh could suffer and die in this way. Likewise only the Son of God could rise again as a resurrected, glorified, immortal being with power to lift others from the grave. Only he could redeem humanity.

Conclusion

Christ is distinct from humanity because of his agency and because he is the "Only Begotten Son in the flesh," but we do not need to believe that he was radically different in terms of his ontological makeup as a premortal being. All human beings are spirit offspring of God, and while all have not used their agency as well as Christ, our belief is that all can receive the fullness of the Father, even as Christ as received the fullness. As Paul stated, our hope is that we may become "heirs of God, and joint-heirs with Christ" (Romans 8:17).

When we see being divine as a choice, we then realize why this inheritance must be chosen rather than given as an irresistible grace. This is where the focus on salvation through faith and obedience becomes operative. In the Doctrine and Covenants we are told by Christ that "if you keep my commandments you shall receive of his fulness, and be glorified in me as I am in the Father; therefore, I say unto you, you shall receive grace for grace" (Doctrine and Covenants 93:20). Out of context, this focus on salvation through obedience sounds like we are asked merely to imitate Christ and thus save ourselves. It is, however, essential to note that in the scripture of the Church of Jesus Christ that came through the revelations of Joseph Smith, "my commandments" consistently refers to believing in Christ and coming unto him.[42] We believe that we are saved by obedience to the laws and ordinances of the gospel, the first of which is faith in the Lord Jesus Christ (see Articles of Faith 1:4).[43]

Christology and soteriology are inseparable. We do believe in obedience because this implies agency, but we do not believe that our obedience alone will save us. Christ's perfect obedience was constant; ours will develop through our faith in him and choosing to receive his power and grace through making and keeping covenants. His perfection and obedience was a choice and a gift to us. Christ is "the resurrection, and the life" (John 11:25); others are resurrected through him. Christ is the way, the truth, and the life, the light and life of the world; others are saved through faith in his name. Christ is the

Firstborn, but he declares that we can be born again: "All those who are begotten through me are partakers of the glory of the same, and are the church of the Firstborn" (Doctrine and Covenants 93:22).[44]

As we choose the path of faith in Jesus Christ, repentance, and making and keeping covenants, our unity with God will also become a unity of purpose and will. Seeing divinity as a matter of choice rather than of essence, we recognize that we can also choose to be submissive to the will of the Father, choosing to trust in Christ and follow him. Our hope is articulated in the intercessory prayer offered in John 17: "That they all may be one; as thou, Father, art in me, and I in thee, that they also may be one in us. . . . And the glory which thou gavest me I have given them; that they may be one, even as we are one: I in them, and thou in me, that they may be made perfect in one" (John 17:21–23). Our hope as Latter-day Saints is in Christ's oneness with the Father, not because of a distinctive divine essence, but because of divine choices, a divine way of being. Because he was always one with the Father, we believe that he has prepared the way for all to be "perfect in one" through him if we desire.

Notes

1. See Jennifer C. Lane, "The Creeds and Councils," in *The Life and Teachings of the New Testament Apostles: From the Day of Pentecost through the Apocalypse*, ed. Richard Neitzel Holzapfel and Thomas A. Wayment (Salt Lake City: Deseret Book, 2010), 299–329.

2. Surveys of the early christological debates can also be found in John McIntyre's *The Shape of Christology: Studies in the Doctrine of the Person of Christ*, 2nd ed. (Edinburgh: T&T Clark, 1998); Roch A. Kereszty's *Jesus Christ: Fundamentals of Christology*, ed. J. Stephen Maddux (New York: Alba House, 1991); and Gerald O'Collins's *Christology: A Biblical, Historical, and Systematic Study of Jesus* (Oxford: Oxford University Press, 1995). A classic treatment of some aspects of this period is J. N. D. Kelly, *Early Christian Creeds*, 3rd ed. (New York: David McKay, 1972).

3. The Oriental Orthodox Churches did not accept the Definition of Chalcedon; these include many Christians in Egypt and Syria and other Eastern Christians. As Robert C. Gregg and Dennis E. Groh have noted, a focus on soteriology was not unique to Chalcedon but had also been central to the concerns of the early Arians in the Trinitarian debates of the fourth century. See Gregg and Groh, *Early Arianism: A View of Salvation* (Philadelphia: Fortress Press, 1981).

4. While it is doctrinally correct, it is significant that the term *Elder Brother* is not found among all the titles given for Christ in "The Living Christ: The Testimony of the Apostles," *Ensign*, April 2000, 2. The title page of the Book of Mormon emphasizes its role in "convincing Jew and Gentile that Jesus is the Christ, the Eternal God."

5. In many post-Enlightenment Christologies these premises have been reevaluated, but so has the belief that Jesus Christ was divine and that he suffered vicariously for the sins of the world. For a broad overview of this issue, see John Macquarrie, *Jesus Christ in Modern Thought* (London: SCM Press, 1990). A survey of recent theological approaches to Christology can be found in McIntyre's *Shape of Christology*.

6. From the "Definition of Chalcedon," in *Documents of the Christian Church*, ed. Henry Bettenson, 2nd ed. (London: Oxford University Press, 1963), 51. As mentioned earlier, the Oriental Orthodox Churches did not accept the Definition of Chalcedon. For clarity of explanation I will focus on this traditional and widely influential formula.

7. I am using the term *ousia* in its philosophical sense as the essence or ground of being from which everything else will result.

8. The question of how God's creation can then be evil becomes a philosophical problem, but the initial assumption about God's nature being good is determined by the assumption of a particular nature or being that is uniquely godly and good and radically different from human beings. Richard J. Mouw, an evangelical theologian very friendly toward the Church, commented that Latter-day Saints "singing Christ-adoring hymns" is internally inconsistent with a belief "that God is on the same ontological level as the human beings he has created." To his mind as an orthodox theologian, there is a "vast ontological gap between Creator and

creature." Richard J. Mouw, "Mormons Approaching Orthodoxy," *First Things* (May 2016): 48. He articulates the traditional belief that "God and human beings are of different orders of 'being'" (44).

9. Givens discusses the term *co-equal* in the King Follett discourse as having the original sense of being "of equal age." Terryl Givens, *When Souls Had Wings: Premortal Existence in Western Thought* (New York: Oxford University Press, 2010), 219.

10. See Doctrine and Covenants 93:30 and Abraham, chapter 3. There are differences of interpretation concerning the few points that we know about our existence before our spiritual birth. Many Latter-day Saints will see this intelligence as differing in degree from one individual to another. Others suggest that differentiation began as we were born as spirits. In either case, this intelligence that seems to be the essence of who we are as beings was "not created or made" (93:29).

11. The full passage reads, "Man was also in the beginning with God. Intelligence, or the light of truth, was not created or made, neither indeed can be. All truth is independent in that sphere in which God has placed it, to act for itself, as all intelligence also; otherwise there is no existence" (Doctrine and Covenants 93:29–30). This is central to our position on agency.

12. While the understanding that all human beings have a component of their being as uncreated intelligence is a standard interpretation of the passages in Abraham 3 and Doctrine and Covenants section 93, other explanations question the degree to which there was individual consciousness within this uncreated intelligence or explore the question of how to distinguish intelligences from spirits. See Paul Nolan Hyde, "Intelligences," in *Encyclopedia of Mormonism* (New York: Macmillan, 1992), 692–93. See also Givens, *When Souls Had Wings*, 217.

13. Misunderstandings of both the Christology and soteriology of the Church of Jesus Christ from within and without have frequently occurred. For members of the Church, there has long been a folk Christology and soteriology not taught by Church leaders that presents ways of thinking about one's own life and the need to be perfect to be saved. This way of thinking emphasizes that in his earthly existence Christ was just like us, having

the same tripartite being of intelligence, spirit, and physical body, and it reasons that Christ obeyed the Father and was saved and, since human beings are just like him—meaning the same kinds of beings—complete and perfect obedience is our only hope as well.

Doctrinally, it is true that we don't believe in total depravity or the bondage of the will, and so theoretically we could obey God the Father just as Christ did. The Book of Mormon gives an important insight into how Christ's Atonement delivers all from the effects of Adam's transgression and allows us to be agents with genuine choices (see 2 Nephi 2:26–29). Practically, however, as we often come to learn through great personal disappointment, it is true that we don't always obey, and so being saved through our works isn't a viable option.

A clarified understanding of doctrinal Christology can help in arriving at a more doctrinal soteriology. In other words, Latter-day Saints believe that salvation comes through the intervention of a God. The more we are grounded in the doctrine of Christ as taught in the Book of Mormon, the more we realize how much we do need Christ and that we can have faith and hope based on his redeeming power that leads us to want to repent and be humble disciples, "relying wholly upon the merits of him who is mighty to save" (2 Nephi 31:19).

14. On the relationship between faith and repentance, the clearest statement is found in Helaman 14:13: "And if ye believe on his name ye will repent of all your sins, that thereby ye may have remission of them through his merits." Another expression of the organic relationship of faith, repentance, baptism, and the gift of the Holy Ghost in Church teaching is found in Moroni 8:25–26: "And the first fruits of repentance is baptism." This passage continues on with a discussion of how this brings the reception of the Holy Ghost and enduring to the end.

15. My reading of the Christology of the Church of Jesus Christ is finally a nonessentialist position. Or, one might say, the essence is choice. As Latter-day Saints we say that God lives, not that God is.

16. In the *Tome of Flavian* that influenced this Definition, Leo describes it thus: "Each nature performs its proper functions in communion with the other; the Word performs what pertains to the Word, flesh what pertains

to the flesh." Bishop Leo of Rome, "The Tome of Leo," in *Documents of the Christian Church*, 51.

17. The docetic position that would have denied these attributes to the person of Jesus Christ was, however, ruled out because of soteriological and scriptural considerations.

18. For an introduction to the doctrine of the impassibility of God in early Christianity, see Joseph M. Hallman, "Impassibility," in *Encyclopedia of Early Christianity*, ed. Everett Ferguson, 2nd ed. (New York: Garland, 1997), 566–67.

19. We take literally Paul's assertion that the premortal Christ, "being in the form of God, . . . took upon him the form of a servant, and was made in the likeness of men: And being found in fashion as a man, he humbled himself, and became obedient unto death, even the death of the cross" (Philippians 2:6–8). We learn in the Book of Mormon that "the Lord Omnipotent who reigneth, who was, and is from all eternity to all eternity, shall come down from heaven among the children of men, and shall dwell in a tabernacle of clay" (Mosiah 3:5). This condescension to "dwell in a tabernacle of clay" is, from a soteriological point of view, an important part of our Christology. The incarnation is referred to in the Book of Mormon as "the condescension of God." The angel asks Nephi, "Knowest thou the condescension of God?" (1 Nephi 11:16). He later explains, telling Nephi, "Behold, the virgin whom thou seest is the mother of the Son of God, after the manner of flesh" (1 Nephi 11:18). The earliest manuscript records this passage as "the mother of God after the manner of the flesh." Royal Skousen, *The Book of Mormon: The Earliest Text* (New Haven: Yale University Press, 2009), 28.

20. This is the sense in which Book of Mormon prophets describe him as the same yesterday, today, and forever (see Mormon 9:7–11; Moroni 10:18–19). In the Book of Mormon this unity of will is seen in Christ's statement that he came into the world "to do the will, both of the Father and of the Son— of the Father because of me, and of the Son because of my flesh" (3 Nephi 1:14). The same theme of bringing his flesh into obedience with his spirit, just as his spirit is in obedience to God the Father can be found in this extremely intricate passage in the Book of Mormon: "because he dwelleth in flesh he shall be called the Son of God, and having subjected the flesh to

the will of the Father, being the Father and the Son—The Father, because he was conceived by the power of God; and the Son, because of the flesh; thus becoming the Father and the Son—And they are one God, yea, the very Eternal Father of heaven and of earth. And thus the flesh becoming subject to the Spirit, or the Son to the Father, being one God, suffereth temptation, and yieldeth not to the temptation" (Mosiah 15:2–5).

21. See Moses 4:2; Matthew 26:42; Mark 14:36; Luke 22:42.

22. In traditional Christianity this idea of Christ being begotten of the Father does not mean that there was ever a time in which he was not—he is seen as eternally spiritually begotten of the Father, always existing as part of the Trinity, but existing in a relationship of being the Son of God.

23. Hebrews 12:23; Doctrine and Covenants 76:92–94. On being joint-heirs with Christ, see Romans 8:14–17. While many Latter-day Saints read this passage as referring to our status as spirit children of God, I believe that it is more accurate to read the text as describing the adoption of covenant and being born again through Christ, becoming his sons and daughters. On this see Mosiah 5:6–8.

24. This role as Creator is elaborated on in some length in Doctrine and Covenants section 93 and John, chapter 1.

25. "There stood one among them that was like unto God, and he said unto those who were with him: We will go down, for there is space there" (Abraham 3:24); "by the Son I created them, which is mine Only Begotten" (Moses 1:33).

26. Here the connection between Christology and soteriology becomes very clear. We believe that salvation comes "with the precious blood of Christ," a being who "was foreordained before the foundation of the world" (1 Peter 1:19–20).

27. Since choices varied in the premortal existence, the degree of light and truth, or intelligence, of spirits also varied (see Abraham 3:18–19). Among these different agents with different degrees of intelligence there stood only "one among them that was like unto God" (Abraham 3:24). It might be argued that these different degrees are products of a different kind of essence. From this perspective, Christ's being the Firstborn and the one that "was like unto God" might suggest a unique generation. While this

would be an understandable way to account for the difference between his character and ours, we do not have any data to support this. In fact, I believe that the idea of a special kind of generation of the Son may be fundamentally problematic. The principle of agency is paramount for Latter-day Saints, and thus we do not agree with Augustine's position in the Pelagian debates. Augustine does, however, make it clear that to the extent that creation is seen as being ex nihilo, the disposition of individuals will ultimately point back to their Creator. The Latter-day Saint understanding of our essence (if you will) being intelligence or light and truth, which is not created or made, means that at our core, we are not the product of a Creator. If our choices and the degree of light that we receive are our own, we must assume the same to be true of Christ.

28. "He was in the world, and the world was made by him, and the world knew him not. He came unto his own, and his own received him not" (John 1:10–11).

29. The Gospel of John testifies that Christ is the source of our life and light and that "as many as received him, to them gave he power to become the sons of God, even to them that believe on his name" (John 1:12; see 1:4–14).

30. We clearly do not believe, as the Arians did, that "there was when He was not." See Kelly, *Early Christian Creeds*, 233. Arius wrote that "before he was begotten or created or appointed or established, he did not exist; for he was not unbegotten." "The Letter of Arius to Eusebius, Bishop of Nicomedia," in *Documents of the Christian Church*, 39. Given the ontological framework of fourth-century Christianity, the Arians were seen as making Christ into a creation and not the Creator. Arius wrote: "We are persecuted because we say that the Son has a beginning, but God is without beginning. For that reason we are persecuted, and because we say that he is from what is not. And this we say because he is neither part of God nor derived from any substance." *Documents of the Christian Church*, 39. The Arians took their position of distinguishing the Father and the Son because they were concerned that if Christ were God there would be a change in God or there would be a "plurality of divine beings." Kelly, *Early Christian Creeds*, 232. We do not have these concerns.

31. "And the Word was made flesh, and dwelt among us, (and we beheld his glory, the glory as of the only begotten of the Father,) full of grace and truth" (John 1:14).

32. See Luke 1:31–35; Alma 7:10; 1 Nephi 11:18–21. Because of the literal sense in which we understand the Sonship of Jesus Christ, some nineteenth-century Church leaders spoke of the conception of Christ in terms that were analogous to all other human conceptions. This has been a favorite point of those seeking to marginalize the Church's position. To hold these statements as binding and true Church doctrine is to refuse to allow insiders to define their own beliefs. A recent Church prophet has, in fact, asked that these nonscriptural speculations not be taught. *The Teachings of Harold B. Lee*, ed. Clyde Williams (Salt Lake City: Bookcraft, 1996), 13–14. In an age of in vitro fertilization it is much easier to understand a conception that follows the scriptural description of a virgin birth. For an additional discussion of this issue, see Craig L. Blomberg and Stephen Robinson, *How Wide the Divide?: A Mormon and an Evangelical in Conversation* (Downers Grove, IL: InterVarsity Press, 1997), 135–36; Robert L. Millet, "What Is Our Doctrine?," *Religious Educator* 4, no. 3 (2003): 15–33.

33. "The Living Christ: The Testimony of the Apostles, The Church of Jesus Christ of Latter-day Saints," *Ensign*, April 2000, 2.

34. See, for example, the discussion of Mary as the source of Christ's body in Carolyn Walker Bynum, *Holy Feast and Holy Fast: The Religious Significance of Food to Medieval Women* (Berkeley: University of California Press, 1988).

35. Isaiah's evocation of the Man of Sorrows is a central passion text for Latter-day Saints. This belief that all of Christ, spirit and body, bore "our griefs, and carried our sorrows" rests on a belief in his capacity and willingness to be "wounded for our transgressions" and "bruised for our iniquities." Isaiah 53:4–5. The Book of Mormon explicitly states that "he shall suffer . . . even more than man can suffer, except it be unto death; for behold, blood cometh from every pore, so great shall be his anguish for the wickedness and the abominations of his people" (Mosiah 3:7).

36. Elder Neal A. Maxwell commented on this: "Imagine, Jehovah, the Creator of this and other worlds, 'astonished'! Jesus knew cognitively what He must do, but not experientially. He had never personally known the exquisite and exacting process of an atonement before. Thus, when the agony came in its fulness, it was so much, much worse than even He with his unique intellect had ever imagined! No wonder an angel appeared to strengthen him!" Maxwell, "Willing to Submit," *Ensign*, May 1985, 72–73.

37. The Book of Mormon refers to this intercession, saying that "there can be nothing which is short of an infinite atonement which will suffice for the sins of the world"; therefore the "great and last sacrifice will be the Son of God, yea, infinite and eternal" (Alma 34:12, 14).

38. It continues, "and would that I might not drink the bitter cup, and shrink—Nevertheless, glory be to the Father, and I partook and finished my preparations unto the children of men" (Doctrine and Covenants 19:18–19).

39. This opposition to Apollinariansim was articulated by Gregory of Nazianus who said that "what he has not assumed he has not healed; it is what is united to his Deity that is saved." *Documents of the Christian Church*, 45. It became a basic principle to connect soteriology and Christology. See, for example, Kereszty, *Fundamentals of Christology*, 192.

40. "No man taketh it from me, but I lay it down of myself. I have power to lay it down, and I have power to take it again" (John 10:18).

41. The purpose for this divine suffering is described in the Doctrine and Covenants: "For, behold, the Lord your Redeemer suffered death in the flesh; wherefore he suffered the pain of all men, that all men might repent and come unto him" (Doctrine and Covenants 18:11).

42. See, for example, 3 Nephi 12:19. Even the context of the preceding verse illustrates this focus on Christ: "I give unto you these sayings that you may understand and know how to worship, and know what you worship, that you may come unto the Father in my name, and in due time receive of his fulness" (Doctrine and Covenants 93:19).

43. Choosing faith in Christ will lead to repentance, a change of heart and nature that will bring obedience.

44. "By him, and through him, and of him, the worlds are and were created, and the inhabitants thereof are begotten sons and daughters unto God"

(Doctrine and Covenants 76:24); "because of the covenant which ye have made ye shall be called the children of Christ, his sons, and his daughters; for behold, this day he hath spiritually begotten you; for ye say that your hearts are changed through faith on his name; therefore, ye are born of him and have become his sons and his daughters" (Mosiah 5:7).

4

Doctrine and Covenants Theology, Eastern Orthodox Terminology
Seeking Clarity about Theosis/Deification

J. B. Haws

My guess is that many, many of us have had a shared experience: the feeling of frustration that comes when you do not feel like you have adequately conveyed to a conversation partner one of your deeply held religious convictions. This feeling, it seems, is something different than experiencing honest *disagreement* with someone over religious beliefs. Somehow that disagreement does not feel as frustrating as the inability to clearly express the belief in the first place. I have often felt that kind of frustration when interfaith conversations have turned to Latter-day Saint beliefs about exaltation—humans' potential to become gods. In theological circles, this belief is often termed *theosis*, or *deification*.[1]

Theosis, for Latter-day Saints, lines up well with the idea of "fulness" in one of Joseph Smith's most remarkable revelations, now contained in section 93 of the Doctrine and Covenants: "I give unto you these sayings that you may understand and know how to worship, and know what you worship, that you may come unto the Father in my name, and in due time receive of his fulness . . . and be glorified in me as I am in the Father" (Doctrine and Covenants 93:19–20).

But section 93 is not alone among Doctrine and Covenants passages in pointing readers in the direction of deification. Sections 76, 84, 88, and 132 all proclaim a similar witness that the ultimate end of the saving work of Jesus Christ is an invitation to share fully in the divine life, to experience theosis. Theosis, simply put, is at the heart of the Latter-day Saint plan of salvation.

It almost goes without saying, though, that while many Latter-day Saints find theosis to be ennobling and awe-inspiring, many other Christians find it to be off-putting and blasphemous. This was, after all, the titular heresy that fueled *The God Makers*, a polemical film produced in the 1980s by the group Ex-Mormons for Jesus. And even the recent musical *The Book of Mormon* takes some similar satirical shots about Latter-day Saints who, in a future glorified state, expect to become gods on their own planets.[2]

This is where the aforementioned kind of frustration can set in. For Latter-day Saints, *The God Makers* and *The Book of Mormon* musical feel off-target in their representations of Latter-day Saint theosis. Polemics and satire aside, what still feels off is the impression that becoming like God for Latter-day Saints implies replacing God or supplanting him or existing independently of him. What often seems most difficult to convey is that Latter-day Saints affirm, perhaps counterintuitively, both the doctrine's boldness and breathtaking scope on the one hand, and its simultaneous call for humility and tentativeness on the other—and in that spirit, this paper is more interested in addressing misunderstandings than in dismissing disagreements. This is where the Doctrine and Covenants can be helpful. To cut to the chase, the key point to be made on this score is that the Doctrine and Covenants is emphatic (as is subsequent related commentary by Latter-day Saint prophets) that theosis for Latter-day Saints does *not* mean a supplanting of God or a detachment from

God or an existence independent of God. Theosis, as understood by Latter-day Saints, is an act of divine grace.

Analogies can often be helpful when coming at concepts that are difficult to communicate in and of themselves—and it is painfully apparent to Latter-day Saints that theosis is a concept that is difficult to communicate. This paper therefore proposes that a comparative lens can be helpful in bringing things into proper focus. There is a potential benefit in turning first, by analogy, to another Christian tradition—Eastern Orthodoxy—that has also felt itself maligned and misunderstood for its beliefs about theosis. Taking this analogy as our starting point might then imbue some key Doctrine and Covenants passages with new significance—and might help Latter-day Saints find "the right words," as Richard Bushman has put it, to "express [our] faith," to "make [ourselves] intelligible to . . . listeners."[3]

A Comparative Analogy: Eastern Orthodoxy, Essence, and Energies

The analogy makes the most sense when we first appreciate how Eastern Orthodox Christians see themselves as distinct from their Western Christian counterparts. The East-West split in Christianity was already well underway, in terms of philosophical approach and theological emphasis and even language (Greek in the East, Latin in the West), long before the ecclesiastical split of 1054, when reciprocal excommunications irredeemably widened the growing rift between Rome and Constantinople. Eminent Orthodox scholar and bishop Kallistos Ware has characterized that difference in mindset this way: Eastern Christians today think of Roman Catholics and Protestants as "two sides of the same coin"[4]—and Orthodoxy, in that view, is a different coin altogether. One key distinguishing feature in Eastern Christianity has been the Orthodox emphasis on theosis, which has been "like a continuous golden thread running throughout the centuries of Orthodoxy's ancient theological tapestry."[5]

The boldness of Orthodox teachings on theosis—even, and especially, *contemporary* teachings—has been a source of surprise for a number of Western Christian commentators. Since Western and Eastern Christianity grew up largely apart from each other, it has only been in the last few decades that Christians in the West (Latter-day Saints included) have discovered/rediscovered both modern Orthodox thought and the writings of early Christian fathers on theosis—and on this point Latter-day Saint and Protestant and Roman Catholic authors have been, at turns, fascinated with, and startled by, Orthodoxy. Many Western Christian authors start their treatises on deification by relating anecdotes about just how "very strange indeed" Orthodox formulations of deification "[sound] to our ears," to use Daniel Clendenin's phrase.[6] Patristics scholar Norman Russell has commented wryly that "it is becoming less necessary in the English-speaking world to apologize for the doctrine of deification. At one time it was regarded as highly esoteric, if it was admitted to be Christian at all."[7] A typical case comes in the preface of David Litwa's 2013 book *Becoming Divine*. Litwa describes a (Protestant) seminary colleague's reaction when the colleague first read Litwa's manuscript, with its frequent quotations from Orthodox writers who spoke of humans becoming gods. The colleague circled passage after passage in red pen and scribbled in the margins with question marks and exclamation points. "What does this *mean?*" his colleague repeatedly asked.[8]

Not so for Latter-day Saints. These statements do not sound foreign; they sound like home. Here are two brief snapshots that illustrate that sentiment.

In my classes at Brigham Young University, I have sometimes put the following quotation on the screen and then asked my students to guess who said it: *"We are each destined to become a god, to be like God himself . . . to become just like God, a true God."* BYU students do not even hesitate to offer guesses like Joseph Smith, Brigham Young, Lorenzo Snow, or another leader of The Church of Jesus Christ of Latter-day Saints. They are always taken aback, however, when they find out that it actually comes from the writings of twentieth-century Greek Orthodox theologian Cristoforos Stavropoulos.[9]

A second snapshot: A couple of years ago, a very articulate Orthodox priest who had relatively little exposure to the Latter-day Saint tradition lectured to BYU's religion faculty on Orthodox beliefs about humans and their potential. In the audience that day was an evangelical Christian pastor who had participated in a number of Latter-day Saint/evangelical interfaith dialogues. When the Orthodox priest finished his lecture, the first comment came from the evangelical pastor. He said, "You sound like my Mormon friends." The look on the faces of *both* the pastor and the priest spoke volumes—neither quite expected what they had just experienced.[10]

Simply put, surprise is a common reaction when it comes to conversations about theosis—and, indeed, in both of these examples surprise was a central element, although for different reasons. For Latter-day Saints, encountering Orthodox writings on theosis brings the pleasant surprise of the familiar: "We didn't know other Christians spoke this way!" For many other Western Christians, though, encountering Orthodox writings on theosis brings the surprise of the *un*familiar, and even the suspect: "We didn't know other Christians spoke this way!"

So, it is probably only natural that Latter-day Saints get excited when they read Orthodox authors on this topic.[11] It is akin to going to watch your national team play at another national team's stadium—you are always relieved to discover a large contingent of your team's supporters walking in at the same time, even if they come from another city. When it comes to defending theosis, the worldwide Orthodox community is just such a large contingent, several hundred million strong. But it is more than a "safety in numbers" issue. While there are a number of areas in which Latter-day Saints and Eastern Orthodox differ in their understanding of theosis, the similarities may also provide Latter-day Saints a sense of theological legitimacy. Latter-day Saint views of deification developed independently of Eastern Orthodoxy; Joseph Smith and his successors (like many patristic writers) wove this doctrinal tapestry with threads of biblical phrases, again and again. But when Latter-day Saints discover that this ancient Eastern church tradition, this self-described guardian of the apostolic faith, has "deification" as the "chief idea of . . . all of [its] theology," it provides a sense of affirmation. It lends credence to the idea that deification is a legitimate way to understand the biblical witness of salvation.[12]

But, of course, not everyone has agreed that this *is* a legitimate way to understand the biblical witness of salvation. Over the centuries of Christian history, Eastern theologians and mystics have been denounced as heretics or as pantheists or as polytheists for their beliefs in theosis.[13] It is in his defense against just such charges that one key fourteenth-century Orthodox thinker, Gregory Palamas, presented the ideas that form the key component of the analogy at hand.

Palamas highlighted two categories that are crucial to Orthodoxy's theosis theology: divine essence and divine energies. In his usage, *divine essence* signifies that aspect or quality or nature of godhood which deified humans will never adopt or assume, and *divine energies* signifies that aspect or quality of godhood in which deified humans can fully participate.

To explore the utility of these categories for Latter-day Saints, we first must understand how they figure into Orthodoxy. These are not categories that are easily defined, especially since Orthodox theology often takes an apophatic (or a negative theology) approach to such questions, acknowledging what can*not* be said about, or attributed to, God more often than what *can* definitively be said. (Latter-day Saint thought typically moves in the opposite direction—and that is often what causes discomfort for other Christians. More on that later.)

Orthodox teachings about theosis start from the place of God's "otherness," and that "otherness" calls for a sacred respect of mystery and transcendence. In Orthodox belief (as in traditional Catholic and Protestant belief), the three persons of the Trinity are wholly distinct from creation. That is, their shared nature or essence is "uncreatedness." There is an unbridgeable gap—a gap of being or ontology—between Creator and creature. No matter how fully divinized all saved humans become, humans will never cross that gap of essence. God alone will be the Uncreated Other; humans will always be essentially different. Christos Yannaras explains the Orthodox understanding that "schematically: God is a Nature and three Persons; man is a nature and 'innumerable' persons. God is consubstantial and in three hypostases, man is consubstantial and in innumerable hypostases."[14] Essence could thus be characterized as that nature which, for the Trinity, is divinity, and that nature which, for humans, is humanity.[15]

But Orthodox writers are repeatedly emphatic that saved humans can enjoy *all* of the divine *energies*—the attributes and activities of godliness—so much so that one Orthodox writer spoke of deified humans being "equal" with God![16] That is a succinct summation, in the Orthodox view, of the remarkable degree to which humans can be invited to participate in the divine life.

Orthodox Christians treat these terms—*essence* and *energies*—with a sophistication and a precision that are not found in Latter-day Saint thought; the terms themselves are not even part of Latter-day Saint discourse—and crucially, Latter-day Saints do *not* hold that God is wholly Other in terms of essence or nature. What I want to suggest, however, is that there is an explanatory utility in these two Orthodox categories for bringing clarity to questions about Latter-day Saint doctrine on deification—what that doctrine is, and what it is *not*. That is, there may be more—practically, functionally—to this essence/energies distinction in Latter-day Saint thinking than meets the eye. This distinction seems especially clear in a number of key passages in the Doctrine and Covenants that emphasize that Latter-day Saints, like Orthodox Christians, believe theosis comes by the grace of Jesus Christ—and *only* by grace. In other words, in the Doctrine and Covenants's framing of this, there will *always* be a uniqueness about God, even when humans are deified. God and his Son, Jesus Christ, are doing the "making equal"—God is the deifier.

And that vision of things can change everything about how we view Jesus Christ as Savior and how we view our relationship to him and his Father.

All of the foregoing prompts a key question, an inescapable question: to what extent do Latter-day Saints and Orthodox Christians mean the same things when they talk about human deification? That is obviously a big question—one that generates different responses based on whom you ask. Most of the responses from outside observers have been dismissive of the viability of such comparisons.[17] Generally speaking, the argument goes, Latter-day Saint conceptions of the nature of God are so radically different as to make Latter-day Saint ideas of deification also radically different. Latter-day Saints, the sense is, believe humans will become what God *is*. While not downplaying the radical difference in beliefs about the nature of God in the two traditions, I think it is worth revisiting that second assumption about becoming what God *is*. The opening line of Norman Russell's seminal book on deification in the writings of early church fathers seems apt here: "All the earlier patristic writers who refer to deification, although sometimes conscious of the boldness of their language, took it for granted that their readers understood what they meant."[18] If Latter-day Saints have likewise taken it for granted that others will understand what they mean when they speak of deification, *The Book of Mormon* musical or *The God Makers* film are jarring reminders that such is not always the case.

It seems that too many comparative conversations about Latter-day Saint and Eastern Orthodox teachings on theosis start and stop at the level of the "divine essence," with reference to Parley P. Pratt's formulation, or some variation of it, that God, humans, and angels are of the same species.[19] For many Christians (and for some Latter-day Saints), the rhetorical question becomes, 'What else is there to talk about?' But the conversations should not stop there, because the richness of the Doctrine and Covenants on this topic challenges easy assumptions and easy dismissals. What I would propose is that despite crucial differences in their theological starting points, both

Orthodox Christians and Latter-day Saints are doing something similar in asserting that a robust view of theosis does not, of necessity, diminish the grandeur of God.

A Doctrine and Covenants Cosmology: Light and Intelligence

What can the Doctrine and Covenants teach us about this notion of a "divine essence" analog in Latter-day Saint cosmology? In Gregory Palamas's hands, this "essence" formulation reminds readers that no matter how complete deification will be—how completely divinized humans will eventually become—there is something about God that will always be essentially different. The contention here is that the Doctrine and Covenants makes an analogous point.

Before getting to that point, though, it is worth repeating that I do not make this argument to downplay the real differences between the Latter-day Saint belief system and that of historic, traditional, creedal Christianity. Latter-day Saints hold to a conception of a corporeal Godhead wherein each person of the Trinity is a tangible personage, a discrete and material individual who nevertheless is infinitely united in purpose and thought with the other persons of the Trinity. Latter-day Saints also reject creation ex nihilo. On one level, Latter-day Saints can agree with other Christians that God *is* uncreated, but they also believe that in some way so *too* are humans, that some kernel of human existence (referred to broadly as intelligence) is coeternal with God—and thus God is *not* wholly Other. Indeed, the May 1833 revelation to Joseph Smith that is now Doctrine and Covenants 93 contains these startling lines: "Ye were also in the beginning with the Father. . . . Man was also in the beginning with God. Intelligence, or the light of truth, was not created or made, neither indeed can be. . . . The elements are eternal" (Doctrine and Covenants 93:23, 29, 33). This is one of the remarkable contributions of the Doctrine and Covenants—it presents a radically new cosmology.

One of Joseph Smith's most moving extrapolations of the implications of this doctrine of coeternality came in his King Follett sermon, wherein he envisioned God this way:

> I might with boldness proclaim from the housetops that God never had the power to create the spirit of man at all. God himself could not create himself.
>
> Intelligence is eternal and exists upon a self-existent principle. It is a spirit from age to age and there is no creation about it. All the minds and spirits that God ever sent into the world are susceptible of enlargement.
>
> The first principles of man are self-existent with God. God himself, finding he was in the midst of spirits and glory, because he was more intelligent, saw proper to institute laws whereby the rest could have a privilege to advance like himself. The relationship we have with God places us in a situation to advance in knowledge. He has power to institute laws to instruct the weaker intelligences, that they may be exalted with Himself, so that they might have one glory upon another, and all that knowledge, power, glory, and intelligence, which is requisite in order to save them in the world of spirits.
>
> This is good doctrine. It tastes good. I can taste the principles of eternal life, and so can you.[20]

This *is* a wholly distinct cosmology, and we must not downplay that difference between Latter-day Saint and Orthodox Christian conceptions of God and the universe. But if that is where the conversation stops, misunderstandings about what Latter-day Saints believe about human deification will persist. This radical "Christian version of materialism," as Stephen Webb called it, has to be part of every discussion about the place deification holds in The Church of Jesus Christ of Latter-day Saints.[21] But one by-product of this Latter-day Saint anthropology is that it can obscure the God/human gap that *is* present in Latter-day Saint theology. That gap, of course, is not as wide, not as absolute, as the ontological gap that is the starting point for Christian Trinitarian thinking, but in Latter-day Saint theology there is nevertheless an emphasis on a gap (especially in Latter-day Saint theology of the past few decades)—perhaps to a degree that many would find surprising.

One way to approach this is to draw from expansive Doctrine and Covenants passages about intelligence, about light. Divine light, we learn, "fill[s] the immensity of space," it "is the law by which all things are governed," and it "giveth life to all things" (Doctrine and Covenants 88:12–13). We also learn about the universal accessibility of light—"the Spirit giveth light to every man that cometh into the world" as an initial extension of divine grace, an initial gift (Doctrine and Covenants 84:46). Then, "he that receiveth light, and continueth in God, receiveth more light—and that light groweth brighter and brighter until the perfect day" (Doctrine and Covenants 50:24). The concept of *light*, with all of its Doctrine and Covenants synonyms—*truth, glory, intelligence, law, the word of the Lord, Spirit* (see Doctrine and Covenants 84:45; 93:36–37)—becomes a beautiful way of thinking ultimately about the aim, the telos, of the Atonement of Jesus Christ: "And if your eye be single to my glory, your whole bodies shall be filled with light, and there shall be no darkness in you; and that body which is filled with light comprehendeth all things" (Doctrine and Covenants 88:67).[22] That phrase—"comprehendeth all things"—also appears just two dozen verses earlier in describing "him who sitteth upon the throne and governeth and executeth all things. *He* comprehendeth all things . . . and all things are by him, and of him, even God, forever and ever" (Doctrine and Covenants 88:40–41; emphasis added). The parallel phrasings are no accident. What they indicate—what the whole of the Doctrine and Covenants indicates—is that the "why" of the Atonement of Jesus Christ is, ultimately, theosis, deification, becoming like God.

That same revelation, Doctrine and Covenants 88, puts the matter in these remarkable terms in a context of eschatological and soteriological culmination: "And again, another angel shall sound his trump, which is the seventh angel, saying: It is finished; it is finished! The Lamb of God hath overcome and trodden the wine-press alone, even the wine-press of the fierceness of the wrath of Almighty God. And then shall the angels be crowned with the glory of his might, and the saints shall be filled with his glory, and receive their inheritance and *be made equal with him*" (Doctrine and Covenants 88:106–7; emphasis added). Being "made equal" with the Lamb of God is the point. The Atonement of Jesus Christ makes little sense in the cosmology of the Doctrine and Covenants without that admittedly breathtaking end in mind.

Being "Made Equal"

A crucial cross-reference must be made here. An earlier revelation (now Doctrine and Covenants 76) used this same "made equal" language: "They who dwell in his [God the Father's] presence are the church of the Firstborn; . . . and he makes them equal in power, and in might, and in dominion" (Doctrine and Covenants 76:94–95). Significantly, God is doing the *making* equal. This is the humility mentioned earlier that the Doctrine and Covenants calls for. Despite all the expansiveness about human potential, the language of the Doctrine and Covenants strongly implies a *qualitative* distinction—perpetually so—between God and deified humanity. It is a distinction of dependence. We must remember that this same revelation, Doctrine and Covenants 76, one of Joseph Smith's earliest revelations on deification, declares that saved and exalted humans "are gods," yes, "even the sons of God," but also that "all things are theirs, . . . and they are Christ's, and Christ is God's" (Doctrine and Covenants 76:58–59). That order signals something important about relationship, about indebtedness, about reliance.

It is telling to see how this scriptural passage was used in an early twentieth-century joint statement of the Church's First Presidency and Quorum of the Twelve Apostles. The statement, called "The

Father and the Son" and issued by Joseph F. Smith and his fellow apostles in 1916, reminded Latter-day Saints that

> those who have been born unto God through obedience to the gospel may by valiant devotion to righteousness obtain exaltation and even reach the status of godhood. Of such we read: "Wherefore, as it is written, they are gods, even the sons of God" (D&C 76:58; compare D&C 132:20, and contrast D&C 132:17 in same section; see also D&C 132:37). Yet though they be gods, *they are still subject to Jesus Christ as their Father in this exalted relationship*; and so we read in the paragraph following the above quotation: "And they are Christ's, and Christ is God's" (D&C 76:59).[23]

The assertion that "gods"—deified humans—will *still* be "*subject* to Jesus Christ" is a point that must not be overlooked and one that echoes ideas in Joseph Smith's revelations.

A similar signal came through clearly in a 1984 general conference address by Elder Boyd K. Packer—and it is apparent that he was mindful of all of the controversy that swirled around Latter-day Saint claims about exaltation as he said this: "The Father *is* the one true God. *This* thing is certain: no one will ever ascend above Him; no one will ever replace Him. *Nor will anything ever change the relationship that we,* His literal offspring, *have with Him.* He is Elohim, the Father. He is God. Of him there is only one. We revere our Father and our God; we *worship* Him."[24]

One proposal here is that it is in this very emphasis on God's fatherhood and on Jesus Christ's saving role that the essence/energies distinction might have the most relevance (and resonance) in Latter-day Saint doctrine. Latter-day Saints, of course, take very literally the words of Jesus when he told Mary that God was "[his] Father, and your Father," or of Paul, who called God the "Father of all" (John 20:17; Ephesians 4:6). Again, admittedly, Latter-day Saint views of that literal parent-child relationship depart from classical theism's Creator-creature formulation in ways that make many other

Christians uncomfortable. But for Latter-day Saints, this parent-child relationship is the very reason that each person has the potential for deification; put another way, it is because we are children of God that we can be joint-heirs with Christ (see Romans 8:16–18).[25] Thus, while this "literal offspring" idea might offend traditional Christian sensibilities, for Latter-day Saints God's *enduring* fatherhood and supremacy and Jesus Christ's *enduring* salvific role resonate with the Orthodox understanding that humans become "gods by grace"—and with the understanding that there is something persistently unique about God. It is thus worth highlighting the words "no one will ever" in Elder Packer's statement.

In the mid-1990s, Church President Gordon B. Hinckley sounded a note from this same refrain, explaining "that this lofty concept [of deification/exaltation] in no way diminishes God the Eternal Father. He is the Almighty. He is the Creator and Governor of the universe. He is the greatest of all *and will always be so.* But just as any earthly father wishes for his sons and daughters every success in life, so I believe our Father in Heaven wishes for his children that they might *approach* him in stature and stand beside him resplendent in godly strength and wisdom."[26] President Hinckley's language seems compatible with another analogy here.

Think of a hyperbola, a curve that infinitely approaches an asymptote or boundary line but never crosses it. For all intents and purposes, the curve—as it is projected toward infinity—is practically equal to the asymptote; yet there will *always* be a difference. By its very mathematical definition, the asymptote and hyperbolic curve cannot be identical. President Hinckley's "*approach* him in stature" formulation suggests that using this metaphor of a hyperbola and its asymptotes as a way to view deification—a metaphor present in other Christian systems—does *not* do injustice to Latter-day Saint beliefs. Of course, the crux here is in defining the asymptote line, that axis—God—that is infinitely approached by the curve—deified humans—but never crossed. For Orthodox Christians, the asymptote is the divine essence: God will "fulfill the mystical act of man's theosis," Panagiotes Chrestou wrote, "by making man like himself *in all ways* except the divine essence."[27] Words that might approximate or point at the divine essence in Orthodoxy—words like eternal Uncreatedness or eternal Otherness—are not part of the vocabulary of Latter-day Saints. But engaging Latter-day Saint thinking in that same definition exercise can be productive in proposing words to capture what is, in Latter-day Saint understanding, God's perpetual, defining distinctiveness vis-à-vis his children—perhaps words like eternal Worshipability, eternal Fatherhood, eternal Supremacy, eternal Irreplaceability. This is the conceptual utility of the essence/energies terminology in comparative conversations like this one—conversations that try to get at just what Latter-day Saints mean when they say humans can become gods, and perhaps more significantly, what they do *not* mean.

Concluding Caveats

Two additional caveats seem important. Recent Latter-day Saint leaders and official publications seem to be recommending more caution and circumspection to Church members when describing just what we know about the look and shape of a deified life. For one example of how this tentativeness has been manifest in Church publications, consider the changes in successive editions of the *Gospel Principles* manual in that book's chapter 47, "Exaltation." In editions prior to the 2009 edition, this is the wording for "What Is Exaltation?": "If we prove faithful to the Lord, we will live in the highest degree of the celestial kingdom of heaven. We will become exalted, just like our Heavenly Father. . . . Those who receive exaltation . . . will have their righteous family members with them and will be able to have spirit children also. These spirit children will have the same relationship to them as we do to our Heavenly Father." However, in the 2009 edition, this is the parallel passage under "What Is Exaltation?": "If we prove faithful to the Lord, we will live in the highest degree of the celestial kingdom of heaven. We will become exalted, to live with our

Heavenly Father in eternal families. . . . Those who receive exaltation . . . will be united eternally with their righteous family members
and will be able to have eternal increase." Notice the absence of the
specific language of "*just like* our Heavenly Father" or "same relationship" in the 2009 edition.[28]

This tentativeness on the precise *meaning* of human deification,
though, does not mean that Latter-day Saints are pulling back from
enthusiastic embrace of the *idea* of human deification. Not at all. In a
January 2020 devotional address at Brigham Young University, Elder
Ronald A. Rasband said, "You have the capacity to become gods and
goddesses in a realm . . . that promises light and goodness and peace
everlasting."[29] With the straightforwardness of statements like that,
what should we make, then, of the tentativeness on display above?

For one thing, it does seem that Church leaders and members
have sensed the need to contextualize and qualify their statements
about theosis, given all of the potential for misunderstanding discussed earlier. A key example of this kind of contextualization and
qualification is an officially produced Church Gospel Topics essay
called "Becoming Like God." That essay includes long passages of
Joseph Smith's crowning King Follett sermon and references to early
Christian luminaries like Clement, Basil, and Dyonisius, as well as
a discussion of Church President Lorenzo Snow's oft-cited couplet:
"As man now is, God once was: As God now is, man may be." The
essay then says, "Little has been revealed about the first half of this
[Lorenzo Snow's] couplet, and consequently little is taught. When
asked about this topic, Church President Gordon B. Hinckley told
a reporter in 1997, 'That gets into some pretty deep theology that
we don't know very much about.' When asked about the belief in
humans' divine potential, President Hinckley responded, 'Well, as
God is, man may become. We believe in eternal progression. Very
strongly.'"[30]

In other words, it seems that Latter-day Saints are now trying to
convey something of their own apophatic approach to this. We are
saying, Here is what exaltation does *not* mean about God or about

us: in the spirit of Elder Packer and President Hinckley, no one will ascend above him; he will always be our God and our Father; Jesus Christ will always be our Savior.

The second caveat is that this is not only a recent phenomenon, even if the tone and the emphasis in these statements do reflect recent paradigm shifts. And that is why attention to the Doctrine and Covenants on this point is crucial. While Latter-day Saints and their leaders have often felt free in the past to speculate about the wonders of eternity, the "asymptotic" view of the God/human relationship in Latter-day Saint thought has been simultaneously present from the beginning, even if it has not always been foregrounded in Latter-day Saint discourse. A point that must be emphasized—and strongly so—is that the clearest exposition in Latter-day Saint scripture of just how expansive the Church's view of deified humans *is* comes in Doctrine and Covenants 132, the revelation about the eternal nature of marriage. This section (and the previous one) highlights that deification is ultimately possible only for married couples; as President Russell M. Nelson has said, "Exaltation is a family matter."[31] Here's what that seminal revelation teaches: sacramentally married couples who hold to their covenants "shall . . . be gods, because they have no end; . . . then shall they be gods, because they have all power" (Doctrine and Covenants 132:20). And yet, after all of that expansiveness, there still is this statement only four verses later: "This is eternal lives—to know the *only* wise and true God, and Jesus Christ, whom he hath sent" (Doctrine and Covenants 132:24; emphasis added). There remains a distinction—the deification of humans does not change the appropriateness of referring to God the Father as the "*only* wise and true God."

I recognize that at first glance, the sense that in Latter-day Saint theology the God-human relationship is one based on a difference of *degree* rather than a difference of *kind* will simply be a nonstarter for some. However, what should not be missed is that this difference in degree is so apparently profound that it will never cease to exist.

What is at stake here seems to be the worshipability or worship-worthiness of God in the Latter-day Saint theological worldview. Can using Orthodox/Palamite distinctions about essence and energies help in assessing that? Can this be profitably employed to emphasize that Latter-day Saints—like Orthodox Christians—do not believe that they will become the *same* as God, if *sameness* is meant to imply that they will ever exist independently of him and his deifying grace, even though they—like Orthodox Christians—talk about being "made equal with him" (Doctrine and Covenants 88:107)? Importantly, God—whom Joseph Smith addressed in a canonized 1836 prayer, as the "Almighty," who "[sits] enthroned, with . . . an infinity of fulness" (Doctrine and Covenants 109:77)—is always the one doing the *making* equal. For Latter-day Saints, God's enduring fatherhood and supremacy imply a resonance with the Orthodox understanding that humans become "gods *by grace*"—and only by grace.

But Orthodox writers before and since Gregory Palamas remind their readers that we should not *under*sell just how remarkable it is to participate in God's energies. They use language like this: "man's main pursuit and ultimate destiny is to become *equal* to God"; humans become "as much a real god as Christ became a real man" (Panagiotes Chrestou); "the *fullness of God* is stamped upon man yet without man thereby being dissolved into God" (Dumitru Stăniloae); "deification is more than the achievement of moral excellence. It is a supernatural gift that transforms both mind and body, making divinity visible" (Norman Russell, paraphrasing Gregory Palamas).[32] Likewise, the most recent (2009) *Gospel Principles* manual still affirms, in precisely the same language as did earlier editions of the manual, that exalted humans "will have everything that our Heavenly Father and Jesus Christ have—all power, glory, dominion, and knowledge (see D&C 132:19–20)."[33] These are words that carry strong resonance with a "divine energies" paradigm.

In that same vein, then, when reading the Doctrine and Covenants with an eye to passages about deification/theosis, two things stand out: from the first years of the Restoration, there is in the revelations of the Doctrine and Covenants a repeated witness that the Savior's atoning grace can make us like him and his Father; and from the first years of the Restoration, there is in the revelations of the Doctrine and Covenants a repeated witness that we cannot do this on our own—we will always be eternally indebted to the deifying power inherent in the Atonement of Jesus Christ, the Savior "whom [the only true and wise God] hath sent" to make all of this possible (Doctrine and Covenants 132:24). This is but one more reason for all of us to sing with deep sincerity, "I stand all amazed."[34]

Notes

1. I am grateful to organizers of panels at meetings of the American Academy of Religion and the International Orthodox Theological Association for opportunities to present versions of this essay.

2. Interestingly, the public attention generated by *The Book of Mormon* musical seems to be one of the prompts behind the "Mormonism 101: FAQ" news release that appears on the Newsroom site of The Church of Jesus Christ of Latter-day Saints, accessed at https://news-my.churchofjesus christ.org/article/mormonism-101#C13. For the purposes of this current essay, it is especially noteworthy to see how the Church's writers handled two related questions: "Do Latter-day Saints believe they can become 'gods'?" and "Do Latter-day Saints believe that they will 'get their own planet'?" The responses to both questions draw on biblical language and are very circumspect in tone in a way that seems consonant with other statements by twenty-first century Latter-day Saint leaders—discussed below in the essay—on the issue of exaltation/theosis. Here are those responses: "Do Latter-day Saints believe they can become 'gods'? Latter-day Saints believe that God wants us to become like Him. But this teaching is often misrepresented by those who caricature the faith. The Latter-day Saint belief is no different than the biblical teaching, which states, 'The Spirit itself beareth witness with our spirit, that we are the children of God: and if children, then heirs; heirs of God, and joint-heirs with Christ; if so be that we suffer with him, that we may be also glorified together' (Romans

8:16–17). Through following Christ's teachings, Latter-day Saints believe all people can become 'partakers of the divine nature' (2 Peter 1:4)." "Do Latter-day Saints believe that they will 'get their own planet'? No. This idea is not taught in Latter-day Saint scripture, nor is it a doctrine of the Church. This misunderstanding stems from speculative comments unreflective of scriptural doctrine. Mormons believe that we are all sons and daughters of God and that all of us have the potential to grow during and after this life to become like our Heavenly Father (see Romans 8:16–17). The Church does not and has never purported to fully understand the specifics of Christ's statement that 'in my Father's house are many mansions' (John 14:2)."

3. Richard Lyman Bushman, "Finding the Right Words: Speaking Faith in Secular Times," in *To Be Learned Is Good: Essays on Faith and Scholarship in Honor of Richard Lyman Bushman*, ed. J. Spencer Fluhman, Kathleen Flake, and Jed Woodworth (Provo, UT: Neal A. Maxwell Institute for Religious Scholarship, Brigham Young University, 2017), 299, 302.

4. Timothy (Bishop Kallistos of Diokleia) Ware, *The Orthodox Church*, new and rev. ed. (London: Penguin Books, 1997), 2.

5. Daniel B. Clendenin, *Eastern Orthodox Christianity: A Western Perspective* (Grand Rapids, MI: Baker Books, 1994), 120.

6. Clendenin, *Eastern Orthodox Christianity*, 119.

7. Norman Russell, *The Doctrine of Deification in the Greek Patristic Tradition* (New York: Oxford University Press, 2004), vii.

8. See the preface to M. David Litwa, *Becoming Divine: An Introduction to Deification in Western Culture* (Eugene, OR: Cascade Books, 2013). Litwa's book also has a really thoughtful chapter on Latter-day Saint deification.

9. Cristoforos Stavropoulos, "Partakers of Divine Nature," in *Eastern Orthodox Theology: A Contemporary Reader*, ed. Daniel B. Clendenin (Grand Rapids, MI: Baker Books, 1995), 184.

10. I mentioned these examples and some of the implications discussed in the essay below in J. B. Haws, "Guest Opinion: Latter-day Saints and the Politics of Human Potential," *Deseret News*, 31 January 2019, https:// deseret.com/2019/1/31/20664640/guest-opinion-latter-day-saints-and -the-politics-of-human-potential.

11. See, for example, David L. Paulsen and Hal R. Boyd, *Are Christians Mormon?* (New York: Routledge, 2017), especially chapter 5, "Deification"; Jordan Vajda, *Partakers of the Divine Nature: A Comparative Analysis of Patristic and Mormon Doctrines of Divinization* (Provo, UT: FARMS, 2002); Stephen E. Robinson, *Are Mormons Christians?* (Salt Lake City: Bookcraft, 1991), 60–65, 68, 70; J. B. Haws, "Defenders of the Doctrine of Deification," in *Prelude to the Restoration: From Apostasy to the Restored Church* (Provo, UT: Religious Studies Center, Brigham Young University; Salt Lake City: Deseret Book, 2004), 70–98.

12. S. L. Epinanovic, as cited in Jaroslav Pelikan, *The Spirit of Eastern Christendom (600–1700)*, vol. 2 of *The Christian Tradition* (Chicago: University of Chicago Press, 1974), 10.

13. See, for example, Russell, *Doctrine of Deification*, 308.

14. Christos Yannaras, *Elements of Faith: An Introduction to Orthodox Theology* (Edinburgh: T&T Clark, 1991), 59.

15. See Yannaras, *Elements of Faith*, 27; Haws, "Defenders of the Doctrine of Deification," 77.

16. Panagiotes Chrestou, *Partakers of God: Patriarch Athenagoras Memorial Lectures* (Brookline, MA: Holy Cross Orthodox Press, 1984), 23.

17. See, for example, Richard N. Ostling and Joan K. Ostling, *Mormon America: The Power and the Promise* (San Francisco: HarperCollins, 1999), 307–14; see also Craig J. Blomberg and Stephen E. Robinson, *How Wide the Divide?: A Mormon and an Evangelical in Conversation* (Downers Grove, IL: InterVarsity Press, 1997), 100–102, as well as 209n12, and 212nn17 and 18.

18. See Russell, *Doctrine of Deification*, 1.

19. See Parley P. Pratt, *The Key to the Science of Theology* (Liverpool: F. D. Richards, 1855), 33.

20. This excerpt from the King Follett sermon comes from a version published in the April 1971 *Ensign*, accessible online at https://churchofjesuschrist .org/study/ensign/1971/04/the-king-follett-sermon. For access to four foundational accounts that became sources for the text of the sermon, as well as the first published amalgamation of those sources in the 15 August

1844 edition of the Nauvoo newspaper, *Times and Seasons*, see https://
josephsmithpapers.org/site/accounts-of-the-king-follett-sermon.

21. Stephen H. Webb, *Mormon Christianity* (New York: Oxford University
Press, 2013), 34.

22. See an important essay along these lines by Jacob Morgan: "The Divine-
Infusion Theory: Rethinking the Atonement," *Dialogue: A Journal of
Mormon Thought* 39, no. 1 (Spring 2006): 57–81.

23. "The Father and the Son: A Doctrinal Exposition of the First Presidency
and the Quorum of the Twelve Apostles" was originally published in
the Church's periodical, *Improvement Era*, August 1916, 934–42; it was
reprinted in the Church's *Ensign*, April 2002, https://churchofjesuschrist
.org/study/ensign/2002/04/the-father-and-the-son; emphasis added.

24. Boyd K. Packer, "The Pattern of Our Parentage," *Ensign*, November 1984,
69. In his address, Elder Packer also noted that "so-called Christians, with
the help of clergymen, belittle in most unchristian ways our teaching that
we are the literal sons and daughters of God. . . . This doctrine [exaltation]
is not at variance with the scriptures. Nevertheless, it is easy to understand
why some Christians reject it, because it introduces the possibility that
man may achieve Godhood. . . . There are those who mock our beliefs in
the most uncharitable ways."

25. For a helpful discussion about two directions of thought in Latter-day
Saint theology about how this parent-child relationship is established
between God and humans—either by "spirit birth" or by "spirit adoption"—see Terryl Givens, *Wrestling the Angel: The Foundations of Mormon Thought; Cosmos, God, Humanity* (Oxford: Oxford University Press,
2015), 156–63. Givens calls "the impossibility of establishing with certainty Smith's position on spirit birth as opposed to spirit adoption . . .
one of the many points of indeterminacy in the Mormon past." But he also
notes that the implications for human potential seem to be the same in
either scenario since both possibilities are fixed on the belief that God and
humans are somehow coeternal, in that "God is not a creator who fashions
humans for his own purposes, as much as a guide and heavenly mentor
who shepherds a pre-existing intelligence toward its highest potential, or
endows spirit matter with the form and conditions conducive to that end:

full emulation of a perfect Father and participation in a celestial community" (163).

26. Gordon B. Hinckley, "Don't Drop the Ball," *Ensign*, November 1994, 48;
emphasis added.

27. Chrestou, *Partakers of God*, 53; emphasis added.

28. *Gospel Principles* (Salt Lake City: The Church of Jesus Christ of Latter-day
Saints, 1978, 1979, 1981, 1985, 1986, 1988, 1992, 1995, 1997), 302; the parallel passage in the 2009 edition of *Gospel Principles* is on page 277.

29. Elder Ronald A. Rasband, "Free to Choose," BYU Devotional Address,
January 21, 2020, https://speeches.byu.edu/talks/ronald-a-rasband/free-to
-choose/.

30. The Church of Jesus Christ of Latter-day Saints, "Becoming like God,"
Gospel Topics Essay, https://churchofjesuschrist.org/study/manual/gospel
-topics-essays/becoming-like-god.

31. Russell M. Nelson, "Salvation and Exaltation," *Ensign*, May 2008.

32. Chrestou, *Partakers of God*, 23, 51; Dumitru Stăniloae, "Image, Likeness,
and Deification in the Human Person," trans. Ioan Ionita and Robert
Barringer, *Communio* 13, no. 1 (Spring 1986): 73; Russell, *Doctrine of
Deification*, 306.

33. *Gospel Principles* (2009), 277.

34. Charles H. Gabriel, "I Stand All Amazed," in *Hymns* (Salt Lake City: The
Church of Jesus Christ of Latter-day Saints, 1985), no.193.

5

The (True) Light of Christ in Joseph Smith's Revelations

Samuel Morris Brown

What is light? This apparently simple question was a major puzzle motivating the development of quantum physics in the early twentieth century. Scientists knew a great deal about light at a practical level— its role in earth life, how to split its wavelengths, how to harness its energy, how to interpret the light radiating from distant stars. What wasn't clear was what light actually is. Generally, light seemed like a wave, such as might strike a seashore. These were the waves of electromagnetism familiar from radio communication. But several experiments suggested that light was more like pellets fired from a gun than it was like a wave on the sea. "Wave-particle duality" was a shorthand for this philosophical conflict for decades, with a more recent turn to "quantum field theory" to try to sidestep the problematic dualism. Physics still isn't entirely sure what light is.[1]

The twentieth-century questions about light were concerned with the study of merely physical matter and the attempt to wrangle light into strictly material terms. But for most of recorded history, physics was only half the story. There was also what stood beside physics, "metaphysics" in the traditional language borrowed from Aristotle. Starting in the early modern period but with dramatic intensification in eighteenth-century Europe and America, Western intellectuals have tended to steer clear of metaphysics. Anti-metaphysical ideologies have come under various banners: Deism, materialism, physicalism, modern paganism. Each of these views and ideologies included different specifics, but most converged on one area of agreement: only the physical world exists. God, if such a word had any meaning at all, was hopelessly far away from the world of human endeavor. The chasm between physics and whatever metaphysics there might be was too great even for God to bridge. Even human beings were merely material objects, best understood as biological machines.[2] According to these ideologies, souls or spirits were illusions at best, exploitive frauds at worst. The philosopher Charles Taylor describes this family of philosophies as commitments to a closed, *immanent* frame for existence, where *immanent* is the opposite of *transcendent*.[3]

Even Latter-day Saints—a faith community notable for its commitments to heaven, angels, and a divine potential for earth and its inhabitants—are often described as modern materialists and strict immanentists when it comes to God's identity.[4] With reference to revelations and sermons from Joseph Smith that actively undermined traditional Christian theologies, writers have often emphasized that in Restoration theology, there is only physicality: Smith described coarse and fine matter, corresponding to the old dualism of body and spirit. This understanding of Restoration theology has emphasized the importance of the world, the immanence of God, and the material reality of spirit.[5] Some observers have classified this version of Smith's account of the integrity of the world as philosophical monism, the opposite of dualism. Others have expressed appropriate skepticism about the equation of Latter-day Saints and materialists or monists.[6]

These traditional accounts of Latter-day Saint theology have been the source of longstanding ideas about inescapable conflict between creedal and Latter-day Saint Christians. One standard story has held that the God of the Christians is wholly other, utterly beyond earthly existence. That God is absolute, perfect, a Platonic Form of goodness, power, and wisdom. Blaise Pascal famously referred to this (in his view, sterile) entity as the "God of the philosophers."[7] The God of the Latter-day Saints, on the other hand, is a deified human, purely immanent, perfectly integrated into the life of the world. That Latter-day Saint God has more in common with the anthropomorphic God of the Bible, what Pascal called more warmly and plaintively "God of Abraham, God of Isaac, and God of Jacob." Both creedal Christians and the Latter-day Saints have tended to agree that divine transcendence is a central point of irreconcilable difference between their competing traditions: creedal Christians embrace divine transcendence, while Latter-day Saints ostensibly reject it.[8]

The significant question is whether that familiar distinction is in fact secure. Revelations from the early 1830s, concerned with the metaphysics of light, suggest that in fact the Latter-day Saints do believe in aspects of divinity that share a great deal with the God of the philosophers. They just don't believe that this divinity exhausts the nature of God, even as they point out the difficulty of separating these aspects from each other. This divine essence is called by various names: law, priesthood, and—crucially—light (see below).

This sense of divine light, generally termed the "light of Christ," has been understood in two complementary ways in Restoration theology. On the one hand, it's the inborn conscience by which humans judge good from evil. On the other, it's a power, essence, or force that exists beyond the merely material world.[9] This light is particularly associated with Jesus, especially in his premortal life, but it appears to also exist beyond Jesus as a matrix in which he and his divine parents live and breathe and have their being.

Four revelations from 1832 to 1833 are crucial to understanding the Light of Christ (also known as the "true light" in the early

Restoration): sections 76, 84, 88, and 93 of the Doctrine and Covenants. These revelations reread, revise, and recast the Gospel of John,
especially its mystical, expansive Prologue (see John 1:1–18).[10]

The Gospel of John argues that Jesus is an entity known from
Jewish tradition, the *Memra Yahweh* or Word of God. This word of
God was a special being, perhaps the generally female divine figure
called Wisdom. This Wisdom existed beside God and carried out
God's will.[11] The Word was a being or essence that could mediate
between God's ultimate remoteness and the mortal world of humans.
This theme of eternal perfection, mortal imperfection, and a sacred
being that mediates between them is at the core of Restoration
Christology.

When John 1 states, "In the beginning was the Word, and the
Word was with God, and the Word was God" (John 1:1), it is repur-
posing traditions about the *Memra Yahweh* to argue that the premortal Jesus was that Word. The subsequent statement, that "all things
were made by him; and without him was not any thing made that
was made" (John 1:3), further connects Jesus and the *Memra Yahweh*
while emphasizing the creative role this Word played at the origins
of the universe. The Prologue then transitions to a discussion of the
ways the Word of God became flesh to dwell among humans. In
this text, the incarnation of Jesus as the Christ bridges the distance
between heaven and earth.

Discussions about light follow. John says that in Jesus "was life;
and the life was the light of men. And the light shineth in darkness;
and the darkness comprehended it not" (John 1:4–5). This special
light overlaps in some important way with Christ as the Word. It
came to earth, and the world could not understand or extinguish it.
(The Greek term, *katalambano*, can mean "apprehend"—in the sense
of either comprehend or seize—take control of, extinguish, or several other concepts. Joseph Smith often sided with the King James
translators' preference for "comprehend," but a complementary reading sees the world trying to extinguish that light, amassing its full
power in the attempt to do so at Golgotha, juxtaposed to the obvious

persistent power of the flame on Easter morning.)[12] A few verses later, John continues to explain that Christ, as opposed to John the Baptist, is "the true Light, which lighteth every man that cometh into the world" (1:9). The Gospel of John moves through many related stories from Jesus's life, death, and new life, exploring what it means for the Word of God to be made human, what it means for the True Light to burn brightly in the universe.

As Joseph Smith reread and retranslated John's Prologue in the early 1830s, he explored the complex relationships between God, Jesus, and the moral order of the universe. In his considerations of the Word and the Light and their relationships to the Godhead, he elaborated a theology of the "true light" that is much more complex than has traditionally been thought. Usual theological and historical writing on the Light of Christ has largely depended on Protestant framings of the questions relevant to the nature of divinity, mostly emphasizing the sense of individual conscience.[13] There is much room for a Restoration-based alternative that is more open to metaphysical richness. Working from within a Restoration worldview, I explore the nature of Christ, divine light, heavenly parents, and the human recipients of the light. I consider the philosophical context, the relevant revelation texts, and then the implications of Smith's theology of light.

Philosophical Contexts: Illumination and Emanation

Questions about the metaphysics of light weren't new with the Latter-day Saint Restoration. Whether it's true or not (and some skepticism on this point is reasonable given precedents in other thinkers), Plato is held to be the key figure in these philosophical debates. He does so both in his writings and more importantly in how others have interpreted those writings over the years, in schools of thought called Platonism or Neoplatonism. The main concept associated with Plato tends to be a duality of perfect, changeless Forms (or Ideas) and the imperfect, changing world where the Forms are manifest. Goodness or beauty or justice for Plato were not just words people use—they were real. They existed as perfect Forms of those attributes. While mortals could manifest goodness, they were not themselves the Good. How Plato understood what we would call God is more complex than many people realize[14]—it's not clear whether God was the Forms taken together, one Form among many, or a being who operated within the cosmic order established by the Forms. Whatever Plato's original intent, in the hands of later Christian interpreters, God was the Forms taken together, an absolute wholeness of perfect being. This was the God without body, parts, or passions (each word carrying the imprint of centuries of theological discussion) that the early Latter-day Saints loved to mock.[15]

The Neoplatonists (in pagan and then Christian variants) emphasized the interplay between Plato's eternal Divine Unity and the temporal world of matter and perception.[16] Some focused on the distance between the Forms and the material world, even veering toward gnostic-sounding notions that the world is inherently evil and our quest as humans is to escape the world.[17] Others, following Plato's teaching about a *demiurge* (the "builder" of the world), saw spanning the distance as important and achievable.[18] This demiurge, a figure in the dialogue *Timaeus,* was the divine worker who was able to mediate between changeless perfection and the changing world of mortals, thus solving a logical puzzle—how could changeless Forms interact with, let alone organize, the world we know?

Especially in pagan Neoplatonism, a vital mode of such connection was light emanating from the divine presence as the force that suffuses the mortal world. Through this emanating light, divine perfection could extend between the divine and human realms.[19] Light, in a manner of speaking, did the work of Plato's demiurge—spanning heaven and earth—on an ongoing basis.

The doctrine of emanations continued in various threads over the centuries, especially in Western esoteric thought. With various complexities, alleys, and tangents, the divine light continued to be a bridge between perfection and imperfection. In parallel it also held open the possibility of a theistic response to pantheism. Where pantheism held that God is only and identically the universe itself, a theist could respond that the pantheist has confused the emanation with its source.

The divine emanations were known well into the nineteenth century, including among African American Protestants, Edwardsians, and contemporary evangelicals.[20] Charles Buck, author of Joseph Smith's preferred theological reference, provided a reasonable summary in his account of mystics, whose Platonic traditions taught that "the divine nature was suffused through all human souls," "the faculty of reason . . . was an emanation from God into the human soul."[21] Some of the ancient sects associated with emanations (thus, for example, Buck's reading of Priscillianists and Sabellians) denied the divinity of Christ, favoring the emanations in his stead.[22] However heretical, these antique sects drew attention to the similar roles played by Christ and the Platonic emanations in spanning the distance between the divine and human realms.

The relationship between the Restoration and Plato/Platonism is complex and usually misunderstood. In the past, many writers assumed that the Latter-day Saints were strict anti-Platonists, and indeed Christian Platonism was the very definition of early Christian apostasy.[23] More recent thought has opened up the possibility that the Restoration has affinities with at least some aspects of Platonic thought. Terryl Givens has recently argued for an emanationist view of Restoration theology, extending work by others who see Platonism as less theologically threatening than it once seemed to be.[24] One Latter-day Saint doctoral dissertation has recently proposed genealogical ties between Christian Platonism and Restoration theology in a celebration of both. While that proposal lacks high-quality documentary evidence, it does draw attention to impressive parallels and points to broader traditions of textual or paratextual connection.[25]

Latter-day Saint resonances with at least some (heavily modulated) strains of Neoplatonism and Western mysticism seem reasonably apparent. Attempts to connect the Restoration with esoteric traditions are longstanding and have generally suffered from a lack of a credible trail of explicit documents.[26] Historically, the approach carried polemical implications, which Latter-day Saints naturally rejected.[27]

The nature of the relationships may benefit from metaphors drawn from biological evolution. Evolutionary theorists distinguish between homology and analogy. Homology means that features derive from the same genetic source (for example, the fins of dolphins and whales), while analogy means addressing similar problems in similar ways without a shared genealogy (for example, the wings of bats and birds). The lack of obvious documentary connections between the Restoration and formal Platonism means that historians cannot prove homology, but at a minimum the analogy seems clear. I thus do not assume that Smith was a formal Neoplatonist, only that at a minimum his theological solutions get at problems that concerned Neoplatonists and use concepts in similar ways. (My personal hunch is that there's at least some homology, but we do not need to solve that evidential problem to appreciate resonances. Theology does not require homology the way history does.)

This context of Platonism, Neoplatonism, emanations, and divine light is important to understanding Joseph Smith's revelations of the early 1830s. While Smith was not himself an obvious or self-avowed Neoplatonist, the background philosophical questions of God, perfection, the human world, and mediation among them are important context for the Restoration theology of divine light. Smith explored these themes in revelations spread over a little more than a year, from 1832 to 1833.

The Vision of February 1832

In early 1832 Joseph Smith and Sidney Rigdon were grappling, as part of their work on the new translation of the Bible, with the possibility of multiple resurrections raised by the spare language of John

THE (TRUE) LIGHT OF CHRIST 107

5:29—people "shall come forth; they that have done good, unto the resurrection of life; and they that have done evil, unto the resurrection of damnation." They had a vision—early Latter-day Saints called it "The Vision"—later canonized as section 76. The Saints and their observers tended to focus on the universalistic implications of the degrees of afterlife glory (a polyphonic amplification of the two resurrections of John 5:29), which said that what the Protestants called hell was actually part of an expansive, multi-tiered heaven. The universalism of the Vision stunned those who heard it, but the revelation was textually as multilayered as the heavenly glories it disclosed.[28]

After a prologue promising enlightenment to those who fear and serve God (see Doctrine and Covenants 76:1–10), Smith and Rigdon clarify that they are illuminating the "things of God . . . which were from the beginning before the world was" (76:12–13), followed immediately by their report of a vision of Jesus (see 76:14). They bear record that "by him, and through him, and of him, the worlds are and were created" (76:24), explicitly echoing John's Prologue. After an excursus on Lucifer's fall and the sons of perdition who follow him (see 76:25–38), Smith and Rigdon then describe at length (76:39–112) and with substantial resonance with other scriptures—especially John's Revelation and Paul's first letter to the Corinthians—the various grades of the afterlife that Protestants called heaven and hell, including the promise that the righteous are "gods, even the sons of God" because "they are Christ's, and Christ is God's" (76:58–59). These verses reveal Restoration universalism, including a promise of equality with God, as mediated in some way by Christ, by whom creation occurred. Light has a role to play as the matrix within which three grades, or degrees, of heaven exist. This is clear in the interwoven treatment of the classes of celestial bodies from 1 Corinthians 15— sun, moon, and stars—itself reflecting Paul's interpretation of Genesis 1–3. The degree of glory in heaven's kingdoms is proportional to the luminosity of the celestial bodies whose creation is a centerpiece of the first three chapters of Genesis. The "highest of all" is God, whose "glory is that of the sun" (76:70). The full glories of heaven and hell are beyond human comprehension, beyond even words (see 76:45–47, 89–90, 114–15). Only the direct revelation of God, making people "able to bear his presence in the world of glory," can facilitate such revelation (76:118). Readers are left, then, with images of an ineffable glory that structures life and afterlife and promises a special relationship between humans and God, mediated by Jesus, who partakes of that ever-ramifying glory. This glory can be described in terms of light.

Within a few months, Smith would draw these revelatory reshapings of Corinthians and Genesis into a more robust exegesis of the Prologue of John. That ultimately came in the Olive Leaf revelation of December 1832 to January 1833. Along the way Smith further developed images of light and order in a revelatory exploration of priesthood in September 1832.

The Oath and Covenant of the Priesthood (Doctrine and Covenants 84)

Doctrine and Covenants 84, a portion of which is sometimes called the oath and covenant of the priesthood, played a role in an early phase of the establishment of Zion, the preparatory work for the Kirtland Temple, the establishment of global evangelism, and the endowment of power. In it Smith predicts that a temple will be built and then filled with glory and priesthood (see 84:4–18). He describes that priesthood, echoing language from the letter to the Hebrews, as "without beginning of days or end of years" (84:17). This priesthood will transform the Saints by sanctifying their bodies until they become the literal children of Moses (see 84:33–34). The text describes a covenant that God makes through priesthood: recipients of the priesthood must obey that covenant. In that context comes an equation of truth, light, and the spirit of Christ (see 84:45–46). The language in these verses sounds both esoteric and assiduously Christian: "Whatsoever is truth is light, and whatsoever is light is Spirit, even the Spirit of Jesus Christ." That "spirit giveth light to every man that cometh into the world: and the Spirit enlighteneth every man through the world." The text doesn't spell out where light ends and spirit begins (and how the two relate to priesthood), but truth, light, and spirit appear to be forces permeating the universe. And those forces are intimately associated with Jesus. Further details regarding the intersection of light and spirit came in the more expansive and thorough Olive Leaf revelation that Christmas season.

The Olive Leaf Revelation (Doctrine and Covenants 88)

The Olive Leaf was part of the ongoing development of the School of the Prophets, the new translation of the Bible, and Smith's work to deepen Restoration theology. More proximately, it was a return to the Vision and the cultivation of seeds sown there, especially the possibilities of salvation and the nature of the light cast by celestial bodies. It also came days after a revelation on the coming war between the states and the miseries that were inevitable before Christ's impending return (Doctrine and Covenants 87). The Olive Leaf is thus a deeply apocalyptic text, worrying over what it means for the world to "comprehend not" (see John 1:5) the Light of Christ.[29]

Smith begins the Olive Leaf with a brief introduction and then a promise of "another Comforter" (Doctrine and Covenants 88:3) that he ties explicitly back to John 14:16. He then says that this Second Comforter is "the promise which I give unto you of eternal life, even the glory of the celestial kingdom" (88:4), with a reference to the "church of the Firstborn" (88:5) that had featured in the Vision's account of the community of the celestial kingdom. This possibility of participation in heaven is mediated by Jesus Christ, who is "in all and through all things, the light of truth" (88:6), thus returning to the image of a permeating force or essence that is inextricable from Jesus. The revelation then moves through the list of celestial bodies that had constituted the backbone of the Vision, describing this "light of Christ" as being "in the sun, and the light of the sun, and the power thereof by which it was made." This "light which shineth, which giveth you light, is through him who enlighteneth your eyes, which is the same light that quickeneth your understandings" (88:7, 11). He then clarifies in perfectly emanationist terms that this "light proceedeth forth from the presence of God to fill the immensity of space" and, crucially, is "the light which is in all things, which giveth life to all things, which is the law by which all things are governed, even the power of God who sitteth upon his throne, who is in the bosom of eternity, who is in the midst of all things" (88:12–13). This light, synonymously law or power, appears to be a matrix or essence within which God exists. In the Olive Leaf, God resides in "the bosom of eternity" rather than himself being that eternity as creedal Christianity would have it. These references to light, power, law, and eternity mark a complex ongoing merger of the God of the philosophers and the God of the Bible within Restoration theology. The revelations both suggest that light is somehow beyond God, and that the light is in some ways synonymous with God (or Christ).

After a return to discussions of resurrection, the Olive Leaf defines the Vision's kingdoms in terms of the "glory by which your bodies are quickened" (Doctrine and Covenants 88:28). The promise is that whereas in life people are animated by "a portion of the celestial glory," the righteous will receive at judgment "even a fulness" of that glory (88:29). For each kingdom, that animating glory will be expanded appropriate to the glory of the kingdom they inherit. One hears both resonances of Paul's first letter to the Corinthians (13:9–10) and the power of divine emanations and their capacity to give life both on earth and in heaven. Light continues to be an essence that structures and animates the cosmos.

Then, after an aside that recurs to the eternal law that exists beyond the heavenly kingdoms (see Doctrine and Covenants 88:34–39), comes a recurrent mention of God's power permeating the cosmos, which is "through all things" (88:41). All bodies in the universe have received a law from God, including their decreed orbits, and "they give light to each other in their times and in their seasons"

(88:44). Of the stars, Smith says in especial eloquence that they "give their light, as they roll upon their wings in their glory, in the midst of the power of God" (88:45). Just as this glorious light intermingles with God and Jesus, so does it permeate, animate, and identify the other bodies that constitute the universe. Once again, light governs celestial hierarchies.

Smith then returns to his exegesis of the Prologue of John. Here he uses the language of John 1:5, clarifying that the world didn't comprehend God (favoring *katalambano*'s resonance with apprehension as comprehension) but that disciples quickened by him and in him would comprehend. Specifically, "then shall ye know that ye have seen me, that I am, and that I am the true light that is in you.... Otherwise ye could not abound" (Doctrine and Covenants 88:50). A few verses later, he lays out the path to the fulfillment of the promise: "if your eye be single to my glory, your whole bodies shall be filled with light, and there shall be no darkness in you; and that body which is filled with light comprehendeth all things" (88:67). Smith thus ties light directly to understanding at the same time that he sees it as an essence or force that can "fill" bodies. He is thereby setting up a possibility he promptly explores further. This light is somehow connected—physically, metaphysically, or both—to the genesis of our mental lives and the eternal substance of our beings. In the connections between Jesus, humans, a permeating cosmic light, moral agency, and the ultimate outcome of human development, the Olive Leaf becomes the story of what later Saints called the plan of salvation, painted with strokes of light rather than sequential moral examinations. As human beings encounter the light of truth, they are drawn into communion with God and cosmic order. Through Christ and in extension of the bare hints in Doctrine and Covenants 76:58, they become gods themselves as they allow their bodies to be filled with light.

This divine light maintained its connection to Jesus, the encompassing universal force, eternal human intelligence, and the moral order of the universe as it continued to develop in Restoration scripture, with an efflorescence the following May in another revelation that even more explicitly and thoroughly engaged the Prologue to John.

The True Light Revelation (Doctrine and Covenants 93)

Smith returned to the themes of the true light in May 1833, in a revelation (Doctrine and Covenants 93) that quibbles with and extends John's arguments. I've proposed that we call this revelation the "True Light," a case I extend here.[30] John largely depicts Christ as the eternal Word and light by which God brings life and truth to humanity, while Smith seems to have proposed a view of Christ as the best and purest vessel for a light beyond us all. Smith thereby seems to have suggested that John had committed a metonymic error: the ancient apostle had unwittingly merged the light and its purest vessel.[31]

Smith's division of the true light into Christ and a power beyond Christ—admitting that bringing their distinction into focus happens in a context in which differences between them are continually blurred—corrects John's mistaken metonymy. The "true light" (Doctrine and Covenants 93:2) exemplifies the *agape*—true, pure love—that unites individuals (see 93:3–4). All power arises as God and Christ dwell in each other (see 93:17), a mutuality made possible by the true light, which appears to have an existence beyond the two divine beings thus united. Smith clarifies that humans can grow toward divinity as they participate in a Christly relationship of mutuality guided by that light (see 93:20–22). He gestures to the concept as the "Spirit of truth" (93:23–24), arguing that light and truth belong together (see 93:29–30, 36) and are uncreated. He then maintains that this light is logically and chronologically anterior to human meaning: "here is the agency of man . . . because that which was from the beginning [the true light] is plainly manifest unto them" (93:31). There must be moral illumination, in other words, or there is no capacity for humans to choose. The light thus suggests a self-revealing moral order. Throughout the revelatory exegesis in Doctrine and Covenants

93, Smith describes true light as both the source and metric of goodness, truth, and morality. This light appears to exist beyond time and beyond any specific incarnation, of which there are many, although Jesus holds pride of place. In Doctrine and Covenants 93, the fresh reassortment of the attributes of the God of the philosophers and the God of Abraham, Isaac, and Jacob moves to another level.

In Doctrine and Covenants 93, Smith revisits the possibility that intelligence—the apparently personal (or personalizable) substance out of which human beings are made in their premortal existence—is a synonym for the true light. "Intelligence, or the light of truth, was not created or made" (93:29). Shortly comes a related reference to the fact that "the glory of God is intelligence, or, in other words, light and truth" (93:36). This intelligence stands outside the flow of creation that depends on the Word, and it also overlaps, perhaps completely, with the "light of truth" somehow synonymous with Christ. This further expansion of uncreated essences places human beings alongside Christ in the flow of true light and mental being.

Then comes a clear interpretation of John 1:5 that indicts modern blindness in another translation of *katalambano*—"that which was from the beginning is plainly manifest unto them, and they receive not the light" (Doctrine and Covenants 93:31). It is not just that they don't comprehend, but they won't allow the light into themselves. Then comes a cryptic line that connects this unreceived intelligence to the "glory of God," which the Book of Moses (1:39) had associated with God in relationship to human beings. In Moses, "the immortality and eternal life" of humanity is God's "work" and "glory." In Doctrine and Covenants 93 God's exalting glory is light. God and humans are brought together in light, intelligence, and glory. There's a lot at play here, drawing on the many different threads of divine light, including human conscience, truth, intelligence, and the essence of divine love in which humans and gods live and breathe and have their being. And that light continues to find its weightiest incarnation in Christ.

The Afterlife of a Doctrine

After this burst of revelatory activity on light in 1832–33, Smith spent less time engaging the true light directly. He seems instead to have explored parallel themes. Smith and Rigdon, in the *Lectures on Faith* in 1834–1835, interpreted the book of Hebrews as an infrastructure for teachings on faith and priesthood. There they used familiar language and ideas to suggest that faith was an essence or force that God could utilize in seeking to achieve God's ends for creation. According to lecture 1, faith is "the first great governing principle, which has power, dominion and authority over all things." The lectures continue to argue that without faith there is no power in the universe, that even God has faith.[32] While they did not connect the dots explicitly, Smith and Rigdon seem in the *Lectures on Faith* to have understood faith as a complementary, uncreated essence that existed beyond the God of the Bible. Faith seems to be an alignment of one's intelligence with the Light of Christ.

A few years later, Smith pursued two threads of related theology, teachings on the Second Comforter and temple priesthood. While those topics are too diffuse for a thorough treatment here, a brief overview will point out continuities. The themes continued those introduced in the early true light revelations, expanding the core themes of light as a force that unites humans with Christ and transforms them.

A key aspect of the true light was the juxtaposition of revelatory knowledge and Christ. Following the hint in the Olive Leaf (Doctrine and Covenants 88:68), in the late 1830s Joseph Smith explained that a Second Comforter (interpreting John 14:16–17, 21–23) was the personal, physical ministry of Christ. Rather than visits from angels or the Holy Ghost (the First Comforter), those who received the Second Comforter would be visited by Christ.[33] More intensely physical and embodied than its precedents, this later doctrine (a Latter-day Saint answer to the Methodist doctrine of sanctification)[34] stayed true to the roots of the true light, with its juxtaposition of truth, intelligence, revelation, and the person of Christ.

As Smith worked to clarify the doctrines and ordinances of salvation, he focused his energies on the Nauvoo Temple. In that temple, Smith brought to fruition the Light of Christ and a specific ritual promise of the Second Comforter as ordinances that brought the Saints as transformed beings into the divine presence together with their kindred. By the end of his life, Joseph Smith was becoming clearer about the interplay of truth, light, priesthood, and power. He was suggesting that in the temple believers could gain access to this power beyond divinity as part of their growth in becoming something greater than merely human. In April 1842 he preached that "if you wish to go whare God is you must be like God or possess the principles which God possesses."[35] Those principles were a structure beyond God, and the mastery of that structure was the promise of Godhood. In the temple these mysteries of Godliness were divulged as manifestations of priesthood and divine intelligence.[36] The temple became the ritual location and sacramental infrastructure for the forces beyond Gods and humans, forces which made them what they were. Through the temple, believers finally and fully comprehended the true light.

Conclusions and Implications

Fundamentally, the Restoration doctrine of the True Light is a vista on an old and important question about the coexistence of perfection and imperfection, divine order and human disorder, personality and impersonality. Many different thinkers and communities over the millennia have proposed solutions to these basic, existential problems. What does it mean to aspire to be better than we are? And what shall we do with the sense that there's more to the cosmos than unrelated tangles of matter? How much of the meaning we see in the universe is impersonal, and how much personal? How does the vast and impersonal affect us as humans?

Classically, Christian theologians taught that God as such was wholly perfect, beyond anything human such as body or emotion. As we've seen, this was the Platonically perfect God we know from Augustine and the Christian creeds. Although many critics (and some proponents) emphasize the entire transcendence of that God, the reality is that the incarnation of Jesus was central to Christianity from the beginning. In Jesus, the transcendent God came to illuminate human life. On the opposing side in current culture wars, contemporary secularist thinkers tend to maintain that they believe only in the immanent world of imperfect humans, denying even the possibility of metaphysics. But most of them will still believe in moral principles and "laws of nature" that have a status beyond any specific tangles of matter. The two main poles of modern thought about the relationship between God and cosmos—that God is wholly transcendent or that God does not exist because there can only be the immanent—thus equivocate substantially. The interdigitation of the transcendent and immanent realms seems impossible to deny, even for the most ardent partisans at the philosophical extremes.

Smith seems to have seen through the equivocations and philosophical blind spots. He did so in his characteristic impulse to harmonize what is discordant by blurring dualisms and uniting a fractured cosmos.[37] He wasn't afraid to assault Protestant clergy and doctrines to make his point, even as he repurposed familiar concepts into new formulations. The doctrine of emanations, modified slightly, seems to have proved a useful mechanism to blur the theological boundaries between persons and essences.

The True Light theology works toward a merger of the God of the philosophers (the Platonic God of perfection) and the God of the Bible (the personal God familiar to most Latter-day Saints). This merger happens alongside and dependent on an elevation of humanity into a status equal with God. The elevation of humans to divine status is mediated by Christ and patterned on him.

Recognizing emanations and interdigitation as moving together dramatically complicates traditional stories about Restoration theology.

Many Latter-day Saints have seen themselves as anti-Platonists—denying the existence of the world of the Forms and embracing a God who is finite and material rather than immaterial and changeless. The True Light theology suggests that the truth is much more complicated than that.

There's a taxonomic question at play—is Restoration theology Platonist or anti-Platonist, and how does Restoration theology compare to creedal Christian understandings? On the one hand, the light and other essences beyond God sound like Plato's world of the Forms, and God the Father of the Latter-day Saints sounds like Plato's demiurge. On the other hand, the emanations aren't only from God but may also come through him. The Latter-day Saints are idiosyncratic Platonists to say the least. As for creedal Christianity, the True Light sounds an awful lot like their God of the philosophers—it appears to be an essence or force that structures and animates the cosmos. But that essence is embodied not only in Christ but in the heavenly parents and human beings as well. And even as this Restoration theology of incarnation radically democratizes the interface, it is still and always tied to Christ.

Restoration theology also runs contrary to common assumptions about the modern world's separation of the heavenly from the earthly, which mostly expresses an ongoing attempt to exile God entirely from the universe. According to Restoration theology, we live in the midst of realms that are complementary and interwoven. Physicality is central to the story, but the merely physical cannot be the whole story. A deep metaphysics also illuminates the world of coarse matter. The question is how to name the realms, how to imagine them, how to orient ourselves within them, and how to unite them in meaningful ways that do not use them up in the process.

As is so often the case, Smith worked fluidly and impressionistically. Many questions remain unanswered. But the True Light theology does raise important questions about the viability of anti-Platonic views of Latter-day Saint theology, whether framed in traditional or postmodern terms. The Restoration proves broader, nimbler, and more interesting than we might otherwise have thought.

Notes

1. Adam Becker, *What Is Real? The Unfinished Quest for the Meaning of Quantum Physics* (New York: Basic Books, 2018) provides a hopeful overview to the ongoing puzzles of quantum physics.

2. On these topics, see especially Charles Taylor, *A Secular Age* (Cambridge, MA: Harvard University Press, 2007); Brad S. Gregory, *The Unintended Reformation: How a Religious Reformation Secularized Society* (Cambridge, MA: Harvard, 2012); Eugene McCarraher, *The Enchantments of Mammon: Capitalism as the Religion of Modernity* (Cambridge, MA: Harvard University Press, 2019); Steven Smith, *Pagans and Christians in the City: Culture Wars from the Tiber to the Potomac* (Grand Rapids, MI: Eerdmans, 2018).

3. Taylor, *Secular Age*, 550–56, 589.

4. Thus, from often opposing perspectives, the thought of Adam Miller, Terryl Givens, and Blake Ostler. Miller operates from the perspective of Continental philosophy, Givens from a kind of Romantic monism, and Ostler as a Christian heretic, using the language of traditional theology repurposed in a contest with creedal Christianity. See Adam S. Miller, *Speculative Grace: Bruno Latour and Object-Oriented Theology* (New York: Fordham University Press, 2013); *Future Mormon: Essays in Mormon Theology* (Salt Lake City: Kofford Books, 2016); and *Rube Goldberg Machines: Essays in Mormon Theology* (Salt Lake City: Kofford Books, 2012); Terryl L. Givens, *Wrestling the Angel: The Foundations of Mormon Thought; Cosmos, God, and Humanity* (Oxford: Oxford University Press, 2015); Blake T. Ostler, *Exploring Mormon Thought* series (Salt Lake City: Kofford Books, 2001, 2006, 2008). For a somewhat more balanced view, see Sterling M. McMurrin, *The Theological Foundations of the Mormon Religion*, Signature Mormon Classics repr. ed. (Salt Lake City: Signature Books, 2000), 5–9, 36; and McMurrin, "The Philosophical Foundations of Mormon Theology," appendix to *Theological Foundations*, 10, 20, 29. Philosopher David L. Paulsen has argued at length for what he terms

Latter-day Saint "finitistic theism"; Paulsen, "Comparative Coherency of Mormon (Finitistic) and Classical (Absolutistic) Theism" (PhD diss., University of Michigan, 1975).

5. See Jordan T. Watkins and Christopher James Blythe, "Christology and Theosis in the Revelations and Teachings of Joseph Smith," 123–56, in this volume.

6. Max Nolan, "Materialism and the Mormon Faith," *Dialogue* 2, no. 4 (1989): 62–75. Sterling McMurrin also noted the complexities of calling Latter-day Saint theology materialist: McMurrin, *Theological Foundations*, 1, 5–7.

7. This famous phrase comes from Pascal's *Memorial*, recovered after his death from the lining of his coat. Martin Buber extended the contrast in his pursuit of religious experience as the encounter of personal beings rather than rationalist theorizing in *The Eclipse of God: Studies in the Relation between Religion and Philosophy* (1965; repr., Princeton: Princeton University Press, 2016).

8. For examples, see Francis J. Beckwith and Stephen E. Parrish, *The Mormon Concept of God: A Philosophical Analysis* (Lewiston, NY: Edwin Mellen, 1991); versus David L. Paulsen and Blake T. Ostler, review of *The Mormon Concept of God: A Philosophical Analysis*, by Beckwith and Parrish, *International Journal for Philosophy of Religion* 35, no. 2 (April 1994): 118–20. See also McMurrin, *Theological Foundations*, 2–3, 9.

9. I introduced my early thinking on this topic in "Mormons Probably Aren't Materialists," *Dialogue* 50, no. 3 (Fall 2017): 39–72. I reuse, revise, and expand aspects of that treatment here.

10. Connections between John and Restoration scripture are a major theme of Nicholas J. Frederick's perceptive *The Bible, Mormon Scripture, and the Rhetoric of Allusivity* (Teaneck, NJ: Fairleigh Dickinson, 2016).

11. Daniel Boyarin, *Border Lines: The Partition of Judaeo-Christianity* (Philadelphia: University of Pennsylvania Press, 2006), 97, 102–9; John Day, *Yahweh and the Gods and Goddesses of Canaan* (Sheffield, UK: Sheffield Academic, 2002), 22, 66–67; William G. Dever, *Did God Have a Wife? Archaeology and Folk Religion in Ancient Israel* (Grand Rapids, MI: Eerdmans, 2008), 199–200, 301–2.

12. I appreciate the urging of an anonymous reviewer to be open to the dual meanings of *apprehend* associated with *katalambano*. I think the connection to crucifixion and resurrection pushes toward the image of extinction, but Joseph Smith's merger of intelligence, truth, and light point toward comprehension. I am comfortable with and see room for both. I'm also echoing N. T. Wright's sense of the meaning of Jesus's life in *How God Became King: The Forgotten Story of the Gospels* (New York: HarperCollins, 2016).

13. Brown, "Mormons Probably Aren't Materialists," 16, 19.

14. And much more complex than McMurrin, *Theological Foundations*, 15, acknowledges.

15. Brown, "Mormons Probably Aren't Materialists," 7–8.

16. Wouter J. Hanegraaff, ed., *Dictionary of Gnosis and Western Esotericism* (Leiden: Brill, 2006), s.v. "Neoplatonism."

17. N. T. Wright, *Surprised by Hope: Rethinking Heaven, the Resurrection, and the Mission of the Church* (New York: HarperCollins, 2008), 88–91.

18. McMurrin maintains, I think correctly, that many Latter-day Saint models of God place the God of the Bible as an equivalent to Plato's demiurge: *Theological Foundations*, 29.

19. On the emanations, see Wouter J. Hanegraaff, *Esotericism and the Academy: Rejected Knowledge in Western Culture* (Cambridge: Cambridge University Press, 2012), 106; and Catherine L. Albanese, *Republic of Mind and Spirit: A Cultural History of American Metaphysical Religion* (New Haven, CT: Yale University Press, 2012), 51, 178, 347, 260, 464.

20. Brett Malcolm Grainger, *Church in the Wild: Evangelicals in Antebellum America* (Cambridge, MA: Harvard University Press, 2019), 4, 8, 98.

21. Charles Buck, *A Theological Dictionary* (Philadelphia: Thomas, Cowperthwaite, 1823), 400. On Smith's preference for Buck, see Matthew Bowman and Samuel Brown, "The Reverend Buck's *Theological Dictionary* and the Struggle to Define American Evangelicalism, 1802–1851," *Journal of the Early Republic* 29, no. 3 (Fall 2009): 441–73.

22. Buck, *Theological Dictionary*, 489, 530.

23. See, for example, Bruce R. McConkie, *Mormon Doctrine* (Salt Lake City: Bookcraft, 1966), s.v. "Logos"; and James E. Talmage, *The Great Apostasy* (Salt Lake City: Deseret News, 1909), 100–101, 110.

24. Terryl L. Givens, *The Pearl of Greatest Price: Mormonism's Most Controversial Scripture* (Oxford: Oxford University Press, 2019), 52–53; Daniel W. Graham and James L. Siebach, "Philosophy and Early Christianity," *FARMS Review of Books* 11, no. 3 (1999): 210–20.

25. Stephen J. Fleming, "The Fulness of the Gospel: Christian Platonism and the Origins of Mormonism" (PhD diss., University of California, Santa Barbara, 2014).

26. The best-known are D. Michael Quinn, *Early Mormonism and the Magic World View* (Salt Lake City: Signature Books, 1987); and John Brooke, *The Refiner's Fire: The Making of Mormon Cosmology, 1644–1844* (Cambridge, MA: Cambridge University Press, 1994).

27. Samuel M. Brown, "The Reluctant Metaphysicians," *Mormon Studies Review* 1 (2014): 115–31.

28. See Gerrit J. Dirkmaat, Brent M. Rogers, Grant Underwood, Robert J. Woodford, and William G. Hartley, eds., *Documents, Volume 3: February 1833–March 1834*, vol. 3 of the Documents series of *The Joseph Smith Papers*, ed. Ronald K. Esplin and Matthew J. Grow (Salt Lake City: Church Historian's Press, 2014), 155, for a contemporary response to the Vision.

29. I thank an anonymous reviewer for urging me to consider this connection.

30. Brown, "Mormons Probably Aren't Materialists," 17.

31. Frederick, *Bible, Mormon Scripture, and the Rhetoric of Allusivity*, chapter 4, is correct that Doctrine and Covenants 93 elaborates a "lower" Christology than John does, albeit without pointing toward the democratized incarnation. Frederick improves upon his initial treatment of the phrase "grace for grace" (64) in his chapter in the present volume, "Incarnation, Exaltation, and Christological Tension in Doctrine and Covenants 93:1–32," 11–41.

32. Robin Scott Jensen, Richard E. Turley Jr., and Riley M. Lorimer, eds., *Revelations and Translations, Volume 2: Published Revelations*, vol. 2 of the Revelations and Translations series of *The Joseph Smith Papers*, ed.

Dean C. Jessee, Ronald K. Esplin, and Richard Lyman Bushman (Salt Lake City: Church Historian's Press, 2011), 321.

33. See, for example, Brent M. Rogers, Mason K. Allred, Gerrit J. Dirkmaat, and Brett D. Dowdle, eds., *Documents, Volume 8: February–November 1841*, vol. 8 of the Documents series of *The Joseph Smith Papers*, ed. Ronald K. Esplin, Matthew J. Grow, Matthew C. Godfrey, and R. Eric Smith (Salt Lake City: Church Historian's Press, 2019), 89; Mark Ashurst-McGee, David W. Grua, Elizabeth Kuehn, Alexander L. Baugh, and Brenden W. Rensink, eds., *Documents, Volume 6: February 1838–August 1839*, vol. 6 of the Documents series of *The Joseph Smith Papers*, ed. Ronald K. Esplin, Matthew J. Grow, and Matthew C. Godfrey (Salt Lake City: Church Historian's Press, 2017), 522, 525, 553.

34. Paul K. Conkin, *The Uneasy Center: Reformed Christianity in Antebellum America* (Chapel Hill: University of North Caroline Press), 70–71.

35. Wilford Woodruff's Journal, 146–47, transcription mine, Church History Library.

36. Samuel Morris Brown, *Joseph Smith's Translation: The Words and Worlds of Early Mormonism* (Oxford: Oxford University Press, 2020), chapter 7.

37. Philip Barlow, "To Mend a Fractured Reality: Joseph Smith's Project," *Journal of Mormon History* 38, no. 3 (Summer 2012): 28–50.

6

Christology and Theosis in the Revelations and Teachings of Joseph Smith

Jordan T. Watkins and Christopher James Blythe

In early 1842 Joseph Smith privately taught that righteous Saints would be saviors. The radical teaching appears in a booklet kept by the apostle Wilford Woodruff in Nauvoo, Illinois. On the book's cover, Woodruff scrawled the title "Book of Revelations," and in its pages he included several of Smith's revelations along with notes from some of Smith's sermons. An entry dated 30 January (1842) reads,

> Joseph the Seer taught the following principles that the God & father of our Lord Jesus Christ was once the same as the Son or Holy Ghost but having redeemed a world became the eternal God of that world he had a son Jesus Christ who redeemed this earth the same as his father had a world which made them equal & the Holy Ghost would do the same in turn & so would all the Saints who inherited a Celestial glory so their would be Gods many & Lords many.[1]

This entry confirms that over two years before Smith publicly revealed the "great secret" of God's history in the King Follett discourse, he was already teaching that God the Father was once mortal and had served as the savior of a previous world. This singular account suggests that Smith not only taught that humans held the potential to become like the Father and the Son but further that the process of deification demanded that they redeem a world as future saviors.

This final teaching—that exalted humans must literally be saviors of worlds—does not appear in the extant records of Smith's public discourses, including the famous King Follett discourse, which raises questions about its place in his thought. Was Smith teaching it as a revealed truth, or was he speculating on the possible destinies of exalted humans? While a historical accounting cannot answer that question in full, it can shed light on the sources of this and related teachings and illuminate their possible meanings. In this paper we track how Smith's revelations seeded concepts that allowed for the development of a robust and radical version of the teaching of theosis—or the process of becoming divine—and trace the flowering of that version in Smith's later teachings. When viewed in light of this history, Smith's January 1842 statements appear less as the beginnings of a late theological change of course and more as the beginnings of an intellectual culmination of prior revelations about Christ and humanity.

Historians have sometimes assumed that Smith's later teachings, particularly those on the nature of God and humans, represent a stark departure from the theology found in his earliest translations and revelations.[2] While Smith's teachings on the history and destiny of Gods and humans developed across time, clear christological and anthropological continuities endured from his early 1830s revelations to his 1840s teachings. Indeed, the 1830s revelations shaped the content of the 1840s teachings. In other words, Smith's Nauvoo pronouncements on the nature of God and his children reflect the maturation of his own views about his earlier revelations. To be sure,

Smith's teachings on theosis upended traditional Christian thought; while the unorthodox Socinians of the sixteenth and seventeenth centuries taught that Christ was more human than divine, the heterodox Smith taught that humans were eternal beings with divine destinies. However, his teachings were rooted in earlier revelations that upheld Christ as the model for how the faithful could obtain godhood. Smith's revelations simultaneously affirmed Christ's role as savior, exemplar, and prototype of salvation while also advancing the idea that humans, as God's children, have the potential to become like Christ.

The Revelatory Foundation of Theosis

The ideas that Smith developed in the 1840s can be found in the revelations he received a decade earlier. In this first section, we look at five revelatory documents that laid the conceptual foundation for the Latter-day Saint version of theosis that began to emerge in the last years of Smith's life. These revelations included statements that challenged the assumption of an ontological—which refers to the nature of being—difference between God, Christ, and humans and explicitly taught that humans could follow the example of Jesus to obtain a divinity and glory that matches that of the Father.

One of Smith's first revelatory writings to introduce these concepts was his June 1830 expansion of Genesis—a vision of Moses that contextualized the creation account. As other scholars have noted, the Book of Moses Christianized Genesis, but it also rejected a core tenet of creedal Christianity—that an unbridgeable ontological distinction separated the Father from his children.[3] In the account, God meets with Moses face to face and reveals that Moses was made in the image of the "only begotten." After this theophany, Moses endures a vision of a different sort. Satan appears and tempts him and calls him a "Son of man," which Moses boldly refutes, declaring that he is "a Son of God in the similitude of his only begotten."[4] The phrases "son of man," "Son of man," and "Son of Man" appear in the Old and New

Testaments, where their referents include a human being, a prophetic and a messianic figure, and Christ himself. While the initial use of the title in the Book of Moses functions as it often does in the Old Testament—to set apart humans from God—subsequent uses, both in the Book of Moses and in Smith's revelations and teachings, align more closely with the New Testament passages in which the phrase refers to Christ.[5] Moreover, the account of Moses's temptation, in its presentation as ancient, *anticipates* Christ's own temptation; at the same time, in its late introduction to nineteenth-century readers, the account narratively *imitates* Christ's temptation. At once, then, the passage rejects Satan's insistence on an ontological distinction between God and man—positing instead an ontological correspondence of the same—while also introducing the idea of a prophetic *Imitatio Christi*, wherein readers discover a familiar prophetic figure who imitates or emulates Christ. In these ways, the account also foreshadows the text's later distinctive use of the phrase "Son of Man."

In the second century some Christian commentators used this descriptor to refine the belief in Christ as both human and divine. For example, Irenaeus referred to passages describing Christ as "the Son of Man" to refute claims that Christ did not take on human flesh and suffer in that flesh.[6] Irenaeus, as well as later Christian commentators such as Saint Augustine, also used the phrase "Son of Man" to make a case for what became known as theosis (that is, deification), insisting that the Son of God became the Son of Man so that believers might partake of his grace. In voicing this belief—which these thinkers asserted rather than fully articulated—they often took care to insist that human participation in the divine came through grace alone and not by nature. In the centuries since Augustine's formulation, Christian theologians who adopted and advanced versions of a belief in theosis remained committed to the idea that ontological difference separates God from humans and that divinization comes only through grace.[7]

Smith's Genesis expansion refuted this reading, in part by overturning some of the traditional understandings of "Son of Man." One passage in particular revealed that "in the language of Adam, Man of Holiness is [God's name], and the name of his Only Begotten is the Son of Man, even Jesus Christ, a righteous Judge, who shall come in the meridian of time."[8] While conveying messianic content that echoed earlier Christian interpretations, the text also indicated that the "Son of Man" refers to Christ and that "Man" refers to God. In teaching that Christ was the son of an exalted "Man," this remarkable formulation suggested that humankind shared in the divine nature. In an apparent rejection of the ontological distinction between God and humans, this passage anticipated the emergence of unique teachings about God's nature and history and a radical version of Christian theosis.

This Book of Moses passage referred to the language of Adam to redefine the terms that described the human and the divine and to reframe the relationship between God and his children. A prior passage had described Adam's effort to maintain a language "which was pure & undefiled."[9] The connection between a pure language and its power to reveal the ontological affinities between Gods and humans continued to intrigue Smith. Sometime around March 1832, he received "A Sample of pure Language" that designated the name of God as "Awmen," and defined Awmen as "the being which made all things." It then labeled the name of the Son of God as "Son Awmen," which it defined as "the greatest of all the parts of Awmen." It also termed men as "Sons Awmen" and defined it as "the human family the children of men the greatest parts of Awmen Sons."[10] Whatever else this text meant, the "Sample of pure Language" joined the Book of Moses in positing that humans shared in the same substance as the Son and the Father.

At the beginning and the end of 1832, Smith dictated two other revelatory documents, both of which aligned postmortal glory with becoming like God. The first was the report of a shared vision experienced by Smith and Sidney Rigdon in February 1832. The righteous inheritors of those "whose bodies are celestial" would be "priests and kings, who have received of his [the Father's] fulness, and of his glory

. . . wherefore," the passage summarized, "as it is written, they are gods, even the sons of god."[11] A later section explained that those who "received of his fulness and of his grace" become "equal in power and in might and in dominion."[12] While the vision of Moses and the pure language document had introduced the idea that Gods and humans were the same kinds of beings and shared the same substance, the vision of Smith seemed to suggest that humans could achieve the same power and glory as God.

A December 1832 revelation affirmed this point. The revelation built on Smith's vision in pointing toward a salvation beyond receiving "celestial bodies"; it explained that those bodies would inhabit a celestial glory or kingdom.[13] Obtaining the Father's fullness appeared to include the inheritance of celestial bodies, powers, and worlds. The revelation reiterated this point in a prophetic passage that described the Saints at Christ's Second Coming. It explained that they would "be filled with his glory and receive their inheritance and be made equal with him."[14] Smith's revelations began to suggest that being made equal with the Son was tantamount to being made equal with the Father. This exalting equation rested in the divine calculus of the Godhead. In a May 1833 revelation Christ declared, "I am in the fathe[r] and the father in me and the fathe[r] and I are one the father because he gave me of his fulness."[15]

The May revelation unveiled the origins and progression of Christ, as well as the origins and possibilities of his followers. In other words, it outlined how Christ received the fullness from the Father, and how his followers could do the same. Nicholas J. Frederick suggests that this revelation "stands as Smith's first and greatest statement on the divine potential of humankind, providing a scriptural justification for the Mormon idea that humanity not only shares its origins with God, but that they can become Gods themselves."[16] While not the first statement on the possibility of human deification, the revelation contains the most explicit description of the process by which believers could, in imitation of Christ, become like God.

As Frederick explains, the revelation radically revised the first chapter of the Gospel of John and with it much of traditional Christian thought.[17] The revision began rather innocuously: "I saw his glory that he was in the begining before the world was therefore in the beg[inn]ing the word was for he was the word even the messenger of salvation the light and the redeemer of the world the spirit of truth, who came into the world."[18] After an unproblematic opening, in which John affirms Christ's magnificent premortal status, he then observes that in mortality Jesus "received not of the fulness at first . . . but continued from grace to grace until he received a fulness and thus he was called the son of God because he received not of the fulness at first."[19] This passage "inverts" the Gospel of John's use of "Son of God," using it not to describe Jesus as God, but rather to show his path toward godhood.[20] The Book of Moses's use of the phrase "Son of Man" pointed toward the humanity of both Son and Father, and the revelation's use of the phrase "Son of God" outlined Jesus's movement toward the Father's fullness. Terryl Givens suggests that this passage "might be construed as indicating—in contradistinction to the council of Chalcedon's pronouncement that Jesus was fully human and fully divine at birth, and 'perfect in his divinity'—a process of total divinization, or Christ's receipt of the Father's fullness, finally achieved through the experience of mortality."[21] These passages countered the prevailing Christian view, not by suggesting that Christ had not always been divine but in describing the process by which a divine being progressed from grace to grace until he received a fullness.

Smith's revelation continued where the portion of John's record finished, moving from a description of the progress of Christ to a discussion of the potential of his followers. Taking the narrative lead, the Lord himself spoke directly to his audience: "I give unto you these sayings that you may understand and know how to worship and know what you worship that you may come unto the fathe[r] in my name and in due time receive of his fulness for if you keep my commandments you shall receive of his fulness and be glor[i]fied in me as I am glor[i]fied in the father, therefore I say <unto> you you shall receive grace for grace."[22] God's children could achieve full divinity by obeying the commandments of Christ, an apparent act of grace that garnered further grace and allowed individuals to progress toward a fullness. In the May 1833 revelation, the Lord revealed a record about himself—"what you worship"—for the purpose of encouraging believers in the revelations to follow his example—"how to worship." In this robust *Imitatio Christi*, the Saints could go on to obtain all that Christ and the Father have.

The revelation seemed to anticipate the audience's question of how they, as mere mortals, could emulate their Savior and become "partakers of the glory of the same." Divulging another heterodox mystery, the Lord explained that his audience and the rest of humanity "were also in the begining with the fathe[r]."[23] This statement, which exploded traditional Christianity's core assumption that Creator existed separate and apart from his creation, drew together the human and the divine. The idea that humans had premortally existed with Christ gave credence to the teaching that they could become like him. This teaching aligned with the emphasis placed on mortality's crucial role in Christ's progress and on the related teaching that bodies were essential to salvation. The 1832 revelations on salvation had described bodies as a defining characteristic of salvation.[24] The May 1833 revelation gave further insight into the importance of bodies in teaching that "the Elements are eternal and spirit and element inseperably connected receiveth a fulness of Joy."[25] In this period, Smith does not appear to have grasped that the exalting connection between spirit and matter had implications for God's embodiment. Even still, the revelation planted the idea that something about humans and the materials that made up their bodies had existed with Christ in a premortal state, which placed them in a position to fulfill the direction to emulate Christ and obtain the Father's fullness.

These revelations laid a conceptual foundation for the development of a new kind of Christian theosis, but that development was not inevitable or automatic. While the ideas, like crude metals, had been made available, they had yet to be forged into useful theological tools. Some forging occurred within months of the May revelation and in the context of Church members' difficulties in Missouri. Whereas most members had little time to consider the exalting power of their bodies while also enduring the effects of mob violence, William W. Phelps managed to do both. Writing to Smith and other Church leaders in Kirtland in December 1833, he asked for guidance "in the midst of [his] solitude" and the Missouri members' "affliction." Those afflictions colored Phelps's reading of Smith's revelations. In his letter to Smith, he wrote that "*the sons of God only* are made equal with Jesus Chrift [Christ] *having overcome*, by righteousness."[26] In attempting to reconcile a revealed promise of divine reward and his harsh temporal reality, Phelps conceptualized suffering as a necessary step toward equality with Christ. With a few exceptions, Missouri persecution and Kirtland opposition appear to have hindered Smith, Phelps, and other Church members from producing much else in terms of direct commentary on these revelations.[27] In the long term, however, persecution became a powerful forge for the refinement of radical ideas about God and his children.[28]

Imprisoned *Imitatio Christi*: 1838–1839

While Smith did not fully cultivate the theological seeds of theosis until the Illinois era, his trials in Missouri prepared him for the work. Other sources of opposition in the late 1830s encouraged the articulation of a Latter-day Saint understanding of theosis. In *A Voice of Warning* (1837), Parley P. Pratt included the revealed teaching that the Saints would "be made equal with" Christ, which drew a critical response from an observant and scandalized Protestant. Instead of backing away from the teaching, Pratt proceeded to defend and declare his belief in theosis.[29] Smith's own interactions with hostile Missourians proved to be an even more effective, if also more painful and less obvious, incubator for these ideas. His imprisonment in the winter of 1838–39 placed him in a space wherein he gained greater insight into the process of becoming like Christ and developed a new mode of teaching the Saints about salvation and exaltation. As Smith sought God from the depths of the human condition, he learned important truths about what it meant to be like Christ.

While issuing his lament from an earthly prison, Smith gained new insight into what Phelps had observed in his December 1833 letter: suffering had exalting power. Smith's contemplation of the Saints' suffering, which added to his own, led him to ask, "O God where art thou?" (Doctrine and Covenants 121:1). This recalled the language of the cross, where the Son asked the Father, "Why hast thou forsaken me?" (Matthew 27:46). No immediate answer was forthcoming for Jesus; the same was true for Smith. In the 1839 letter to the Saints that contained his plea, the Lord does not immediately reply. Instead, Smith's mundane comments on public perception, personal correspondence, and suffering Saints precede his report of the Lord's response. Only in Orson Pratt's truncated version, which he prepared for inclusion in a later edition of the Doctrine and Covenants, does the Lord instantly respond to Smith's Christlike petition (see Doctrine and Covenants 121:1–7). By removing portions of the text and thereby fusing together question and answer, Pratt's canonized account highlights but also simplifies the dialogue with the divine.[30] Smith had to wait for the Lord to speak these comforting words: "My son pease be unto thy soul thine adivrsity and thy afflictions shall be but a small moment and then if thou indure it well God shall exalts the[e] on high."[31] The original letter's quotidian interlude, more than Pratt's canon-making ellipses, underscores the Lord's promise that exaltation would follow endurance. This teaching corresponded with Phelps's earlier equation and with the revealed teaching about receiving "grace for grace."

Smith's isolation gave him a deeper understanding of the expansive nature of salvation that had been introduced in his revelations. There was something poetic about this development; the telestial prison setting encouraged a prophet to develop celestial ideas. In a portion of the letter that Pratt later edited out, Smith wrote, "Thy mind O Man, if thou wilt lead a soul unto salvation must streach [stretch] as high as the utmost Heavens, and sink sear[c]h in to and contemplate the loest [lowest] consideatins [considerations] of the darkest abyss, and Expand upon the broad considerations of Eternal Expance, he must commune with God."[32] Pratt's redactions uncomplicated the processes of salvation and revelation, and it was those very processes that had power to activate the promises in Smith's earlier revelations. In one of those revelations the Lord explained that "he that assended up on high, as also he, deceded below all things; in that he comprehended all things, that he might be in all, and through all things; the light of truth."[33] In his moment of need, Christ himself had wondered where God had gone and in that supreme condescension he came to comprehend all things. In prison, Smith learned that growing from grace to grace involved Christlike suffering and learning. In these ways, Smith's prison experience was an *Imitatio Christi* in microcosm.

In another March 1839 letter that he wrote two days after the first, Smith continued to record the Lord's response to his plea, which included this question: "The Son of Man hath descended below them all art thou greater than he?"[34] On the surface, the interrogation put Smith in his place, but in light of his prior revelations, including the description of "Son of Man" in Moses, the question might be read as an instance of the Lord instructing Smith on how he could become like him.

Smith emerged from prison with an enhanced prophetic confidence born from a new closeness to God. This was evident in the content of his teachings, which Smith foreshadowed in more than one of his prison letters. In a 15 March letter to Presendia Buell, who had visited the Prophet earlier that day, Smith expressed his desire to "once more lift my voice in the midst of the Saints," noting "I never have had opportunity to give them the plan that God has revealed to me." Smith proceeded to suggest that his understanding of the things of God and his desire to explain them to the Saints had developed in relationship to his trials. "[Our trouble]," he noted, "will only give us that knowledge to understand the minds of the Ancients for my part I think I never could have felt as I now do if I had not suffered the wrongs that I have suffered."[35] Suffering, Smith had learned, cultivated the knowledge needed to ascend toward God.

In his 20 March letter to the Church, Smith forecast a flood of revelation. He noted that while some Saints had "tasted a little" of the "mistres [mysteries]" of God, many more "of them are to be pored down" upon the faithful. He promised the persecuted Saints that if they endured, they would receive knowledge "that has not been revealed since the world was untill now." This included an answer to the question of "whither there be one god or many god's," and information regarding "all thrones dominions principalities and powers" and the times and revolutions of the planets.[36] The statements in Smith's March 1840 letters highlight the forging power of his imprisonment and anticipated the theological developments in Illinois.[37]

Smith's new prophetic confidence was also evident in the method of his teaching, both in terms of how and whom he taught. In Nauvoo he dictated relatively few revelations in the voice of the Lord; he had developed a prophetic voice that no longer depended on the familiar form of his prior revelations. Instead, Smith conveyed core teachings about God, Christ, and humanity in numerous private meetings and, later, in public discourses. The records of those meetings and discourses indicate that Latter-day Saint audiences received these instructions as revealed truth. Smith first shared those instructions among intimate friends. Sharing close quarters with fellow sufferers seems to have conditioned him to reveal new teachings in secluded settings with trusted associates before later gaining the confidence to share those same teachings in public.

So when guards allowed Smith to escape from Missouri in spring 1839, he was liberated in two ways; it gave him freedom over his body, and it also gave him a kind of intellectual freedom to cultivate the theological seeds contained in his earlier revelations. Intellectual freedom followed from bodily freedom, as Smith's escape provided him opportunities to develop ideas in both private and public settings. Before his imprisonment, the practicalities of church organization, the logistics of ecclesiastical governance, and the enervating influence of persecution had militated against theological development. Such challenges followed Smith to Illinois, but he had become accustomed to them. In 1842 he wrote that "deep water is what I am wont to swim in, it all has become a second nature to me."[38] The physical lows of Smith's confinement spurred and shaped the spiritual highs of his postconfinement life.

Saints as Saviors: 1839–1841

Only months after his escape to Illinois, Smith began to privately instruct his most trusted friends and Church leaders. In June and July of 1839 he met with the Quorum of the Twelve Apostles to help them prepare for their imminent mission to Europe. Smith taught them about the "keys of the kingdom of God," which included the first principles of the gospel, such as faith and repentance, but also the detection of false spirits and making one's calling and election sure. He revealed that they could use a handshake to distinguish between the devil and a divine messenger, whether a disembodied "just man made perfect" or an embodied angel of God.[39] He also explained that the second comforter spoken of in John 14 "is no more or less than the *Lord Jesus Christ* himself" and clarified that those who make their calling and election sure would be taught by him "face to face," and he would introduce them to the Father.[40] These instructions built on Smith's earlier scriptural productions about spirits, salvation, and Moses's vision.[41] Wilford Woodruff later copied his notes of these and other discourses into his "Book of Revelations," a title that demonstrates how Woodruff received Smith's instructions.[42]

In the same way that early Saints had made copies of Smith's revelations, they made copies of his later discourses. Willard Richards, who was preaching in England at the time, obtained access to notes of Smith's sermons and recorded them in his "Pocket Companion."

In one such discourse, Smith again taught about discerning spirits, as well as the relationship between the priesthood and "the coming of the Son of Man."[43] He described the priesthood as eternal and also asserted that "the Spirit of Man is not a created being; it existed from Eternity. . . . Any thing created cannot be Eternal & earth, water &c—all these had their existence in an elementary state from Eternity."[44] This radical rejection of creation ex nihilo (out of nothing) and provocative assertion of humankind's coeternal status with God had been planted in Smith's May 1833 revelation. Now, six years later and in light of the Saints' experiences in Missouri and Smith's time in prison, the ideas began to flower in Smith's private discourses. While introducing these ideas to Church leaders, he nonetheless urged them "to preach among the first principles of the gospel of Jesus Christ."[45] Smith wanted the apostles to teach basic principles for practical proselytizing purposes, but perhaps he also wanted to be allowed to develop the ideas more fully before reading about them in the publications of his followers.

And yet, not long after Smith had revealed the idea of the soul's eternal existence among his closest followers in private, he was ready to test the idea in public. In February 1840, while pursuing redress for Missouri wrongs in the nation's capital, he gave a public sermon to correct false reports about the Saints' beliefs. He affirmed core Christian tenets, including belief in a God with "all the attributes ascribed to him by Christians of all denominations," and in "nothing but what the Bible teaches," including the "fall of man" and redemption through Christ.[46] But Smith also went beyond these widely held views and "entered into some details" about original sin and predestination, which he rejected. While these beliefs were still debated, many American Protestants had also set aside Calvinist creeds for Arminian faith. Smith then moved on to more radical teachings. In discussing the nature of God, he affirmed the traditional belief that "God is Eternal" and then added "that the *Soul* is Eternal." Smith did not discuss this topic at length, but "entered into some Explanations," which newspaperman Matthew Davis "could not perfectly comprehend."[47] In the same discourse Smith dismissed rumors that he had pretended to "be a Saviour" and confessed that "he was but a man."[48] While Smith described himself as a *man* to dismiss the notion that he was a *savior*, both terms had multiple valences among the Latter-day Saints. In 1840 Smith began to publicize teachings that closed the gap between the human and the divine.

He continued to teach Church leaders about the eternal nature of things during his trip to the eastern United States. In his autobiography, Parley Pratt wrote that while in Philadelphia Smith introduced him to "the idea of eternal family organization."[49] Smith also preached with Parley's brother Orson in New Jersey and may have taught him newer principles related to the nature of God, his creation, and the salvation of his children.[50] Regardless, within months of these interactions, both Pratts began to publish pamphlets that expanded on these topics. As noted above, a few years earlier Parley had articulated a version of theosis based on Smith's December 1832 revelation.[51] For a time Parley and his brother Orson took the initiative in introducing Smith's teachings on the topic to the world.

In a piece Parley published while in New York, he asserted that "matter and spirit are the two great principles of existence." Drawing on Smith's revelations and teachings, which had raised base matter to the level of sacred spirit, Parley emphasized the "physical nature" of Christ's body "both before and after he arose from the dead."[52] While explaining that Christ rose with a glorified body, Parley insisted that it was the same body he had in life. His focus on Christ's physical body highlighted the similarities between his existence and human existence. Parley extended this discussion to the material earth, which also awaited purification and glorification. The glorified earth, he explained, would become the inhabitation of "Jesus and the saints."[53] In these phrases, Parley flattened out existence and charted a similar destiny for all existing things. In doing so, he relied on Smith's revelations and teachings, but while Smith focused on the nature of the human and the divine in his public teachings during this period,

Parley continued to publicly consider what those teachings meant for human potential.

Parley continued to write about Christ's body in England. "The Father and Son are in the express *image* of each other," he wrote, "and both have '*hands, feet, eyes, ears, nose*, and *mouth*.' . . . And man is created in their *image*, or *likeness*." Parley held "that the Son has flesh and bones, and that the father is a spirit," while adding that "a personage of spirit has its organized formation, its body and parts . . . although not composed of such gross materials as flesh and bones."[54] Whether taken from Smith's prior revelations, his later private instructions, or both, the ideas in Parley's writings underscored the similarities between Father and Son, and between Son and Saints, in terms of both their essential nature and their ultimate destination.

Orson also published on related ideas while preaching in the British Isles. In the first published account of Smith's early encounters with the divine, Orson outlined the Saints' most definitive beliefs. He first addressed basic teachings, which aligned with traditional Christian tenets, before turning to transgressive ideas. Near the conclusion of his pamphlet, Orson voiced the belief in continuing revelation and described the end result of ongoing instruction. "God will continue to give revelations," he asserted, "until the saints are guided unto all truth," and when they arrive "in their immortal and perfect state" and "are made perfect in one, and become like their Savior, then they will be in possession of all knowledge, wisdom, and intelligence: then all things will be theirs."[55] Orson's statement echoed a passage in Smith's December 1832 revelation and built on his brother's 1838 defense of the same. In equating learning with godhood, Orson also made explicit what had been implicit in Smith's prison teachings.

While the Pratt brothers began to teach the world that becoming like Christ involved acquiring divine knowledge and earthly inheritance, Smith introduced the Nauvoo Saints to a practice with power to make them "saviours . . . on mount Zion" (Obadiah 1:21).[56] In August 1840 he taught living members that they could be baptized on behalf of their kindred dead. Smith's willingness to teach baptism for the dead to the general membership without first explaining it to the Church leadership attests to a deepening confidence in his new revelatory mode. When Smith wrote the Twelve about the subject months later, he warned that he could not "in this letter give you all the information you may desire on the subject."[57] Perhaps the introduction of the teaching served to remind the Twelve, including the Pratt brothers, that the Lord revealed his truths through Smith.

The unexpected and exciting new practice had ties to Smith's teachings on embodiment, matter and spirit, and the nature of God and his creation. The same month in which Smith introduced baptism for the dead, he preached on "the Eternal Duration of matter."[58] About six months later, and just a few weeks after writing to the Twelve about the new practice, Smith again discussed the eternal nature of matter at the organization of a "school of instruction." In doing so, he affirmed that God had formed the earth out of existing materials and stated that "the elements are eternal," a direct quote from his May 1833 revelation. As indicated in that revelation, teachings on the nature of matter impinged on teachings about the nature of the human soul. Echoing what he had said in Washington, Smith taught that "Spirits are eternal." While these ideas were present in Smith's earlier revelations, his later cultivation of them brought into the open the idea that humans were like Gods. It also indicated that Gods were like humans; Smith asserted that "there is no other God in heaven but that who has flesh and bones."[59] Though his revelations pointed in this direction, and while Parley had been moving toward the same conclusion, this seems to have been the first time that Smith explicitly taught that God had a body.[60] In these teachings, Smith developed ideas that had lain mostly dormant in his revelations. In making it clear that human souls are eternal and that Christ and his Son are embodied, he cast aside the Creator/created divide at the center of Christian thought.

Having set aside a core Christian teaching, Smith proceeded to add a heretical corollary. He taught that God the Father, like his Son, had a history. Elucidating John 5:26, Smith stated that "God

the father took life unto himself precisely as Jesus did." Like Father,
like Son, Smith taught. In this statement, Smith made an unknow-
able known; he made shape and temporality essential to, rather than
departures from, godliness. According to this theology, embodiment
was not the formation of a hapless creature, but a step in an eternal
soul's bid to become like God. Continuing his apparent explication of
the May 1833 revelation, Smith stated that "we came to this earth that
we might have a body," and building on his earlier teachings to the
Twelve, explained that "all beings who have bodies have power over
those who have not." Following the implications of his earlier revelations, Smith imbued bodily existence with ultimate significance.
In pitting embodied beings against a disembodied devil, he was also
aligning humans with God. As in Parley's writings, the value Smith
placed on matter included both bodies and the earth they inhabited,
which, he explained, "will be rolled back into the presence of God and
crowned with Celestial Glory."[61] This teaching echoed his December
1832 revelation.[62] While prior teachings had suggested that humans
could become like the Son, these statements implied that to become
like the Son was to become like the Father, while also revealing that
the Father was a being like the Son, a being that existed in both space
and time.

All of this related to Smith's teaching on baptism for the dead,
which affirmed the value of the physical body, as well as the spaces
those bodies inhabited. On 19 January 1841, in one of the few formal
revelations that Smith received in Nauvoo, the Lord urged the Saints
to build a temple so they "may be baptized for those who are dead."[63]
While the body could be imprisoned, as Smith had learned, it also
had power to perform sacred acts in sacred spaces to liberate cap-
tive spirits. In this way, the Saints could, in imitation of Christ and
God, use their bodies to become "saviours . . . on mount Zion."[64] The
teaching suggested that because disembodied spirits were fundamentally unlike embodied Gods, they needed the assistance of embodied
Saints to move toward an exalted destination. During an October
1841 conference, while speaking on the topic at the request "of some

of the Twelve," many of whom had returned from the British Isles, Smith "presented 'Baptism for the Dead' as the only way that men can appear as saviors on mount Zion." He clarified that it was "not men that saved" the dead, but "by actively engaging in rites of salvation substitutionally," he explained, the living "became instrumental in bring[ing] multitudes of their kin into the kingdom of God."[65] Throughout Smith's ministry, he remained committed to the teaching at the heart of his salvation revelations—that Christ was the singular Savior of the human family—even as he gradually introduced the doctrine that Christ saved beings who had the power to perform feats that would make them like him.

As Smith introduced this teaching and related practices to the general Church audience, his critics took note of what they viewed as mounting heresies. In an 1841 publication, "anti-Mormon" editor Thomas C. Sharp cited Parley Pratt's earlier defense of the revealed statement that "the saints shall be made equal with Christ." Perhaps knowing of Parley's and Orson's other writings on the topic, along with something of the content of Smith's recent sermons, Sharp asserted that the Saints "believe that they will have power to create worlds, and that those worlds will transgress the law given, consequently they will become saviors to those worlds, and redeem them; never, until this is accomplished," Sharp reported, "will their glory be complete; and then there will be 'Lords many, and Gods many.'"[66] Despite Sharp's stinging bias, records indicate that he actually had a pulse on radical developments in Latter-day Saint thought.

Making Gods: 1842–1844

In late January 1842, Smith met with a small group inside his home in Nauvoo and instructed them on the histories of Gods and the future of humankind. Just over a month before, in mid-December, he had held a similar meeting. According to Woodruff's record of that gathering, Smith instructed them that if "we kept the commandments of God we Should bring forth fruit & be the friends of God &

know what our lord did & he would reveal his secrets unto us."[67] A few weeks later, Smith made good on his promise. On that occasion, he taught that what the "lord did" on this earth was what God the Father had done on another earth. In teaching this, Smith put flesh on the theological bones he had unveiled a year before, but he did not end with the histories of Gods. He proceeded to trace the destinies of their righteous believers: "The Holy Ghost would do the same in his turn & so would all the Saints who inherited a Celestial glory so their would be Gods many & Lords many."[68] According to Woodruff's account, Smith appears to have taught that exalted Saints had similar destinies as the Father, Son, and Holy Ghost. It seems that Sharp had not been far off in his account of "heretical" Latter-day Saint beliefs.

While Smith was anxious to teach these mysteries, and although related ideas about eternal existence, the plurality of Gods, and human potential appeared the next month in published selections of the Book of Abraham, Smith became frustrated when some of his secret instructions were made public before he thought prudent.[69] In an April 1842 discourse given to the Female Relief Society of Nauvoo, he chastised some Church leaders, including Parley and Orson Pratt. Smith described them, along with Orson Hyde and John E. Page, as "great big elders" and charged them with repeating certain principles taught in "private counsel . . . as their own revelations."[70] In light of the fact that Smith often taught about theosis and corresponding concepts in private, he appears to have had those teachings in mind in these statements to the Relief Society. While Smith seemed most concerned about the source of these teachings, he also might have been just as concerned about when and in what setting they were taught.

Despite this frustration, or perhaps even because of it, Smith continued to unveil teachings on becoming like God and proceeded to introduce new practices meant to actualize the deification process.[71] Within days of chastising the Pratts and others, he spoke to the Saints about the elders being "endued with power," and then, a few days later, he introduced nine men to the endowment, the purpose of which was to bring initiates into "the prese[n]ce of Eloheim in the eternal worlds."⁷² In a Sunday sermon given in 1843, the same year in which he introduced the ritual of the endowment to women, Smith described the similar histories of Father and Son and noted that some of God's children "are resurrected to become gods by such revelations as god gives in the most holy place."⁷³ Smith's statement seemed to indicate that the endowment was essential to the process of becoming like God.

While introducing new practices, Smith continued to elucidate teachings about the natures and destinies of God and humans. In an April 1843 meeting in Macedonia, Illinois, he corrected Orson Hyde's interpretation of a passage in 1 John that reads, "When he shall appear, we shall be like him" (1 John 3:2). In a prior meeting, Hyde had taught that Christ "will appear on a white horse.—as a warrior" and proposed, "May be we shall have some of the same spirit." Smith clarified that the passage referred more to Christ's nature than how he would appear at that moment, explaining that "we shall see that he is a man like ourselves." In the same meeting, Smith also corrected Hyde's reading of the scripture in John 14 regarding the appearance of the Father and the Son. Hyde had taught that "it is our privilege to have the father & son dwelling in our hearts," but Smith dismissed the idea as "an old Sectarian notion," explaining that the appearance written of "is a personal. appearance."⁷⁴ Before the day was over, Smith again referred to Hyde's mistake and explained that "the Father has a body of flesh & bones as tangible as mans the Son also."⁷⁵ Smith may have relished the opportunity to correct one of the "great big elders," but in any case he used the occasion to reiterate divine embodiment and human potential.

While Smith had begun to include veiled references to these teachings in sermons, he continued to follow the pattern of explaining deifying practices and principles to his most trusted friends before preaching them in public. This was particularly the case with related revelations on the new and everlasting covenant of marriage.

For instance, in May 1843 Smith met with Benjamin F. Johnson and explained the concept of marital sealings. According to his scribe William Clayton, who was present at the time of the teaching, "He said that except a man and his wife enter into an everlasting covenant and be married for eternity while in this probation by the power and authority of the Holy priesthood they will cease to increase when they die (i e) they will not have any children in the resurrection."[76] This suggested that exaltation involved not just glorified bodies, but also the ability to propagate children in eternity.

Smith's revelation on plural marriage, which he revealed two months later, confirmed that godhood involved eternal families and eternal increase. It declared that the righteous who did not enter the new and everlasting covenant of marriage would "remain separately and Singly without exaltation in their Saved Condition to all eternity and from henceforth are not Gods, but are angels of God forever and ever." In contrast, those who abided the covenant, would receive "a fullness and Continuation of the Seeds for ever and ever. Then Shall they be Gods, because they have no End."[77] These statements added to the prior teachings on becoming like God. God's children had eternal souls that would inhabit and create eternal bodies on eternal worlds.

All of Smith's teachings on the topic came together in a sermon he gave on 7 April 1844 at the funeral of King Follett. Follett had spent time imprisoned with Smith in Missouri, an experience that contributed to the development of teachings Smith now shared at his friend's funeral. The concepts contained in this sermon had been introduced in revelations given fourteen years earlier and developed in meetings and discourses preached during the prior half decade. While Smith had introduced these teachings and related practices first in private, he now distilled all that he had learned about the nature of God, Christ, and man, before a large body of Saints.

Smith grounded his sermon in New Testament passages to show that these teachings had been sown long before his early 1830s revelations. "What did Jesus say," Smith asked, "as the father hath power in himself even so hath the son power. to do what why what the father did To lay down his body and took it up again." After teaching that Christ had died as his Father had, Smith went on to tell his audience, "You have got to learn how to be a god yourself."[78] Such statements, like the passages in Smith's revelations, might have raised the question of how mere mortals could become like God. Anticipating the queries, Smith followed his revelations in providing an answer that placed humans on the same ontological plane as God. "The mind of man—the intelligent part is coequal with God himself," he stated, "their spirit exists coequal with God." Smith concluded that because "intelligence exists—upon a self existent principle" and there is "no creation about it . . . all the spirits that God ever sent into the world are susceptible of enlargement."[79] The exalted ontological status of humans made eternal progression and eventual perfection possible. Smith followed these statements with a call for the Saints to save their dead, again linking the practice of baptism for the dead to the process of theosis. These teachings represented Smith's latest reflections on the revealed teaching that, in emulation of Christ, the righteous could grow from grace to grace until they obtained a fullness.

Conclusion

Smith's last public reflections on the teaching came a few months later in his Sermon at the Grove, given just over a week before he was killed. Prior to speaking, Smith sang "Mortals, awake!" with the Saints, perhaps in anticipation of his message about Gods and men. Once again, opposition encouraged the articulation of mature theological concepts. In this case, the publication of the *Nauvoo Expositor* drew Smith's radical rejoinder. Rather than refute the newspaper's claim, Smith dug in his heels, insisting that he had preached on "the plurality of Gods" for fifteen years. Backing the teaching from the Bible, he declared that he had "always" preached that God, Christ, and the Holy Ghost were "distinct" personages, a necessary qualification to his assertion. In what was perhaps an acknowledgement of a newer teaching, Smith then indicated his intention to preach "the doctrine [of] there being a God above the" Father of Christ. Smith might have had in mind the King Follett discourse when he insisted that he had taught "all the strong doctrines publicly—& always stronger than what I preach in private," or maybe he was signaling to the audience that the present occasion would evidence the truth of his assertion.[80]

Smith proceeded to preach the plurality of Gods from both the Old and New Testaments. He explained that a proper reading of the Hebrew Bible showed that Gods organized the heavens and the earth and made man in their own image, and that "the heads of the Gods appointed one God for us."[81] Setting aside the Trinitarian formulation as an absurdity, Smith reasoned that if Christ had a Father, then the Father "had a [Father] also." Smith made this point from the Bible, but he also directly drew on a passage from the Book of Abraham. In the passage, wherein the Lord described a hierarchy of intelligent spirits to Abraham, he noted, "I am the Lord thy God, I am more intelligent than they all."[82] Smith understood the scripture to mean that "intelligences exist one above ano[ther and] that there is not [an] end to it." Refusing to be "scared to death" of these teachings, he proceeded to explain that as the Father "wrought precisely in the same way as his [Father] had done," so Christ "laid down his life & took it up."[83] Another account of the discourse indicates that Smith taught that "the holy ghost is yet a spiritual Body. and waiting to take to himself a body as the savior did or as god did or the gods before them took bodies."[84] As in the revelations and Smith's prior sermons, when he thought and taught about the nature of Gods, he also thought and taught about the destinies of God's children.

Smith's radical views of the Father and the Son, whom he described as beings with bodies and histories, directly related to his radical teachings about humans, whom he described as beings with premortal pasts and immortal futures. Citing a passage from Romans that had begun to appear with more regularity in his discourses, Smith explained that to become joint heirs with Christ, "we then also took Bodies to Lay them down and take them up again." As the passage in Romans taught, this required suffering "with him in the flesh that we may be also glorified together."[85] These statements suggest that perhaps Smith had reconsidered the unique teaching that exalted saints needed to become saviors; perhaps it was enough that they suffered with Christ in this life, a lesson that harkened back to his experience in prison. Such suffering meant that "we shall see as we are seen & be as God—& be as the God of his Fa[ther]."[86] Smith had once taught that when Christ appears the righteous would see that he was a man, like unto them; now he chose to emphasize that the Saints would be seen as Gods. While Smith grounded these teachings in biblical passages, he had also cited the Book of Abraham and even made mention of the Book of Mormon and the Doctrine and Covenants. Indeed, he spoke specifically of "the vision" of 1832, wherein he had learned of differing glories and multiple gods, to emphasize that "every man who reigns is a God."[87]

Smith's last formulations on theosis might be interpreted as a threat to the Christology that had been at the heart of Latter-day Saint theology, but this interpretation fails to recognize the christological continuities between Smith's 1830s revelations and his 1840s teachings. The close reading of early revelations yields a contextual understanding that should limit and constrain how we understand Smith's late teachings. While those teachings spurned much of traditional Christian theology, they rested on revelations that simultaneously emphasized salvation through Christ and the potential to achieve exaltation in imitation of Christ. In other words, from beginning to end, the articulation of a Latter-day Saint theosis depended on a robust Christology.

This had been made clear in the 1832 vision, which taught that through Jesus, who "came in to the world . . . to be crucified for the world and to bear the sins of the world," the righteous Saints could become "Gods even the sons of God." The vision indicated that these, who "the father hath given all things . . . are priests and kings."[88] Over fourteen years later, in one of his last public statements on the topic,

Smith again taught that Jesus Christ "hath by his own blood made us [Kings and Priests] to God."[89]

Notes

1. Wilford Woodruff, 30 January 1842, "Book of Revelations," Church History Library (hereafter cited as CHL).

2. For instance, John Turner notes that while Christology "was not one of the points of contention between early Mormons and their many antagonists," during the next quarter century Latter-day Saints "embraced a different metaphysics and a new way of interpreting God's 'plan of salvation.'" John G. Turner, *The Mormon Jesus: A Biography* (Cambridge, MA: Belknap Press of Harvard University Press, 2016), 154–55.

3. See, for example, Richard Lyman Bushman, *Joseph Smith: Rough Stone Rolling* (New York: Knopf, 2005), 134.

4. Visions of Moses, June 1830 [Moses 1], in Michael Hubbard MacKay, Gerrit J. Dirkmaat, Grant Underwood, Robert J. Woodford, and William G. Hartley, eds., *Documents, Volume 1: July 1828–June 1831*, vol. 1 of the Documents series of *The Joseph Smith Papers*, ed. Dean C. Jessee, Ronald K. Esplin, Richard Lyman Bushman, and Matthew J. Grow (Salt Lake City: Church Historian's Press, 2013), 154.

5. See, for example, Old Testament Revision 2, pp. 21, 23–25, 40 [Moses 7:24, 47, 54–56, 59, 65]; Revelation ca. 7 March 1831 [D&C 45:39], in *JSP*, D1:278; Revelation, 7 May 1831 [D&C 49:6, 22], in *JSP*, D1:301–2; Revelation, 1 August 1831 [D&C 58:65], in Matthew C. Godfrey, Mark Ashurst-McGee, Grant Underwood, Robert J. Woodford, and William G. Hartley, eds., *Documents, Volume 2: July 1831–January 1833*, vol. 2 of the Documents series of *The Joseph Smith Papers*, ed. Dean C. Jessee, Ronald K. Esplin, and Richard Lyman Bushman (Salt Lake City: Church Historian's Press, 2013), 21; Revelation, 12 August 1831 [D&C 61:38], in *JSP*, D2:44; Revelation, 30 August 1831 [D&C 63:53], in *JSP*, D2:54; Revelation, 30 October 1831 [D&C 65:5], in *JSP*, D2:93; Vision, 16 February 1832 [D&C 76:16], in *JSP*, D2:184; Revelation, ca. June 1835 [D&C 68:11], in Matthew C. Godfrey, Brenden W. Rensink, Alex D.

Smith, Max H Parkin, and Alexander L. Baugh, eds., *Documents, Volume 4: April 1834–September 1835*, vol. 4 of the Documents series of *The Joseph Smith Papers*, ed. Ronald K. Esplin and Matthew J. Grow (Salt Lake City: Church Historian's Press, 2016), 357; Letter to the Elders of the Church 30 November–1 December 1835, in Brent M. Rogers, Elizabeth A. Kuehn, Christian K. Heimburger, Max H Parkin, Alexander L. Baugh, and Steven C. Harper, eds., *Documents, Volume 5: October 1835–January 1838*, vol. 5 of the Documents series of *The Joseph Smith Papers*, ed. Ronald K. Esplin, Matthew J. Grow, and Matthew C. Godfrey (Salt Lake City: Church Historian's Press, 2017), 98–99; Blessing to Alvin Winegar, 7 February 1836, in *JSP*, D5:167; Minutes and Prayer of Dedication, 27 March 1836 [D&C 109:5], in *JSP*, D5:195, 199.

6.   Jason R. Combs, "'Christ' after the Apostles: The Humanity and Divinity of the Savior in the Second Century," in *Thou Art the Christ, the Son of the Living God: The Person and Work of Jesus in the New Testament*, ed. Eric D. Huntsman, Lincoln H. Blumell, and Tyler J. Griffin (Provo, UT: Religious Studies Center, Brigham Young University, 2018), 321–25.

7.   See Stephen Finlan and Vladimir Kharlamov, eds., *Theōsis: Deification in Christian Theology* (Eugene, OR: Pickwick Publications, 2006). On the history of this belief among the Church Fathers and in Christian thought, see Norman Russell, *The Doctrine of Deification in the Greek Patristic Tradition* (New York: Oxford University Press, 2004); and Michael J. Christensen and Jeffery A. Wittung, *Partakers of the Divine Nature: The History and Development of Deification in the Christian Tradition* (Grand Rapids, MI: Baker Academic, 2007). For comparative studies on early Christian and Latter-day Saint theosis, see Jordan Vajda, *"Partakers of the Divine Nature": A Comparative Analysis of Patristic and Mormon Doctrines of Divinization* (Provo, UT: Foundation for Ancient Research and Mormon Studies, 2002); Grant Underwood, "Justification, Theosis, and Grace in Early Christian, Lutheran, and Mormon Discourse," *International Journal of Mormon Studies* 2 (Spring 2009): 206–23, and Adam J. Powell, *Irenaeus, Joseph Smith, and God-Making Heresy* (Teaneck, NJ: Fairleigh Dickinson University Press, 2015).

8. "Old Testament Revision 2," p. 18 [Moses 6:57], The Joseph Smith Papers, https://josephsmithpapers.org/paper-summary/old-testament-revision-2/22. See also, "Old Testament Revision 1," p. 14 [Moses 6:57], The Joseph Smith Papers, https://josephsmithpapers.org/paper-summary/old-testament-revision-1/16.

9. "Old Testament Revision 1," p. 11 [Moses 6:5–6], The Joseph Smith Papers, https://josephsmithpapers.org/paper-summary/old-testament-revision-1/13.

10. Sample of Pure Language, between ca. 4 and ca. 20 March 1832, in JSP, D2:215.

11. Vision, 16 February 1832, in JSP, D2:188–89 [D&C 76:58].

12. Vision, 16 February 1832, in JSP, D2:190 [D&C 76:91].

13. Revelation, 27–28 December 1832, in JSP, D2:337–38 [D&C 88].

14. Revelation, 27–28 December 1832, in JSP, D2:344 [D&C 88:107].

15. Revelation, 6 May 1833 [D&C 93:3–4], in Gerrit J. Dirkmaat, Brent M. Rogers, Grant Underwood, Robert J. Woodford, and William G. Hartley, eds., Documents, Volume 3: February 1833–March 1834, vol. 3 of the Documents series of The Joseph Smith Papers, ed. Ronald K. Esplin and Matthew J. Grow (Salt Lake City: Church Historian's Press, 2014), 86.

16. Nicholas J. Frederick, The Bible, Mormon Scripture, and the Rhetoric of Allusivity (Teaneck, NJ: Fairleigh Dickinson University Press, 2016), 97.

17. Frederick, Bible, Mormon Scripture, and the Rhetoric of Allusivity, 95–130.

18. Revelation, 6 May 1833, in JSP, D3:86 [D&C 93:7–8].

19. Revelation, 6 May 1833, in JSP, D3:88 [D&C 93:12–14].

20. Frederick, Bible, Mormon Scripture, and the Rhetoric of Allusivity, 112–13.

21. Terryl L. Givens, Wrestling the Angel: The Foundations of Mormon Thought; Cosmos, God, Humanity (New York: Oxford University Press, 2015), 120–21.

22. Revelation, 6 May 1833, in JSP, D3:88 [D&C 93:19–20].

23. Revelation, 6 May 1833, in JSP, D3:88–89 [D&C 93:22–23].

24. See Vision, 16 February 1832, in JSP, D1:189–90 [D&C 76:70, 95]; Revelation, 22–23 September 1832, in JSP, D2:297 [D&C 84:33]; and Revelation, 27–28 December 1832, in JSP, D2:338 [D&C 88:20, 28].

25. Revelation, 6 May 1833, in JSP, D3:89 [D&C 93:33].

26. Letter from William W. Phelps, 15 December 1833, in JSP, D3:383.

27. In a series of theological discussions in Kirtland, Ohio, held in the winter of 1834–35, Joseph Smith and other Church leaders discussed matters relating to the nature of God and salvation. While their scriptural references pointed toward the Bible rather than Smith's revelations, the fifth, sixth, and seventh lectures emphasize that Christ obtained a fullness of the Father and further insist that righteous Saints could also obtain a fullness of perfection through Christ. Doctrine and Covenants, 1835 ed., 52–74, in Robin Scott Jensen, Richard E. Turley Jr., and Riley M. Lorimer, eds., *Revelations and Translations, Volume 2: Published Revelations,* vol. 2 of the Revelations and Translations series of *The Joseph Smith Papers,* ed. Dean C. Jessee, Ronald K. Esplin, and Richard Lyman Bushman (Salt Lake City: Church Historian's Press, 2011), 362–84.

28. Adam Powell posits a relationship between persecution and a belief in deification among early Christians and Latter-day Saints. See Powell, *Irenaeus, Joseph Smith, and God-Making Heresy.*

29. See Jordan Watkins, "'All of One Species': Parley P. Pratt and the Dialectical Development of Early Mormon Conceptions of the Theosis," in *Parley P. Pratt and the Making of Mormonism,* ed. Gregory K. Armstrong, Matthew J. Grow, and Dennis J. Siler (Norman, OK: Arthur H. Clark, 2011), 201–18.

30. See Kathleen Flake, "Joseph Smith's Letter from Liberty Jail: A Study in Canonization," *Journal of Religion* 92, no. 4 (October 2012): 515–26.

31. Joseph Smith to the Church and Edward Partridge, 20 March 1839, in Mark Ashurst-McGee, David W. Grua, Elizabeth Kuehn, Alexander L. Baugh, and Brenden W. Rensink, eds., *Documents, Volume 6: February 1838–August 1839,* vol. 6 of the Documents series of *The Joseph Smith Papers,* ed. Ronald K. Esplin, Matthew J. Grow, and Matthew C. Godfrey (Salt Lake City: Church Historian's Press, 2017), 312–16.

32. Joseph Smith to the Church and Edward Partridge, 20 March 1839, in *JSP,* D6:319.

33. Revelation, 27–28 December 1832, in *JSP,* D2:337.

34. Joseph Smith to Edward Partridge and the Church, ca. 22 March 1839, in *JSP,* D6:342.

35. Letter to Presendia Huntington Buell, 15 March 1839, in *JSP,* D6:355.

36. Joseph Smith to the Church and Edward Partridge, 20 March 1839, in *JSP*, D6:369.

37. For an illuminating contextual analysis of Smith's prison letters, including a discussion of the relationship between suffering and revelation, see David W. Grua, "Joseph Smith's Missouri Prison Letter and the Mormon Textual Community," in *Foundational Texts of Mormonism: Examining Major Early Sources*, ed. Mark Ashurst-McGee, Robin Scott Jensen, and Sharalyn D. Howcroft (New York: Oxford University Press, 2018), 124–53.

38. Letter to "All the Saints in Nauvoo," 1 September 1842 [D&C 127], The Joseph Smith Papers, https://josephsmithpapers.org/paper-summary /letter-to-all-the-saints-in-nauvoo-1-september-1842-dc-127/1.

39. Discourse, 27 June 1839, in *JSP*, D6:510.

40. Discourse, between ca. 26 June and ca. 2 July 1839, in *JSP*, D6:525.

41. Revelation, ca. 8 March 1831-A, in *JSP*, D1:282 [D&C 46:7]; and Revelation, 9 May 1831, in *JSP*, D1:306 [D&C 50:2]; Revelation, 27–28 December 1832, in *JSP*, D2:336-337 [D&C 88:1-5].

42. Historical Introduction to Discourse, 27 June 1839, in *JSP*, D6:509.

43. Discourse, between ca. 26 June and ca. 4 August 1839-A, in *JSP*, D6:542-48.

44. Discourse, between ca. 26 June and ca. 4 August 1839-A, in *JSP*, D6:543.

45. Discourse, between ca. 26 June and ca. 2 July 1839, in *JSP*, D6:521. See Letter to Heber C. Kimball and Brigham Young, 16 January 1839, in *JSP*, D6:315.

46. Discourse, 5 February 1840, in Matthew C. Godfrey, Spencer W. McBride, Alex D. Smith, and Christopher James Blythe, eds., *Documents, Volume 7: September 1839-January 1841*, vol. 7 of the Documents series of *The Joseph Smith Papers*, ed. Ronald K. Esplin, Matthew J. Grow, and Matthew C. Godfrey (Salt Lake City: Church Historian's Press, 2018), 177.

47. Discourse, 5 February 1840, in *JSP*, D7:178.

48. Discourse, 5 February 1840, in *JSP*, D7:179. Parley P. Pratt wrote that while in custody in Missouri the prior year, a women had asked "which of the prisoners was the Lord whom the Mormons worshipped?" and that Smith, after being singled out by a guard, "professed to be nothing but a man, and a minister of salvation sent by Jesus Christ." P[arley] P. Pratt,

History of the Late Persecution Inflicted by the State of Missouri upon the Mormons (Detroit: Dawson & Bates, 1839), 45.

49. *The Autobiography of Parley Parker Pratt, One of the Twelve Apostles of the Church of Jesus Christ of Latter-day Saints* (New York: Russell Brothers, 1874), 329.

50. Orson Pratt to Sarah Marinda Bates Pratt, 6 January 1840, in *Times and Seasons*, February 1840, 1:61.

51. See Watkins, "'All of One Species,'" 205–9.

52. P[arley] P. Pratt, *The Millennium, and Other Poems: To Which Is Annexed, A Treatise on the Regeneration and Eternal Duration of Matter* (New York: W. Molineux, printer, 1840), 128.

53. Pratt, *Millennium, and Other Poems*, 147–48.

54. Parley P. Pratt, *An Answer to Mr. William Hewitt's Tract against the Latter-Day Saints* (Manchester: W. R. Thomas, printer, 1840), 5, 9. See Parley P. Pratt, *A Reply to Mr. Thomas Taylor's "Complete Failure," &c., and Mr. Richard Livesey's "Mormonism Exposed"* (Manchester: W. R. Thomas, printer, 1840), 9–10.

55. O[rson] Pratt, *A[n] Interesting Account of Several Remarkable Visions, and of the Late Discovery of Ancient American Records* (Edinburgh: Ballantyne and Hughes, 1840), 30.

56. On this practice, and its development, see Ryan G. Tobler, "'Saviors on Mount Zion': Mormon Sacramentalism, Mortality, and the Baptism for the Dead," *Journal of Mormon History* 39, no. 4 (2013): 182–238.

57. Letter to Quorum of the Twelve, 15 December 1840, in *JSP*, D7:470.

58. John Smith, Journal, 1840 July–1841 March, 30 August 1840, in John Smith Papers, CHL.

59. Accounts of Meeting and Discourse, 5 January 1841, in *JSP*, D7:494.

60. On the development of embodiment in Latter-day Saint thought, see Benjamin E. Park, "Salvation through a Tabernacle: Joseph Smith, Parley Pratt, and Early Mormon Theologies of Embodiment," *Dialogue: A Journal of Mormon Thought* 43, no. 2 (Summer 2010): 1–44.

61. Accounts of Meeting and Discourse, 5 January 1841, in *JSP*, D7:494, 95.

62. Revelation, 27–28 December 1832, in *JSP*, D2:338–39 [D&C 88:17–20].

63. Revelation, 19 January 1841, in *JSP*, D7:517 [D&C 124:29].

64. In an 1834 revelation, the Lord described "his people" as "saviours of men," and in subsequent statements Smith and other Church leaders applied the terms "saviour" and "savior" to those who participated in preaching the gospel and the work of Zion. (See, for example, Revelation, 24 February 1834, in *JSP*, D3:460 [D&C 103:9]; Minutes, Discourse, and Blessings, 1 March 1835, in *JSP*, D4:275; Joseph Smith Sr. to Rebecca Swain Williams, Blessing, 14 September 1835, in Patriarchal Blessings, 1:30–31; and Discourse, ca. 19 July 1840, in *JSP*, D7:337, 341). After Smith introduced baptism for the dead in 1840, the phrase most often appeared in references to that practice and the connected passage in Obadiah 1:21. See, for example, Discourse, 16 May 1841, in Brent M. Rogers, Mason K. Allred, Gerrit J. Dirkmaat, and Brett D. Dowdle, eds., *Documents, Volume 8: February–November 1841*, vol. 8 of the Documents series of *The Joseph Smith Papers*, ed. Ronald K. Esplin, Matthew J. Grow, Matthew C. Godfrey, and R. Eric Smith (Salt Lake City: Church Historian's Press, 2019), 152; "The High Council of the Church of Jesus Christ, to the Saints of Nauvoo, Greeting," *Times and Seasons*, 15 February 1842, 3:699; "Discourse, 21 January 1844, as Reported by Wilford Woodruff," p. [182], The Joseph Smith Papers, https://josephsmithpapers.org/paper-summary/discourse-21-january-1844-as-reported-by-wilford-woodruff/2; "Conference Minutes," *Times and Seasons*, 15 August 1844, 5:616; and "Discourse, 12 May 1844, as Reported by George Laub," p. 21, The Joseph Smith Papers, https://josephsmithpapers.org/paper-summary/discourse-12-may-1844-as-reported-by-george-laub/3.

65. Minutes and Discourse, 1–5 October 1841, in *JSP*, D7:287. See Discourse, 3 October 1841, in *JSP*, D7:300–302.

66. William Harris, *Mormonism Portrayed: Its Errors and Absurdities Exposed, and the Spirit and Designs of Its Authors Made Manifest* (Warsaw: Sharp & Gamble, 1841), 22–23. Sharp's paper later indicated that he, the paper's editor, had written *Mormonism Portrayed* "from materials furnished by Mr. Harris." "Monsieur Violet and the Mormons," *Warsaw Signal*, 11 September 1844, [1].

67. Woodruff, 19 December 1841, "Book of Revelations," CHL.

68. Woodruff, 30 January 1842, "Book of Revelations," CHL.

69. Book of Abraham Excerpt and Facsimile 2, 15 March 1842, in Alex D. Smith, Christian Heimburger, and Christopher James Blythe, eds., *Documents, Volume 9: December 1841–April 1842*, vol. 9 of the Documents series of *The Joseph Smith Papers*, ed. Ronald K. Esplin, Matthew J. Grow, and Matthew C. Godfrey (Salt Lake City: Church Historian's Press, 2019), 225–26.

70. Minutes, 28 April 1842, in *The First Fifty Years of the Relief Society*, ed. Jill Mulvay Derr, Carol Cornwall Madsen, Kate Holbrook, and Matthew J. Grow (Salt Lake City: Church Historian's Press, 2016), 55.

71. Samuel Morris Brown, *In Heaven as It Is on Earth: Joseph Smith and the Early Mormon Conquest of Death* (New York: Oxford University Press, 2012), 268.

72. Discourse, 1 May 1842, in Elizabeth A. Kuehn, Jordan T. Watkins, Matthew C. Godfrey, and Mason K. Allred, eds., *Documents, Volume 10: May–August 1842*, vol. 10 of the Documents series of *The Joseph Smith Papers*, ed. Matthew C. Godfrey, R. Eric Smith, Matthew J. Grow, and Ronald K. Esplin (Salt Lake City: Church Historian's Press, 2020), 7; Historian's Office, Joseph Smith History, draft notes, 4 May 1842, CHL.

73. "Discourse, 11 June 1843–A, as Reported by Willard Richards," p. [250], The Joseph Smith Papers, https://josephsmithpapers.org/paper-summary /discourse-11-june-1843-a-as-reported-by-willard-richards/11.

74. JS, Journal, 2 April 1843, in *JSP*, J2:324.

75. JS, Journal, 2 April 1843, in *JSP*, J2:326.

76. "Instruction, 16 May 1843, as Reported by William Clayton," p. [14], The Joseph Smith Papers, https://josephsmithpapers.org/paper-summary /instruction-16-may-1843-as-reported-by-william-clayton/2.

77. "Revelation, 12 July 1843 [D&C 132]," p. 3, The Joseph Smith Papers, https:// josephsmithpapers.org/paper-summary/revelation-12-july-1843-dc-132/3.

78. "Discourse, 7 April 1844, as Reported by William Clayton [26]," p. 14 [26], The Joseph Smith Papers, https://josephsmithpapers.org/paper-summary /discourse-7-april-1844-as-reported-by-william-clayton/4.

79. "Discourse, 7 April 1844, as Reported by William Clayton [28]," p. 16 [28].

80. "Discourse, 16 June 1844–A, as Reported by Thomas Bullock," p. [1], The Joseph Smith Papers, https://josephsmithpapers.org/paper-summary/discourse-16-june-1844-a-as-reported-by-thomas-bullock/1.

81. "Discourse, 16 June 1844–A, as Reported by Thomas Bullock," p. [2].

82. Book of Abraham Excerpt and Facsimile 2, 15 March 1842, in *JSP*, D9:225.

83. "Discourse, 16 June 1844–A, as Reported by Thomas Bullock," p. [3].

84. "Discourse, 16 June 1844–A, as Reported by George Laub," p. 30, The Joseph Smith Papers, https://josephsmithpapers.org/paper-summary/discourse-16-june-1844-a-as-reported-by-george-laub/2.

85. "Discourse, 16 June 1844–A, as Reported by George Laub," p. 31. For examples of references to Romans 8:16–17 in Smith's discourse, see "Discourse, 14 May 1843, as Reported by Wilford Woodruff," p. [32], The Joseph Smith Papers, https://josephsmithpapers.org/paper-summary /discourse-14-may-1843-as-reported-by-wilford-woodruff/3; "Discourse, 27 August 1843, as Reported by James Burgess," p. [13], The Joseph Smith Papers, https://josephsmithpapers.org/paper-summary/discourse-27-august -1843-as-reported-by-james-burgess/4; "Discourse, 7 April 1844, as Re-ported by Wilford Woodruff," p. [135], The Joseph Smith Papers, https://josephsmithpapers.org/paper-summary/discourse-7-april-1844 -as-reported-by-wilford-woodruff/3; and "Discourse, 12 May 1844, as Reported by Thomas Bullock," p. [2], The Joseph Smith Papers, https:// josephsmithpapers.org/paper-summary/discourse-12-may-1844-as -reported-by-thomas-bullock/2.

86. "Discourse, 16 June 1844–A, as Reported by Thomas Bullock," p. [3].

87. "Discourse, 16 June 1844–A, as Reported by Thomas Bullock," p. [4].

88. Vision, 16 Feb. 1832, in *JSP*, D2:188 [D&C 76:56].

89. "Discourse, 16 June 1844–A, as Reported by Thomas Bullock," p. [5].

7

Praxis Makes Perfect

Christian Perfection and *Imitatio Christi* in Joseph Smith's Temple Pedagogy

Richard Sleegers

It is necessary in the ushering in of the dispensation of the fulness of times, which dispensation is now beginning to usher in, that a whole and complete and perfect union, and welding together of dispensations, and keys, and powers, and glories should take place, and be revealed from the days of Adam even to the present time. And not only this, but those things which never have been revealed from the foundation of the world, but have been kept hid from the wise and prudent, shall be revealed unto babes and sucklings in this, the dispensation of the fulness of times.[1]

The Nauvoo period in Latter-day Saint history was a time of welding for Joseph Smith: bringing together previous revelatory teachings and actively shaping rituals into "a whole and complete and perfect union."[2] He believed he was opening a dispensation, or a pouring out of knowledge and authority from heaven, and was

anxious to finish it. He had a vision—at least in the down-to-earth
sense of a goal—of all Saints being educated in the knowledge prerequisite for a salvation he coined exaltation.

This exaltation can be seen as a unique form of Christian
perfection,[3] as the end goal toward which followers of Christ
strive—in this life or the next—to achieve a wholeness or degree of
refinement that would bring them salvation. Most early nineteenth-
century Christian denominations were seeking after salvation, differing in forms and degrees, but united in their desire for certainty.
Denominations based on Calvinism found surety of salvation in
God-given grace to a select few, while Arminian-based theologies,
such as that found in Methodism, believed that all who chose Christ
as their Savior could be saved. Universalists, like Joseph Smith's
grandfather,[4] believed that Christ would (eventually) save all. The
basic premise of Christian theology—forgiveness of sins through
Christ's Atonement—seemed undebated, though. Each acknowledged that a power went forth from the atoning sacrifice of Christ.
The debate centered on how to access that power—how one could be
certain that power was manifest, and hence whether salvation was
sure.

Joseph Smith revolutionized the idea of and prerequisites for salvific surety into a perfectionism that was both concrete and attainable but to most people was quite unfathomable: becoming as God,
or becoming gods.[5] The rationale is that to be certain one can reenter
the presence of God, one should strive to know or see God and progress to be like him.[6] In other words, Joseph saw theophany (encounter with God) as a precursor to theosis (becoming like God). This
is *imitatio Christi* in its purest form: striving to become as Christ as
a means to become godlike, by "receiv[ing] his image in [our] coun-
tenances" (Alma 5:14), and by "becom[ing] sons [and daughters] of
God; [so] that when he shall appear we shall be like him [theosis], for
we shall see him [theophany]" (Moroni 7:48).

Some of Joseph's teachings during the Nauvoo period indicate that
spiritual education and personal development were a prerequisite to

meeting/seeing God (theophany) and to becoming like him (theosis). How were these teachings to be transposed into praxis and what was the place to prepare to meet God?— in God's temple through sacred ordinances. But what was Joseph Smith's pedagogy? How should a Latter-day Saint progress as it were "from grace to grace"[7] toward this exaltation? What educational means or pedagogic devices did Smith and his contemporaries in the Church devise to make this perfectionism comprehensible and tangible? And how were these dispensed?

In this chapter I will answer these questions by first sketching the cultural religious context within which Joseph's view on salvation as exaltation took shape. Next I will draw from Joseph's teachings about gaining certainty of exaltation found in his revelations, public sermons, and more private teachings. Then I will examine the pedagogy, the modes of teaching, and the associated (temple) ordinances and how Joseph Smith planned to dispense these, first to the Twelve Apostles and then to all the Saints. I will conclude by applying these findings to Latter-day Saints seeking surety of salvation as exaltation in our time.

Historical Context: Protestant Perfectionism and the Search for Certainty of Salvation

Joseph Smith's contemporary religious teachers and reformers were united in their search for salvific certainty[8] and taught various versions of Christian perfectionism to achieve it.[9] One could say that, as Protestants, they had left the security of Catholic sacramentalism behind and had all proposed different substitute doctrines to achieve perfection and salvation.[10] Joseph himself describes the Methodists, Presbyterians, and Baptists as three of the main sects he and his family were in contact with. He said he "attended their several meetings as occasion would permit" and that his "mind became somewhat partial to the Methodist sect."[11] Christopher Jones documents further that Methodism was one of the most expansive and influential sects in antebellum America.[12] Many early converts to the Church, as

Jones shows, came from a Methodist background, such as Brigham Young, John Taylor, and Thomas B. Marsh. Many of them stayed sympathetic toward the Methodist founder John Wesley and—while engaged in missionary activities—saw Methodist teachings as a sound basis upon which converts could add in their conversion to the restored Church. Even Joseph Smith reportedly said that "if the Methodists would only advance a step or two further, they would take the world. We Latter-day Saints are Methodists, as far as they have gone, only we have advanced further."[13] This begs the question: how much did the soteriology and perfectionism of the Methodists (and others) influence or even shape Smith's own search for a personal and later doctrinal surety of salvation?

Despite the doctrinal differences of these Christian sects, there was some consensus on the idea that humanity's fallen and sinful state had to be overcome through the mediation and power of Jesus Christ's atoning sacrifice. As mentioned earlier, the debate focused on how to access that power and how one could be certain that power was manifest and hence that salvation was sure. The sectarian landscape was also divided over the question of individual choice in salvation. For Calvinistic Presbyterians, there was no choice: God had to elect you and make it known in a spiritual outpouring of grace. For Arminian-Wesleyan Methodists, individuals could choose to accept Christ's Atonement and exercise faith to bring about good works and confirming spiritual experiences. For Universalists, the choice to believe in Christ was relevant only for the moment you were saved, for eventually—at the last judgment—all were saved. The divide was present in Joseph Smith's own family, where mother, brothers, and older sister joined the Presbyterian Church and father turned from a Universalist to a more neutral standpoint and did not adhere then to a particular church.[14] Joseph's quest, most likely sparked by a Methodist camp meeting,[15] was an individual endeavor to gain certainty of forgiveness for his sins, an endeavor that hinged on deciding which church to join in this pursuit of justification. He attended meetings but did not seem to have the same level of excitement, nor experience the physical sensations that others had.[16] This set Joseph in dire need of a different confirmation or source of certainty.[17]

Methodists looked for certainty through scripture,[18] full devotion to a Christian life, and spiritual manifestations, or what they called works of grace. These were commonly sought after and celebrated when received, confirming to faithful seekers that God corroborated their efforts with an "outpouring" of his power. The most well-known spiritual manifestations, mainly derived from biblical reports, were speaking in tongues, healings, dreams, and visions. Also, very physical effects were seen, like "people [who] went into trances, jerked, rolled and crawled on the ground," or were, in Joseph Smith's time, at least "crying, mourning, and sighing."[19] The feeling of being "touched upon" or "recognized" or "accepted" by God was mostly a communal experience. Among the Methodists, camp meetings were predominant in bringing about this communal excitement, aimed at a spiritual "revival" or a bringing of souls "from darkness to light."[20]

This begs the question: once such an "acceptance" took place, did those in the congregation who were part of this group experience feel secure about their standing before God; did they feel they were "forgiven of their sins"? If so, this must have been more of an individual certainty, for not all present experienced it. The ecclesiastical counterpart of that experience was the power or authority of a church to extend the right doctrines and means whereby its adherents could have these reviving experiences.[21] If false doctrine were preached or one adhered to a corrupt faith, there was danger of damnation, or at least—as Joseph Smiths portrayed it—such things were being preached in an effort to dissuade converts from one sect to another.[22]

Christopher Jones also points out that Methodists were very likely to accept dreams and visions, like Joseph Smith's First Vision, to be authoritative revelations from God.[23] Joseph's vision, seen through a Methodist lens, can be seen as a conversion experience whereby God answers a prayer by an apparition of sorts, invoking spiritual gifts and/or forgiving sins. Brigham Young's older brother Phineas, also a Methodist who later converted to the Church of

Jesus Christ, had a similar experience as Joseph when he prayed to be "made holy" to fulfill his recent calling.[24] From the earliest account of Joseph Smith's First Vision we learn that his initial effort was indeed a search for confirmation of forgiveness of personal sin. His prayer, he writes, was answered by God appearing and saying, "Joseph, my son, thy sins are forgiven thee."[25] This was the first certainty Joseph longed to experience.

Pertaining to authority as a church, Joseph sought additional certainty about which church to join, a church that would be "accepted of God." Wesleyan teachings on power derived from "spiritual witness" were indicative of the certainty needed to be a "living church." When denied, Wesley taught, "there is a danger lest our religion degenerate into mere formality; lest, 'having a form of godliness,' we neglect if not 'deny, the power of it.'"[26] This resembles a statement of the Lord in Joseph Smith's 1838 account of his First Vision and was part of the answer and instruction Joseph received to join none of the churches he was in contact with.[27] What was truly remarkable and very decisive for his later perfectionism—as we will see below—is that Joseph professed to receive these confirmations from God the Father and Jesus Christ in person. The accompanying conclusion, one that up to this day continues to make many other Christian denominations feel uneasy, is that Joseph claimed that the church he was asked to organize was not his own, but the Lord's, and the gospel he proclaimed was not his own, but restored by the Lord himself.

With regard to perfectionism among Methodists, John Wesley wrote three works with "perfection" prominent in their title.[28] In his treatise on perfection he defines it as

> that habitual disposition of the soul which, in the sacred writings, is termed holiness; and which directly implies being cleansed from sin, "from all filthiness both of flesh and spirit"; and, by consequence, being endued with those virtues which were in Christ Jesus; being so "renewed in the image of our mind," as to be "perfect as our Father in heaven is perfect."[29]

Wesley describes perfection in another sermon as

> a restoration not only to the favour, but likewise to the image
> of God, implying not barely deliverance from sin, but the
> being filled with the fullness of God.[30]

Phrases such as "holy," "cleansed from sin," "endued with
Christlike virtues," and "renewed in mind" all imply a change brought
about by the exercise of faith and the working of grace, but which
make the human believer only "as to be" perfect as God. Receiving
the image of God or being filled with his fullness seems to point more
to *imitatio Christi* in the form of a refinement of Christian character, but not leading to eventual achievement of godhood in the more
literal sense Joseph Smith later adopted. Methodist perfection can
more readily be incorporated with its teaching of entire sanctification, as shown in two other quotes from Wesley, stating that perfection is "deliverance from inward as well as from outward sin" and
"a Christian is so far perfect as not to commit sin."[31] Joseph clearly
also taught about the need to be cleansed from sin but added that
we then need to move forward—even beyond the grave—to attain
godlike qualities that would enable us to inherit the kind of life God
lives.[32] We see here that Smith's teachings—drawing upon both
his Protestant heritage, study of the Bible, and his continuing revelations—employ similar language but pointed toward different or
added meanings. Joseph's understanding of perfection and salvation
as exaltation, as already explained, developed over many years. As
these doctrines of exaltation became clearer, Joseph gathered elements of temple ritual (literally and spiritually cleansing our bodies
as a preparation to enter the temple or God's presence) leading up to
the Nauvoo era, where doctrine and ritual came together.

A lesser-known influence on Joseph Smith was that of the
Universalist Society, originating in Boston but present in most
of New England, a movement to which Joseph's grandfather and
father adhered.[33] Asael Smith had moved away from orthodox
Congregationalism to the Universalist teachings of John Murray.[34]

Murray rejected the Calvinist idea of election and damnation and universalized the idea that Jesus was "from everlasting ordained to be the savior of all." Through unity with Christ, everyone could be justified through his vicarious Atonement.[35] Similar teachings on perfection can be found with the related Unitarians. William Ellery Channing, the latter movement's dominant minister, taught that "likeness to God is a good so unutterably surpassing all other good, that whoever admits it as attainable, must acknowledge it to be the chief aim of life."[36] He even talks about exaltation but in a broader sense of a God who cares for his children so much that he does everything for their "recovery and exaltation." Channing also strongly believes that God and all of his attributes can be known because man himself carries the knowledge of God in his own soul, and that through the influence of the Holy Ghost and a Christian life of service, these godly attributes can be brought to perfection.[37] It is unclear how much Universalist or Unitarian teachings passed from Joseph's grandfather and father to him. One Universalist idea Asael Smith certainly taught, which can be recognized in Joseph's soteriology, is its anti-Calvinistic conception of God's universal salvific love: a desire to save all his children.[38] It is likely that Joseph accepted this desire that God could save all, while also adhering to the Methodist requirements of agency and exercise of faith to bring about saving grace. Having established this context, we will now investigate how Joseph situated this reciprocal desire for human and God to reunite in perfect unity in an almost Catholic sacramental covenant theology with accompanying temple ordinances.

Joseph Smith's Own View on Salvific Surety through Perfection: The Pinnacle of Salvation

> If you wish to go where God is, you must be like God, or possess the principles which God possesses. . . . A man is saved no

faster than he gets knowledge, . . . Hence [we] need revelation
to assist us, and give us knowledge of the things of God.[39]

Notwithstanding his historical background and surroundings,
Joseph took a different course—guided by the revelations he received—in restoring teachings on what salvation meant and how it
was to be achieved. Starting from the earliest period, while translating the Book of Mormon, and moving into the Kirtland/Missouri
period and on to the Nauvoo period, this process can be described
as a process of consolidation and dissemination. By *consolidation* and
dissemination, I mean the bringing together (*con*) of principles of salvation into tangible (*solid*) ordinances that can be experienced and
teaching them to more and more of the Saints (*dis*) to eventually bear
much fruit (*seminate*). Teaching the Quorum of the Twelve, building
the Kirtland Temple, later teaching a Quorum of the Anointed, and
building the Nauvoo Temple all illustrate these purposes.

I argue that the two forms of certainty Joseph sought after, as
explained earlier as doctrinal (ecclesiastical) and personal certainty,
also came together as (1) the presence of God's power, acceptance by
God, authority, and (2) surety of salvation.

First, the presence of God's power and authority took form in
the priesthood, which had to accompany all performed ordinances.
While translating the Book of Mormon, Joseph Smith and Oliver
Cowdery explained, they had received the Aaronic Priesthood from
John the Baptist. At a later time they also claimed to have received the
Melchizedek Priesthood from Peter, James, and John. Several revelations on Church and priesthood organization (for example, Doctrine
and Covenants 20, 84, 88, 107, 110, 131, 132) gradually explained and
clarified the different offices and uses of those priesthoods. Even
before any temple ordinances were revealed, people were baptized
and confirmed and received the sacrament, drawing upon these two
priesthoods to perform such acts with authority.

In Kirtland, however, a new priesthood was installed—after the
order of the ancients—namely the "High Priesthood."[40] Within a

few months of ordaining elders to this priesthood for the first time, Joseph taught that "the order of the High priesthood is that they have power given them to seal up the Saints unto eternal life."[41] As David Buerger suggests, Joseph was teaching what "strict Calvinists reserved solely to God."[42] Subsequently, he introduced accompanying ordinances that were later incorporated into the temple endowment.[43] *Sealing* is another word connoting certainty and can be seen in connection with the sealing or binding power Peter and Nephi received "to bind on earth as in heaven" and later in the reception of the sealing keys of Elijah in the Kirtland Temple.[44] Zebedee Coltrin in 1831, Jared Carter in 1832, and Orson Pratt in 1833 all testified of the outpourings of the Spirit, not only on individuals, but on entire groups that Joseph gathered in his School of the Prophets to "seal them up" "to the Lord" "unto eternal life" "by the power of the Holy Ghost."[45] These greatly resembled Methodist communal outpourings but in a completely new doctrinal context of apostles and prophets (see Doctrine and Covenants 88:127–38) called to the ministry (see Doctrine and Covenants 95:4–5). Authority thus came from being called and then receiving the(se) priesthood(s).[46]

Second, Joseph Smith's first quest for personal salvation was answered by a personal visitation[47] of the Father and the Son, which is exactly the theophany that he later posed as the end goal of temple practice. I say "practice" because Joseph merged gaining knowledge, exercising faith, and producing works in a development toward perfection or godhood. The temple was to be a place to meet God and a place of learning in preparation for that.[48] These can be seen as original additions to the Methodist faith and works required for spiritual approval from God—searching for the mysteries of god(liness) by study and by faith made education into a mode of worship. We could redefine the word *worship* now as "a mode to approach God," a reciprocal act to return to him.[49] God had asked Joseph and the early Saints to build a temple to be able to receive the knowledge requisite for salvation, and now they had to respond. Joseph started first by organizing (on divine command) the previously mentioned School of the Prophets in Kirtland. It was in this school, and later—upon its completion—in the Kirtland Temple, that Joseph started preparing others to meet the Lord, preparatory for their missions as literal witnesses of Christ. In this school they taught one another by posing and answering questions (almost in a Socratic manner):

> How do men obtain a knowledge of the glory of God, his per-fections and attributes? By devoting themselves to his service, through prayer and supplication incessantly strengthening their faith in him, *until*, like Enoch, the Brother of Jared, and Moses, they obtain *a manifestation of God* to themselves.[50]

This resembles the Methodist method of receiving entire sanctifica-tion up to the point when the word *until* appears, after which Joseph refers to other prophets in the scriptures who were called by God in person.

To make that viable, the Kirtland Temple needed to be built. The twelve apostles were charged "not to go to other nations . . . [but to] tarry at Kirtland until [they were] endowed with power from on high."[51] Oliver Cowdery gave them this charge:

> The ancients passed through the same. They had this testi-mony, that they had seen the Saviour after he rose from the dead. . . . You must bear the same testimony, that there is but one God and one Mediator; he that has seen him will know him and testify of him. . . . You have been indebted to other men in the first instance for evidence, on that you have acted. But . . . you will, therefore see the necessity of getting this tes-timony from Heaven. Never cease striving until you have seen God, face to face. Strengthen your faith, cast off your doubts, your sins and all your unbelief and nothing can prevent you from coming to God. Your ordination is not full and complete till God has laid his hand upon you.[52]

This ordination refers to their calling as apostles to be witnesses, which flows from having seen God. In other words, the Twelve had to make their calling and election as apostles sure. Here we witness another shift in meaning of the word *calling* and the added *election*. Apostles needed to be called and elected to their ministry through the laying on of hands (literally or symbolically) by the Lord himself in a theophany that resembled Joseph's First Vision. The event of seeing God the Father and his Son occurred (at least for most of the Twelve)[53] "at one of these meetings after the organization of the school (the school being organized on the 23rd of January, 1833)."[54] Afterwards the prophet Joseph said: "Brethren, now you are prepared to be the apostles of Jesus Christ, for you have seen both the Father and the Son and know that they exist and that they are two separate personages."[55] Similar to the vision and calling he personally received in Palmyra, Joseph also deemed such a witness necessary for the Twelve and others sent out to the ministry from Kirtland. It is interesting to see that many also received a blessing by the laying on of hands whereby their "sins were forgiven them."[56]

Here we see a complete unity of the two lines of authority in Joseph's search for salvific surety: (1) priesthoods were restored, including the sealing power, and (2) the "most sure" way of getting salvation is by meeting God, but this was also a way of having the apostles' calling and election made sure—to enable them to teach with authority as witnesses of Christ. Nevertheless, this theophany to the Twelve in preparation of their ministry was only a precursor to what was about to come. Their calling and election did not deal explicitly with surety of salvation. They were still learning and repenting, confessing their sins to one another, bearing one another up. Theophany as a means whereby one could be sure of salvation, being sealed unto eternal life or exaltation, is something Joseph would start teaching in Nauvoo.

In a sermon delivered at the Nauvoo Temple grounds on 12 May 1844, Joseph pleaded with all Saints present there: "I am going on in my progress for eternal life. . . . Oh! I beseech you to go forward, go

forward and make your calling and election sure."[57] Surely Joseph had
been adamant in his search for knowledge: the inspired or explanatory translation of the Old and New Testaments, the discussions in
the School of the Prophets, the ongoing revelations, receiving the
sealing keys of Elijah, the discovery of the Abraham papyri, and join-
ing the Masonic Lodge were all sources of knowledge—ancient and
new—that Joseph employed to construct his theology of exaltation.
All were being consolidated, brought together: the knowledge and
principles needed to guide all Saints to meet God in his holy house,
the temple, and thus to become sure of salvation.

Joseph named this surety of salvation after Peter's "calling and
election made sure" (see 2 Peter 1:10, 19). He explained on 17 May
1843, "The more sure word of prophecy means a man's knowing
that he is *sealed up unto eternal life*, by revelation and the spirit of
prophecy, through the power of the Holy Priesthood" (Doctrine and
Covenants 131:5). The Protestants around him used these scriptures
too. For example, Calvinists talked about them, using scriptures on
sealing to corroborate their doctrine of predestination. Methodists,
like John Wesley, as we saw above, had teachings on sanctification
and even perfection. But none went as far in teaching perfection as
reaching a point in spiritual development where God—in person—
seals a person unto eternal life. Moreover, Smith also devised temple
ordinances to mediate these sealings, through one holding the priesthood power to seal both on earth and in heaven.[58] What Calvinists
could only assume based on professed faith and Methodists hoped
to derive from spiritual witness, Latter-day Saints could obtain by
revealed knowledge coupled with a priesthood ordinance.

Joseph made one more addition unique to Latter-day Saint theology to his concept of exaltation—eternal marriage, and for some
plural marriage. One day before his 17 May explanation on the more
sure word of prophecy, Joseph taught:

> In the celestial glory there are three heavens or degrees; and in
> order to obtain the highest, a man must enter into this order

of the priesthood [meaning the new and everlasting covenant of marriage]; and if he does not, he cannot obtain it. He may enter into the other, but that is the end of his kingdom: he cannot have an increase.[59]

Joseph's February 1832 vision already showed him that heaven was divided into three kingdoms of glory (see Doctrine and Covenants 76). The celestial kingdom now had three degrees. The eternal increase mentioned points to similar blessings Abraham received pertaining to his posterity, "both in the world and out of the world" (Doctrine and Covenants 132:30; see Abraham 2:11). This revelation on both the sealing power and the covenant of eternal (and plural) marriage, made exaltation and perfection—becoming gods—more explicit: all gods are married—or sealed to one another—and continue in procreation in the eternities. Any lesser form of salvation (a "saved state" or obtaining a place in (one) heaven, as most Christian sects would see it), would be a limitation to eternal progression:

> For these angels did not abide my law; therefore, they cannot be enlarged, but remain separately and singly, without exaltation, in their saved condition, to all eternity; and from henceforth are not gods, but are angels of God forever and ever. (Doctrine and Covenants 132:17)

Later on this revelation shows that exaltation entails knowing who God is and being able to live where and how he lives:

> For strait is the gate, and narrow the way that leadeth unto the exaltation and continuation of the lives, and few there be that find it, because ye receive me not in the world neither do ye know me. But if ye receive me in the world, *then shall ye know me*, and shall receive your exaltation; that *where I am ye shall be also*. (Doctrine and Covenants 132:22–23; emphasis added)

Joseph was now doctrinally prepared to make these highest blessings available to all who were "spiritual[ly] minded" and "prepared to receive" them.[60] This spiritual preparation was of course the purpose of the Church in general and of the priesthood quorums and the newly established Female Relief Society of Nauvoo as well. In preparing the Saints, Joseph wanted to make haste, as he expected to be taken from this world and felt the need "to instruct the [Relief] Society and point out the way for them to conduct, that they might act according to the will of God . . . delivering the keys to this society and the church."[61] This sermon reflected the need for the women to be instructed in the same knowledge as the men. This anticipated Smith's presentation of the endowment a few days later and the emergence of the Quorum of the Anointed, in which—logically—women played an equal part. This Quorum of the Anointed was different in the sense that it focused on couples preparing for the newly completed temple rituals. There Joseph eventually revealed all these ordinances of exaltation (keys), which were later to be disseminated to the entire church. Joseph started with the initiation of a select few, twenty-four couples and seventeen others to be exact,[62] but with a broader view ahead:

> In this Council [Quorum] was instituted the Ancient order of things for the first time in these last days. . . . and there was nothing made known to these men, but what will be made known to all <the> Saints of the last days, so soon as they are prepared to receive, and a proper place is prepared to communicate them, even to the weakest of the Saints.[63]

That proper place was the (Nauvoo) temple, but it was still under construction, so Joseph went ahead and set up the upper room of his red brick store to serve as an ordinance room. Two more essential elements were part of the ordinance: marriage and generations. By adding marriage, the gospel of Adam and Eve one could say, the full meaning of the word *sealing* was established: this sealing of couples to one another and to God now extended—through the Abrahamic covenant and the keys of the sealing power of Elijah (see Doctrine and Covenants 110:13–16)—to all progenitors and progeny, both living and dead, so that the entire human family could be bound together on earth and in heaven. This bonding of generations ties in to an element of perfection Joseph had already introduced in 1840 and further developed in 1842: that "neither can we without our dead be made perfect" (Doctrine and Covenants 128:15; see Hebrews 11:40). Hence, all the ordinances that Joseph had instituted would eventually also be performed by proxy for ancestors. This adds a small Universalist element—namely, that God's salvific love extends to the entire human family, back to Adam and Eve, and that he gives a chance to all who have lived to accept his covenant. And here we find the complete fitting together of all aspects of salvation as exaltation as are now found and taught in The Church of Jesus Christ of Latter-day Saints.

Praxis: Joseph Smith's Search for Fitting Ordinances, A Pedagogy of Perfection

> And without the ordinances thereof, and the authority of the priesthood, the power of godliness is not manifest unto men in the flesh; for without this no man can see the face of God, even the Father, and live. (Doctrine and Covenants 84:21–22)

> The question is frequently asked: Can we not be saved without going through with all these ordinances &c. I would answer: No, not the fullness of Salvation, . . . any person who is exalted to the highest mansion has to abide a Celestial law & the whole law to.[64]

Now that the doctrines were in place, or consolidated, they were ready to be passed on, or disseminated. How? Orally and performatively. An oral canon of scripture was about to be opened, expounded upon, clothed in symbolic scenes and acts, all fitted to the envisioned purpose that every Saint who was prepared to receive the temple endowment should receive it in preparation to meet God in person and be assured of exaltation. Oral and performative transmissions of sacred truths, which were "not to be riten,"[65] serve several important purposes, as we will see below. This mode of ritual transmission was performed by the Jews, Egyptians, Masons, and as far as we can infer from the limited canon of the New Testament, also in the days of the early apostles.[66]

Joseph considered many plain and precious things from the gospel to have been lost,[67] mostly from scripture, but much, he believed, had been preserved through these other traditions. Through his study and "inspired translation" of the Old and New Testaments, Joseph learned (among other things) about priesthood and the nature of salvation. Joseph's discovery of the Egyptian papyri brought back teachings (among others) on the premortal life and the Abrahamic covenant. His involvement in the Masonic temple and his own revelations concerning the rituals there helped him discover precious parts of that (lost) ritual tradition. Although it is very hard to trace back exactly and chronologically each of the building blocks that formed the Nauvoo temple ceremony, one could accept the idea that ofttimes information precedes inspiration. Gathering all these pieces of knowledge and tradition and seeking revelation about their meaning and purpose led at least to certain clear doctrines and covenants, around which the much more culturally or even biographically infused ritual forms and language took shape.[68] Following his pattern of dissemination, he introduced them to the Twelve Apostles as well as to others and expounded on them in his public sermons. In Nauvoo he urged the apostles and hundreds of Church members to join the Masonic lodge[69] to learn what he had learned and help him bring it into one revealed whole.

The next step Joseph took was to fit all these saving principles into a mode of teaching that would, on the one hand, be instrumental in revealing unto the participant all knowledge necessary to reenter God's presence. On the other hand, since it was sacred knowledge, he had to safeguard it. This put Joseph in a delicate position, and the way he went about it was to create a tradition of knowledge by initiation. The Masonic temple rites are the most exemplary for this mode of teaching.[70] The important point about this teaching approach is how Joseph Smith envisioned it and its purposes. This method of teaching resembles Jesus's use of parables—to communicate hidden knowledge to those who had "ears to hear" (Matthew 13:9) but conceal at the same time the pearls from the swine (see Matthew 7:6). Masons would express the principle as being hidden in plain sight. This approach requires a specific form of pedagogy between a master or mentor and a learner.

Education[71] and pedagogy[72] are in their Latin and Greek roots almost interchangeable. *Educare* ("leading out") is mostly associated with training the powers of the mind, oriented more toward the transmittal and sharing of knowledge. Παιδαγογία, or *paidagōgía* ("leading a child"), is more relational, associated with mentoring and aiding in the development of a child. By combining these concepts, we perceive the need for teaching both principles and knowledge and for the leading, guiding, or mentoring that is part of initiation and providing certain experiences necessary for development. This method also resembles the way Jesus taught his disciples. As a rabbi he explained to them the scriptures, taught them principles, and expanded their knowledge. But he also wanted the apostles to experience certain things, so as a Master he gave them assignments and performed rituals with them like the Last Supper and the washing of feet.

Hidden knowledge of principles, and the experiences necessary to internalize these principles "deeply into the bone,"[73] are made into a whole by initiation into rituals or ordinances. Ordinances are not only tools in teaching, but—like Catholic sacraments—are also binding rituals. A ritual can be defined as a symbolic act meant to bridge a distance, to initiate a passage, or to symbolize a relationship of belonging.[74] In a Christian context, binding or sealing both refer to a covenant relationship between humans and God that is meant to bridge the gap between them: the gap in refinement of character (perfection) and the gap between earth and heaven (salvation) or between the mortal life we live now and the eternal life that gods enjoy (exaltation). One can view the temple ritual in both Methodist and Calvinist senses of surety of salvation: it can be instrumental both in receiving spiritual outpourings and in confirming one's holiness or standing before God. Another Methodist or Arminian element, one could say, is that the relationship is entered into of one's own free will and choice.

All these functions can be applied to the temple ordinances, which for Joseph Smith and the early leaders were seen as parts of one ritual. Perhaps with the exception of baptism for the living—the first initiation rite to become a member of the Church—all other ordinances were done in the temple setting: sacrament,[75] washings and anointings, endowment, marriage sealing, washing of feet, and so forth (see Doctrine and Covenants 88:75, 138–41). The new (Nauvoo) additions to the endowment and marriage ordinances were introduced in the upper room of Joseph's red brick store. He had asked five men who were Masons to prepare the room according to his instructions. Eight people were the first to receive this improvised endowment on 4 May 1842. It is illustrative to consider how Joseph later apologized for the improvised quarters, saying to Brigham Young:

> This is not arranged right, but, we have done the best we could under the circumstances in which we are placed, and I wish you take this matter in hand . . . organize and systematize all these ceremonies . . . [Brigham Young:] We performed the ordinances under Joseph's supervision numerous times and each time I got something more so that when we went through the Temple at Nauvoo I understood and knew how to place them there. We had our ceremonies pretty correct.[76]

It was an evolving ceremony, and frankly, it has been evolving ever since,[77] which tells us something about its instrumental nature. Symbols, by their metaphorical nature, are meant to "carry over" (μετα-φέρειν) from one realm of reality to another. For example, the story of Adam and Eve can have meaning within the context of their dealings with God but at the same time can carry over meaning for all men and women going through mortal life. The portrayal of the stories and symbols—with the exception of some key elements—does not have to be exact every time. There is constant interpretation: some (though little) by the persons portraying the symbols (live performance) and even more by the persons receiving them. In fact, every individual receiving them can make his or her own interpretations and apply them in his or her life.

These new temple ordinances bring initiates into higher knowledge and ritual experiences and prepare them for meeting God and becoming like God. They can be seen as steps on a ladder, a pedagogy toward perfection, as Joseph explained:

> Here then is eternal life, to know the only wise and true God. You have got to learn how to be Gods yourselves; to be kings and priests to God, the same as all Gods have done; by going from a small degree to another, from grace to grace, from exaltation to exaltation, until you are able to sit in glory as doth those who sit enthroned in everlasting power; . . . When you climb a ladder, you must begin at the bottom and go on until you learn the last principle; it will be a great while before you have learned the last. It is not all to be comprehended in this world; it is a great thing to learn salvation beyond the grave.[78]

Joseph Smith seemed eager to prepare the Saints to meet God in this life and have the promised blessings sealed upon them. All his temple instructions point to that.

Washings and anointings were among the first temple ordinances to be performed in this dispensation. An important part of these rituals are the references to our own bodies and the blessings connected to them. So, one's own body becomes an instrument in sanctification by overcoming the natural tendencies of the flesh and instead by using the body to acquire these spiritual blessings. One could say the Methodist sense of perfection, becoming entirely clean of (the blood and) sins (of this generation), took on this sacramental form in Joseph's perfectionism. Again, internalization through the ritual is very prominent, as these blessings are memorized and one's own body—and the symbolic garment it is clothed with—serve as daily reminders. It also has a communal aspect of great trust since the washings and anointings are performed by a brother or sister, who symbolically touches the parts of the body being blessed, thus providing the experience that internalizes the ritual.

The endowment is even closer to a ladder of sanctification, as the initiate is literally taken from one phase to the other, symbolized by the different rooms one passes through, the increasing brightness of light, and the ever deeper commitments entered into. Deeper commitments also lead to a closer connection with the divine in anticipation of reuniting with God at the end of the ceremony, where one ritually steps into God's presence by passing through a veil (see Ether 3:20).

Temple marriage is, of course, a direct symbol of uniting man and woman in God and having these relationships sealed beyond the grave. Children of parents who have been sealed are born in the covenant, and covenant relationships can be extended vicariously to ancestors. Blessings pertaining to offspring in this world and the next are pronounced and are found in symbolic representations of fertility.[79] Unity in marriage as a way to grow nearer to Heavenly Father and Mother sets up family life as a learning environment as well, one that allows us to practice becoming gods and to have an "increase" (Doctrine and Covenants 131:4).

We could go on expanding on the symbolism of these ordinances, but I noted only some that had relation to the perfectionism Joseph taught. The Latter-day Saint temple ritual is deeply pedagogical: anyone can learn new things relevant to one's current phase of development and as the Holy Spirit may direct. This, one can say, is the perfect mode of learning: tailored, deeply spiritual, and experiential. On the one hand it brings personal revelation to the individual by communal symbolic rites and experiences, and on the other hand the sacredness of these teachings is safeguarded by the principle of initiation and the promises entered into. I identify this mode of teaching with Joseph's pedagogy of perfection. In essence this model allows all Saints, of their own free will and choice, to participate in ordinances as a means to experience spiritual maturation, to the end purpose of meeting and becoming like God.

The early Saints who first received these ordinances were still innovating and learning to apply this new mode of teaching to their development and spiritual life. I would like to show, from their own experiences, how they thought these teachings were to be applied and disseminated. Just as Joseph had openly preached many of the principles pertaining to exaltation and making one's calling and election sure, partakers of the ordinances discussed their experiences in the temple. Helen Mar Whitney recorded Amasa Lyman's insights and experiences of the temple ordinances he received on 21 December 1845, which reveal some keys to the perceived purposes of temple pedagogy:

> These things [are] to put you in possession of the means of salvation, and be brought into a *proper relationship to God*. . . . It is the key by which you *approach* God. No impression which you receive here should be lost. It was to rivet the recollections of these things in your *memory*, like a nail in a sure place *never to be forgotten*. The scenery through which you have passed is actually laying before you a picture or *map*, by which you are *to travel through life* and obtain entrance into the celestial Kingdom hereafter.[80]

According to this statement, the ritual accomplishes three things: First, it is meant to bridge the gap between humans and God, to establish a "covenant relation." Second, it provides a specific goal to internalize the oral scripture by memorizing the proceedings of the ordinances and even to imprint them in our bodies through gestures. Third, there is a close relation between our symbolic journey through the temple and our everyday travel through life.

Nowhere in any ordinance or covenant is there such a clear connection with the everyday, or Christian, life. We are to imitate Christ, we put on Christ, we become as Christ as we advance in his priesthood, we take his name upon us and we even pass through him—which symbolically sanctifies us to be ready to meet him—so that we, as "true followers of his Son, Jesus Christ; . . . may become the sons of God; that when he shall appear we shall be like him, for we shall see him as he is; that we may have this hope; that we may be purified even as he is pure" (Moroni 7:48).

Easily overlooked, but to me very poignant, is the fact that Amasa Lyman's experience quoted above comes from minutes of meetings held just after the performance of the ordinances. This was like a temple testimony meeting, with seventy-five brothers and sisters present and where several shared their views on what they had just experienced. These early Saints, under the direction of Heber C. Kimball, helped each other understand and get a testimony of these important saving ordinances. They were actively making that connection with real life and following and becoming like Christ, and that is what Saints today are asked to do.

Conclusion: Teaching Joseph's Perfectionism and Temple Pedagogy in Our Time

> God's earthly kingdom is a school in which the saints learn the doctrines of salvation. Some members of the Church are being taught elementary courses; others are approaching graduation and can do independent research where the deep and hidden things are concerned. All must learn line upon line and precept upon precept.[81]

As in Joseph's time, we too hope to progress—and help fellow members progress—and to be initiated further and further into the prerequisite knowledge, moving from grace to grace in our lives, onto exaltation and making our calling and election sure. But are all the modes of teaching that the early Saints had at their disposal still present and intact? We have some institutionalized ways to prepare, initiate, and perform temple ordinances for members who are ready to receive them. There is an official temple preparation class, and up until 1990 there was a summary at the conclusion of the endowment ceremony that provided some explanation about the symbolism involved. Systematic teaching and mentoring about the temple ceremony, as in the School of the Prophets or like the temple testimony meetings of 1845, have been discontinued.

Education is still the most dominant form of worship in Latter-day Saint Church meetings and homes, with Church members being encouraged to keep rereading the standard works of scripture, aided by Sunday School and seminary and institute classes. But does this bring about sufficient development? If one is to learn line upon line, ascending Joseph's ladder, advancing from the preparatory gospel to the temple university, one needs constant hints leading to new and deeper meanings and insights[82] into knowledge beyond one's current understanding. I argue that the same goes for the oral scripture hidden in the proceedings and performances of the temple. Progress without mentoring is difficult.

Just recently Elder Bednar stressed the importance of teaching about the temple in the home and announced the release of a new specialized website about temples. He reiterated President Benson's guidelines to speak about the temple with care and reverence, but he underscored the need to indeed teach about it.[83] And the home is a fitting place, closely connected to the temple, both to teach about the principles and covenants of the temple and to share experiences or even revelations received in the temple. But are other more communal schools of prophets outside the home imaginable?

True, Joseph's pedagogy of perfection is quite a unique form of salvation theology, adding elements that Joseph deemed to be lost in most traditional Christian theologies he was surrounded with and that he thus sought to restore. It made the restored Church, with its emphasis on temple praxis, stand out more than it blended in. This gave rise to a paradox,[84] even in Joseph's time, of stressing the newly revealed points of doctrine (including premortal existence, eternal marriage, and exaltation as theosis) on the one hand and wanting to be accepted as a Christian religion on the other. But this now seems to have changed as the temple—and all that it stands for—is moved more to the forefront, for example, in the Church's message of hastening the work of salvation on "both sides of the veil."[85] The temple offers a tangible and achievable way to prepare faithful believers in Christ to the point where they are ready to meet him. We could take the same pride in these teachings as did the early Saints who announced it in bold terms:

> These teachings of the Savior [in 1 John 3:2–3; 1 Peter 1:15–16; Matthew 5:48; John 14:12; 17:20–24] most clearly show unto us the nature of salvation, and what He proposed unto the human family when He proposed to save them—that He proposed to make them like unto himself, and He was like the Father, the great prototype of all saved beings; and for any portion of the human family to be assimilated into their likeness is to be saved.[86]

And we could recognize, as did Bruce R. McConkie, that to continually advance toward God is an innate human desire:

> Among those who have received the gospel, and who are seeking diligently to live its laws and gain eternal life, there is *an instinctive and determined desire to make their calling and election sure*. Because they have tasted the good things of God and sipped from the fountain of eternal truth, they now seek the divine presence, where they shall know all things, have all power, all might, and all dominion, and in fact be like Him who is the great Prototype of all saved beings—God our Heavenly Father. (Doctrine and Covenants 132:20.) *This is the end objective, the chief goal of all the faithful*, and there is nothing greater in all eternity, "for there is no gift greater than the gift of salvation." (Doctrine and Covenants 6:13.)[87]

Notes

This paper resulted from research done during the Neal A. Maxwell Institute for Religious Scholarship 2015 Summer Seminar, "Organizing the Kingdom: Priesthood, Church Government, and the Forms of LDS Worship." This adaptation is shortened and focuses more on soteriology as *imitatio Christi* and the role temple practice and worship play in the development of the Saints as Joseph Smith envisioned it. A broader version of this paper was published earlier as "Pedadogy of Perfection: Joseph Smith's Perfectionism, How It Was Taught in the Early LDS Church, and Its Contemporary Applicability," *Dialogue* 51, no. 4 (2018): 105–43.

1.   From a letter by Joseph Smith "to the Church of Jesus Christ of Latter-day Saints," 6 September 1842, in Andrew H. Hedges, Alex D. Smith, and Richard Lloyd Anderson, eds., *Journals, Volume 2: December 1841–April 1843*, vol. 2 of the Journals series of *The Joseph Smith Papers*, ed. Dean C. Jessee, Ronald K. Esplin, and Richard Lyman Bushman (Salt Lake City: Church Historian's Press, 2011). See also Doctrine and Covenants 128:18.

2.   Joseph Smith, "To the Church of Jesus Christ of Latter-day Saints," 6 September 1842.

3.   For a definition of Christian perfection, with an etymology and all its shades, see Thomas A. Noble, *Holy Trinity: Holy People; The Theology of Christian Perfecting* (Eugene, OR: Wipf and Stock, 2013), 22–25. For an extensive treatise of precedents to Latter-day Saint perfectionism (or *theosis*), see Terryl L. Givens, *Wrestling the Angel: The Foundations of Mormon Thought; Cosmos, God, Humanity* (New York: Oxford University Press, 2014), chapter 21.

4.   Richard L. Anderson, *Joseph Smith's New England Heritage*, rev. ed. (Salt Lake City: Deseret Book; Provo, UT: Brigham Young University Press, 2003), 162, 133–35.

5.   Becoming as God is to this day the single most-contested doctrine upon which mainstream Christianity disavows The Church of Jesus Christ of Latter-day Saints as a Christian religion. An example of disputing this doctrine is "Response to the 1982 anti-Mormon film *The God*

Makers," FairMormon, https://fairmormon.org/answers/ Criticism_of
_Mormonism/Video/The_God_Makers.

6. "Discourse, 10 April 1842, as Reported by Wilford Woodruff," p. [146],
    The Joseph Smith Papers, https://josephsmithpapers.org/paper-summary
    /discourse-10-april-1842-as-reported-by-wilford-woodruff/1.

7. "Discourse, 7 April 1844, as Reported by *Times and Seasons*," p. 614, The
    Joseph Smith Papers, https://josephsmithpapers.org/paper-summary
    /discourse-7-april-1844-as-reported-by-times-and-seasons/3. See also Doc-
    trine and Covenants 93:12–13.

8. I will distinguish two lines of certainty: The first is about believers who
    looked for certainty that the power of God was present, and that by that
    presence God showed his acceptance of the exercise of their faith—in
    other words, that their religious acts or rites were recognized by God and
    that they administered them—as a church—with (a degree of) authority.
    The second line is about surety of salvation, expanding on the first line
    because it has to do with reassurances received in this life about our ability
    to transfer to the next life in a saved state. We will see that the definition
    of that saved state determines to a great extent the reassurances and the
    authority needed.

9. For example, Methodist evangelist and cofounder of the Holiness move-
    ment Phoebe Palmer, in her book *The Way of Holiness*, taught that to be a
    Bible Christian one must "travel the way of holiness," being fully obedient
    to and a "co-worker with God" by being true to the "Spirit's operations
    on the heart" and fully open to "the direct teachings of the Spirit" as the
    only way to be forgiven and "cleanse[d] from all unrighteousness" "for the
    attainment of the salvation promised in the Gospel of Christ." See Phoebe
    Palmer, *The Way of Holiness* (New York: Lane & Tippett, 1845 [1843]), 59.
    Additionally, the Presbyterian revivalist Charles G. Finney taught about
    "Growth in Grace" as "exhibit[ing] the character of God more and more,
    to reflect as many rays of image of God possible . . . to obey more and more
    perfectly and constantly the Law of God." See Charles G. Finney, *Lectures
    on Revivals of Religion* (New York: Leavitt, Lord, 1835), lecture 22, 416.

10. However, not all Protestants left sacramentalism. Some reformists
    like Calvin and followers (for example, Theodore Beza and Théodore

Turrettini) viewed sacraments as instruments of grace (albeit not in the same way as Catholicism [for example, the Council of Trent]).

11. "History, 1838–1856, volume A-1 [23 December 1805–30 August 1834]," p. 2, The Joseph Smith Papers, https://josephsmithpapers.org/paper -summary/history-1838-1856-volume-a-1-23-december-1805-30-august -1834/2. There is some evidence also that Joseph did indeed attend Methodist meetings; see Richard Lyman Bushman, *Joseph Smith: Rough Stone Rolling* (New York: Knopf, 2005), 37.

12. Christopher C. Jones, "We Latter-day Saints Are Methodists: The Influence of Methodism on Early Mormon Religiosity" (master's thesis, Brigham Young University, 2009), 14–24.

13. *Autobiography of Peter Cartwright*, with an introduction by Charles L. Wallis (Nashville: Abingdon Press reprint, 1984), 225–26. Christopher Jones warns though that "there is no record that authenticates Cartwright's attributed statement to Joseph Smith," although it does strengthen the suggestion that Joseph and his contemporaries believed "that Methodism contained more truth than other religions of the era." See Jones, "We Latter-day Saints Are Methodists," 25.

14. "History, 1838–1856, volume A-1 [23 December 1805–30 August 1834]," p. 2; Steven C. Harper, *Joseph Smith's First Vision: A Guide to the Historical Accounts* (Salt Lake City: Deseret Book, 2012), 14–21.

15. Orsamus Turner, a former printer's apprentice at the *Palmyra Register*, records in 1851 that he remembered that Smith caught "a spark of Methodism in the camp meeting, away down in the woods, on the Vienna road" and that he later became "a very passable exhorter in the evening meetings." See Orsamus Turner, *History of the Pioneer Settlement of Phelps and Gorham's Purchase, and Morris' Reserve* (Rochester, NY: William Alling, 1851), 214.

16. Alexander Neibaur, in a journal excerpt of 24 May 1844, recorded that "Br Joseph tolt us the first call he had a Revival Meeting his Mother & Br & Sister got Religion, he wanted to get Religion too wanted to feel & shout like the Rest but could feel nothing." "Alexander Neibaur, Journal, 24 May 1844, extract," p. [23], in Andrew H. Hedges, Alex D. Smith, and Brent M. Rogers, eds., *Journals, Volume 3: May 1843–June 1844*, vol. 3 of the Journals

series of *The Joseph Smith Papers*, ed. Ronald K. Esplin and Matthew J. Grow (Salt Lake City: Church Historian's Press, 2015).

17. Harper, *Joseph Smith's First Vision*, 23–25.

18. Methodists also clung to *sola scriptura*—whatever revelation was received must be in accordance with scripture.

19. Milton V. Backman Jr., "Awakenings in the Burned-Over District: New Light on the Historical Setting of the First Vision," in *Exploring the First Vision*, ed. Samuel Alonzo Dodge and Steven C. Harper (Provo, UT: Religious Studies Center, Brigham Young University; Salt Lake City: Deseret Book, 2012), 177–78.

20. William Neill, "Thoughts on Revivals of Religion," *Christian Herald*, 7 April 1821, 708–11, in Backman, "Awakenings," 186.

21. The partaking of the sacrament in Latter-day Saint theology can also be seen as a weekly reviving spiritual experience.

22. "History, 1838–1856, volume A-1 [23 December 1805–30 August 1834]," p. 2.

23. Jones, "We Latter-day Saints Are Methodists," 32–33.

24. The similarities are quite striking. In Young's own words: "I prayed continually to God to make me holy. . . . While in this state of mind I had a very singular manifestation, . . . when all of a sudden I saw the Heavens open and a body of light above the brightness of the sun descending towards me, . . . I then felt satisfied that the Lord had heard my prayers and my sins were forgiven." Phinehas Young, "Life of Phinehas Howe Young— Written by Himself," L. Tom Perry Special Collections, Harold B. Lee Library, Provo, Utah (hereafter Perry Special Collections). Quoted in Jones, "We Latter-day Saints are Methodists," 33.

25. "Letterbook 1," p. 3, The Joseph Smith Papers, https://josephsmithpapers .org/paper-summary/letterbook-1/9.

26. John Wesley, "Sermon 11, The Witness of the Spirit II," 1, no. 2 (1767), in *The Works of John Wesley*, ed. Thomas Jackson (Grand Rapids, MI: Zondervan, 1872), 1:285, quoted in Jones, "We Latter-day Saints Are Methodists," 42.

27. "They teach for doctrines the commandments of men, having a form of Godliness but they deny the power thereof.'" "History, 1838–1856, volume

A-1 [23 December 1805–30 August 1834]," p. 3. See Isaiah 29:13; Matthew 15:9.

28. *On Perfection* (Sermon 40, 1739), *Christian Perfection* (Sermon 76, 1784). These were sermons on sanctification, which hints at how Wesley understood "perfection." See "A Plain Account of Christian Perfection" (treatise, 1739).

29. John Wesley, "A Plain Account of Christian Perfection," in *The Works of John Wesley* 11, no. 29, 1:366–446.

30. John Wesley, "The End of Christ's Coming" (Sermon 62), Wesley Center, available at http://wesley.nnu.edu/john-wesley/the-sermons-of-john -wesley-1872-edition/sermon-62-the-end-of-christs-coming/.

31. Wesley, "Plain Account of Christian Perfection," 366–446.

32. Like Smith taught in the King Follett discourse. "Discourse, 7 April 1844, as Reported by *Times and Seasons*," p. 614, The Joseph Smith Papers, https://josephsmithpapers.org/paper-summary/discourse-7-april-1844 -as-reported-by-times-and-seasons/3.

33. Harper, *Joseph Smith's First Vision*, 17. Also, Richard L. Bushman makes a strong claim of Universalism present in the New England area and influence on Asael Smith's religious beliefs, in Bushman, *Joseph Smith and the Beginnings of Mormonism* (Urbana: Illinois University Press, 1984), 27–28. See also his more recent *Rough Stone Rolling*, 17.

34. Bushman, *Rough Stone Rolling*, 17.

35. E. Brooks Holifield, *Theology in America: Christian Thought from the Age of the Puritans to the Civil War* (New Haven, CT: Yale University Press, 2003), 221–22.

36. William Ellery Channing. "Likeness to God: Discourse at the Ordination of the Rev. FA Farley, Providence, RI, 1828," in *The Complete Works of William E. Channing* (Whitefish: Kessinger, 2010), 230. The connection to the topic of theosis was also made by Givens in *Wrestling the Angel*, 263. For further discussion on Channing, see Nicholas J. Frederick's paper "Incarnation, Exaltation, and Christological Tension in Doctrine and Covenants 93:1–20," in this volume, 11–41.

37. As exemplified in this quote: "To hold intellectual and moral affinity with the Supreme Being, to partake his spirit, to be his children by derivations

of kindred excellence, to bear a growing conformity to the perfection which we adore, this is a felicity which obscures and annihilates all other good." Channing, "Likeness to God," 230.

38. Anderson, *Joseph Smith's New England Heritage*, 136. See also Bushman, *Rough Stone Rolling*, 17.

39. "Discourse, 10 April 1842, as Reported by Wilford Woodruff," pp. 146–47, The Joseph Smith Papers, https://josephsmithpapers.org/paper-summary /discourse-10-april-1842-as-reported-by-wilford-woodruff/2.

40. "Minutes, circa 3–4 June 1831," p. 4, The Joseph Smith Papers, https:// josephsmithpapers.org/paper-summary/minutes-circa-3-4-june-1831/2. The historical introduction notes that "this conference marked the first time elders in the church were '"ordained to the High Priesthood."'

41. "Minutes, 25–26 October 1831," p. 11, The Joseph Smith Papers, https:// josephsmithpapers.org/paper-summary/minutes-25-26-october-1831/2.

42. David John Buerger, *The Mysteries of Godliness: A History of Mormon Temple Worship* (San Francisco: Smith Research Associates, 1994), 5. He further explains, "Key players in the sixteenth-century Reformation used many of these sealing passages [in the Bible] as evidence for their belief in predestination. Liberal reaction to Calvinist doctrine arose early in the seventeenth century when Arminians rejected this view, asserting that God's sovereignty and human free will were compatible, that such sealings depended on choices of the individual believer."

43. This Kirtland "endowment" during the solemn assembly held on 30 March 1836 included washings and anointings of kinds, the washing of feet (and face), and the sacrament. "Minutes, 30 March 1836," pp. 187–88, The Joseph Smith Papers, https://josephsmithpapers.org/paper-summary/minutes -30-march-1836/2. See also Doctrine and Covenants 88:127–41.

44. See Matthew 16:19; Helaman 10:4–7; and Doctrine and Covenants 110:13–16; and Joseph Smith's explanation in Doctrine and Covenants 128:5–18.

45. See Zebedee Coltrin Diary, 15 November 1831, Church History Library (hereafter CHL); Journal History of the Church of Jesus Christ of Latter-day Saints, 27 September 1832, CHL; and Journal of Orson Pratt, 26 August and 8 September 1833, CHL.

46. Later, Joseph Smith would express this in the Wentworth Letter as one of the central characteristics of the Church; it was later canonized as the fifth article of faith: "We believe that a man must be called of God, 'by prophecy, and by the laying on of hands' by those who are in authority, to preach the Gospel and administer in the ordinances thereof." "*Times and Seasons,* 1 March 1842," p. 709, The Joseph Smith Papers, https://josephsmithpapers .org/paper-summary/times-and-seasons-1-march-1842/7. See also Pearl of Great Price, Articles of Faith 1:5.

47. Actually several visitations, because three years after his First Vision he again prayed to know his standing before God, and as an answer angel Moroni appeared: "I often felt condemned for my weakness and imperfections; when on the evening of the above mentioned twenty first of September, after I had retired to my bed for the night I betook myself to prayer and supplication to Almighty God for forgiveness of all my sins and follies, and also for a manifestation to me that I might know of my state and standing before him. For I had full confidence in obtaining a divine manifestation as I had previously had one." "History, circa June 1839–circa 1841 [Draft 2]," p. 5, The Joseph Smith Papers, https://josephsmithpapers.org/paper-summary/history-circa-june-1839-circa-1841-draft-2/5.

48. Doctrine and Covenants 88:68 says, "He will unveil his face unto you," and verse 119 says, "Organize yourselves; prepare every needful thing; and establish a house, even a house of prayer, a house of fasting, a house of faith, a house of learning, a house of glory, a house of order, a house of God."

49. As Joseph once stated, "A man is saved no faster than he gets knowledge." "Discourse, 10 April 1842, as Reported by Wilford Woodruff," p. 147. Being brought back into God's presence by gaining knowledge is an idea also found in the Book of Mormon: "And because of the knowledge of this man [brother of Jared] he could not be kept from beholding within the veil; . . . wherefore, having this perfect knowledge of God, he could not be kept from within the veil; therefore he saw Jesus; and He did minister unto him" (Ether 3:19–20).

50. Lectures on Faith, Second lecture; emphasis added. "Doctrine and Covenants, 1835," p. 35, The Joseph Smith Papers, https://josephsmithpapers .org/paper-summary/doctrine-and-covenants-1835/43.

51. "Minute Book 1," p. 162, The Joseph Smith Papers, https://josephsmith papers.org/paper-summary/minute-book-1/166. Note the resemblance to Luke 24:49.

52. "Minute Book 1," pp. 156a–b; 159; 162.

53. "There were members as follows: Joseph Smith, Hyrum Smith, William Smith, Frederick G. Williams, Orson Hyde (who had the charge of the school), Zebedee Coltrin, Sylvester Smith, Joseph Smith, Sr., Levi Hancock, Martin Harris, Sidney Rigdon, Newel K. Whitney, Samuel H. Smith, John Murdock, Lyman Johnson and Ezra Thayer." As related by Zebedee Coltrin in "Minutes, Salt Lake City School of the Prophets," 3 October 1883.

54. This remark by Zebedee Coltrin obscures the date when this took place. He doesn't state the date, only the date of the organization of the School. The apostolic charge was given in 1835 and the temple dedicated 27 March 1836.

55. As related by Zebedee Coltrin in "Minutes, Salt Lake City School of the Prophets," 3 October 1883.

56. "Minute Book 1," p. 154.

57. "Discourse, 12 May 1844, as Reported by Thomas Bullock," p. 2, The Joseph Smith Papers, https://josephsmithpapers.org/paper-summary/discourse -12-may-1844-as-reported-by-thomas-bullock/2.

58. "Sealed by the Holy Spirit of promise, of him who is anointed, both as well for time and for all eternity, and that too most holy, by revelation and commandment through the medium of mine anointed, whom I have appointed on the earth to hold this power (and I have appointed unto my servant Joseph to hold this power in the last days, and there is never but one on the earth at a time on whom this power and the keys of this priesthood are conferred)." "Revelation, 12 July 1843 [D&C 132]," p. 1, The Joseph Smith Papers, https://josephsmithpapers.org/paper-summary /revelation-12-july-1843-dc-132/1. See Doctrine and Covenants 132:7; see also 132:46.

59. "History, 1838–1856, volume D-1 [1 August 1842–1 July 1843]," p. 1551, The Joseph Smith Papers, https://josephsmithpapers.org/paper-summary /history-1838-1856-volume-d-1-1-august-1842-1-july-1843/194. See also Doctrine and Covenants 131:1–4.

60. "History, 1838–1856, volume C-1 [2 November 1838–31 July 1842]," p. 1328, The Joseph Smith Papers, https://josephsmithpapers.org/paper-summary /history-1838-1856-volume-c-1-2-november-1838-31-july-1842/502.

61. "Nauvoo Relief Society Minute Book," p. 37, The Joseph Smith Papers, https://josephsmithpapers.org/paper-summary/nauvoo-relief-society -minute-book/34.

62. See table with list of initiated in Andrew F. Ehat, "Joseph Smith's Introduction of Temple Ordinances," in Andrew F. Ehat and Lyndon W. Cook, eds., The Words of Joseph Smith (Provo, UT: Religious Studies Center, Brigham Young University; Salt Lake City: Deseret Book, 1980), 102.

63. "History, 1838–1856, volume C-1 [2 November 1838–31 July 1842]," p. 1328, The Joseph Smith Papers, https://josephsmithpapers.org/paper-summary /history-1838-1856-volume-c-1-2-november-1838-31-july-1842/502.

64. "History, 1838–1856, volume E-1 [1 July 1843–30 April 1844]," p. 1866, The Joseph Smith Papers, https://josephsmithpapers.org/paper-summary /history-1838-1856-volume-e-1-1-july-1843-30-april-1844/238.

65. From Heber C. Kimball, in a letter to Parley and Mary Ann Pratt, dated 17 June 1842, Church History Archive: "We received some pressious things though the Prophet on the preasthood that would caus your Soul to rejoice. I can not give them to you on paper fore they are not to be riten. So you must come and get them fore your Self. We have organized a Lodge here. Of Masons. Since we obtained a Charter. That was in March since that thare *has near two hundred been made masons* Br Joseph and Sidny was the first that was Received in to the Lodg. All of the twelve have become members Exept Orson P. . . . thare is a similarity of preast Hood in Masonry. Bro Joseph ses masonry was taken from preasthood but had become degenerated but menny things are perfect"; emphasis added. Actually, the temple ceremonies were not written down until the year before Brigham Young's death.

66. A complete study of aspects of the Latter-day Saint temple ritual that can be traced back to Jewish, Egyptian, and Masonic sources, as well as the early apostles lies far beyond the scope of this paper. Hugh Nibley's extensive work on this can be consulted. I have focused, for the latter part of this paper, on the intended purposes of the mode of teaching that was devised.

67. See 1 Nephi 13:20–29. Verse 26 says, "For behold, they have taken away from the gospel of the Lamb many parts which are plain and most precious; and also many covenants of the Lord have they taken away."

68. See Armand L. Mauss, "Culture, Charisma, and Change: Reflections on Mormon Temple Worship," *Dialogue: A Journal of Mormon Thought* 20, no. 4 (1987): 79–80.

69. Also from Heber C. Kimball's letter to Parley P. Pratt, dated 17 June 1842, Church History Archive.

70. There are many excellent sources on the comparison and evolvement of Masonic and Latter-day Saint temple ordinances; for example, Buerger compares them in *Mysteries of Godliness*. See Michael W. Homer, "Similarity of Priesthood in Masonry: The Relationship between Freemasonry and Mormonism," *Dialogue: A Journal of Mormon Thought* 27, no. 3 (1984): 1–113. See also Matthew B. Brown, *Exploring the Connection between Mormons and Masons* (American Fork, UT: Covenant Communications, 2009), a recent article by Jeffrey M. Bradshaw, "Freemasonry and the Origins of Modern Temple Ordinances," *Interpreter: A Journal of Mormon Scripture* 15 (2015): 159–237, and again Hugh Nibley, *Temple and Cosmos* (Salt Lake City: Deseret Book and FARMS, 1992).

71. Educate (v.) mid-15c., "bring up (children), to train," from Latin *educatus*, past participle of *educare* "bring up, rear, educate," which is a frequentative of or otherwise related to *educere* "bring out, lead forth," from ex- "out" (see ex-) + *ducere* "to lead" (see duke (n.)). Meaning "provide schooling" is first attested 1580s. Related: Educated; educating. According to "Century Dictionary," *educere*, of a child, is "usually with reference to bodily nurture or support, while *educare* refers more frequently to the mind," and "There is no authority for the common statement that the primary sense of education is to 'draw out or unfold the powers of the mind,'" from http://etymonline.com/index.php?term=educate&allowed_in_frame=0.

72. Pedagogue (n.) late 14c., "schoolmaster, teacher," from Old French *pedagoge* "teacher of children" (14c.), from Latin *paedagogus*, from Greek *paidagogos* "slave who escorts boys to school and generally supervises them," later "a teacher," from *pais* (genitive *paidos*) "child" (see pedo-) + *agogos* "leader," from *agein* "to lead" (see act (n.) from http://etymonline.com/index.php?term=pedagogue&allowed_in_frame=0.

73. Ronald L. Grimes, *Deeply into the Bone: Re-inventing Rites of Passage* (Berkeley: University of California Press, 2000), 16.

74. See Grimes, *Deeply into the Bone*, 121.

75. The sacrament, of course, was also performed outside of the temple in regular Sunday meetings. It seems to have been an ordinance to remember Christ's sacrifice on any occasion the early brethren seemed fit. For an extensive treatise on the sacrament, see Ugo A. Perego, "The Changing Forms of the Latter-day Saint Sacrament," *Interpreter: A Journal of Latter-day Saint Faith and Scholarship* 22 (2016): 1–16. Available online at https://journal.interpreterfoundation.org/the-changing-forms-of-the-latter-day-saint-sacrament/.

76. L. John Nuttall, diary, typescript entry for 7 February 1877, Vault MSS 790; Journals of L[eonard] John Nuttall, 1857–1904, 19th Century Western and Mormon Americana, Special Collections.

77. In January 2019 the First Presidency announced the new changes to the temple ceremony using these words: "Over these many centuries, details associated with temple work have been adjusted periodically. . . . Prophets have taught that there will be no end to such adjustments as directed by the Lord to His servants" (First Presidency Statement on Temples, 2 January 2019, available at https://newsroom.churchofjesuschrist.org/article/temple-worship). The previous major changes in the endowment date from 1990; some minor changes in the initiatories were made in between, diminishing the communal part of touching at the pronouncement of blessings. See below and John-Charles Duffy, "Concealing the Body, Concealing the Sacred: The Decline of Ritual Nudity in Mormon Temples," *Journal of Ritual Studies* 21, no. 1 (2007): 1–21. A full account of all policy and content changes can be found in the works of Buerger, *Mysteries of Godliness*, and Buerger, "'The Fulness of the Priesthood': The

Second Anointing in Latter-day Saint Theology and Practice," *Dialogue: A Journal of Mormon Thought* 16, no. 1 (1983): 10–44.

78. "Discourse, 7 April 1844, as Reported by Times and Seasons," p. 614; emphasis added.

79. This is most obvious in the Salt Lake Temple where the celestial room is adorned with many fertility symbols.

80. Helen Mar Whitney, "Scenes in Nauvoo, and Incidents from H.C. Kimball's Journal," *Woman's Exponent* 12 (1 and 15 August 1883), 26, in Ehat, "Joseph Smith's Introduction of Temple Ordinances," 115–16; emphasis added.

81. Bruce R. McConkie, *Doctrinal New Testament Commentary* (Salt Lake City: Bookcraft, 1965), 2:323.

82. In the literal meaning of "looking into" or "peeking." So "dropping hints" and letting others "take a peek" becomes part of the teaching skill. In Dutch there is a phrase that comes even closer to this skill: Een tip van de sluier oplichten, "lifting up a tip of the veil."

83. David A. Bednar, "Prepared to Obtain Every Needful Thing," *Ensign*, May 2019, 101–4.

84. The fourth paradox as explained by Terryl Givens in *People of Paradox: A History of Mormon Culture* (New York: Oxford University Press, 2007), 53–62.

85. President Russell M. Nelson and Sister Wendy W. Nelson, "Hope of Israel," Worldwide Youth Devotional, 3 June 2018, Conference Center, Salt Lake City, Utah, at https://churchofjesuschrist.org/study/broadcasts/worldwide-devotional-for-young-adults/2018/06/hope-of-israel?lang=eng&cid=rdb_v_hope-of-Israel.

86. Lectures on Faith, Seventh lecture, verse 16. "Doctrine and Covenants, 1835," p. 701; emphasis added.

87. McConkie, *Doctrinal New Testament Commentary*, 2:325; emphasis added.

8

"Thou Art an Elect Lady"

How Christ Includes and Empowers
Women in Doctrine and Covenants 25

Carter Charles

If *praxis*, here defined as Christian living, is a fruit, it would seem logical to assume that it tells something about the tree from which it stems. Such a deduction may seem validated by Christ's allegorical teaching to help discern false prophets from good ones (see Matthew 7:15–20; Luke 6:43–45). However, the deduction quickly becomes untenable if we assume that the tree metaphorically stands for Christ and if we swap *prophets* for *disciples*. We will inevitably notice that while *praxis* is important, it is not a conclusive statement about Christ. Because of our nature (see Mosiah 3:19), we somehow always "come short of the glory of God" (Romans 3:23) or fail to fully manifest who Christ really is. *Praxis* then helps to know "them" (Matthew 7:20), meaning disciples in general, but it is always a filtered, and therefore imperfect, indicator of "what [we] worship" (Doctrine and Covenants 93:19). It does not follow, for instance, that what Christ has revealed and continues to reveal is false because some of us have failed, and may yet fail, to live up to those revelations. Christ and his gospel, for instance, do not cease to be inclusive and empowering because some disciples may prove, willfully or not, to be intolerant.

While *praxis* is partly rooted in faith, Doctrine and Covenants 93:19 suggests that its quality also depends on what the Latter-day Saints "understand and know" of the revelations that Christ gave to Joseph Smith. In the specific area of inclusion and empowerment of women, some Latter-day Saints may be like the Ethiopian eunuch (see Acts 8:26–36) in that they may lack the tools, including secular ones,[1] that have the potential to illuminate their study and facilitate a greater outpouring of the Spirit. The example of the Ethiopian eunuch also illustrates that although revelation may be hard to understand, the way of the disciple is still to engage it fully and to expect that external help will come to further clarify the revelation. It seems to be in that spirit that President Russell M. Nelson invited the women of the Church in October 2019 "to study prayerfully section 25 of the Doctrine and Covenants,"[2] in which Christ refers to Emma Smith as "an elect lady."

President Nelson's subsequent remarks to the men of the Church in the same sermon suggest that they will also benefit from a greater understanding of section 25. The contextual and interpretive reading proposed here is not as authoritative as Phillip's exegetical assistance to the Ethiopian eunuch. I am hopeful, however, that it will help readers come to a greater realization that section 25 is an innovative, revolutionary revelation in that it reveals a Christ who gives pastoral functions to Emma and, through her, all the women of his Church at a time when some were arguing that women should not be allowed to pray or even raise questions directly during worship services.

Of course, there have been previous attempts in Sperry symposiums and publications to contextualize and explicate Doctrine and Covenants 25.[3] I endeavor in this paper to present one more perspective.[4] I will postulate and argue in particular that Christ continues in section 25 the dynamic of inclusion and of religious empowerment of women that he had started in the New Testament, and that—for the

Saints, at least—he also resolved in the revelation the biblical misunderstanding that was being used in nineteenth-century America to justify the exclusion of women from pastoral functions. Three aspects of the revelation will be considered in support of these claims, namely Emma's callings (1) as wife, (2) as "elect lady," and (3) as teacher and exhorter. Ultimately, I will argue that through Doctrine and Covenants 25, Christ establishes Emma as a type and a reflection to show that all women can be empowered and elevated through religious functions in The Church of Jesus Christ of Latter-day Saints.

Context is one of the tools needed to understand the profound social and spiritual implications of Doctrine and Covenants 25. Because of that, I will take great care throughout this paper to situate the revelation within the history of the Restoration and the larger history of religion in the United States.

The General Context of Doctrine and Covenants 25

Within the Church, the date of the revelation, July 1830, directs our thoughts to its immediate Restoration framework. The Book of Mormon was published the previous March, and the Church was incorporated in April. This means that Emma, who was baptized toward the end of June, was by today's standards even a younger "new convert" compared to those who had been baptized in April. The priesthood power necessary to perform the rituals of baptism and of confirmation had been restored in the months leading to the revelation.

For the larger context, it is safe to assume that the revelation was given when the effects of the "unusual excitement on the subject of religion" Joseph had experienced in the early 1820s were still very much present (Joseph Smith—History 1:5).⁵ As Joseph describes, the religious landscape was very much an open market of offer and demand with preachers from competing religious groups like the Methodists, the Presbyterians, and the Baptists "crying, 'Lo, here!'

and others, 'Lo, there!'" and where "great multitudes united themselves to the different religious parties" (Joseph Smith—History 1:5).

The idea of a "free religious market" did not mean the competitors gladly welcomed others and accepted conversion to other churches. The context of the "awakening" of America to God was "bitter in its divisions," as one historian puts it;[6] in the words of Joseph, it was a context of "bad feeling" and "strife" among the churches (Joseph Smith—History 1:6). Members of the nascent Church also suffered from this context of religious pluralism, which paradoxically favored the emergence of the Church: for instance, persecutions, which intensified prior to the publication of the Book of Mormon, had delayed the confirmation of Emma and of other people baptized at the same time.[7]

Aside from affiliation, as Joseph indicates, the bitterness and strife covered a broad spectrum of issues including, of course, theology with intense and protracted debates on Christology,[8] the procedures and disciplines of religious life with questions on acceptable forms of worship,[9] and the role women could play, if any at all, in these areas.

A Comfort unto My Servant: When Christ Reconstructs Matrimonial Duties

The first calling extended to Emma in the revelation is a confirmation of her matrimonial responsibilities toward her husband. Christ stipulates that "thy calling shall be for a comfort unto my servant, . . . thy husband, in his afflictions, with consoling words, in the spirit of meekness" (Doctrine and Covenants 25:5). There is no contesting that matrimony was an important part of the calling. Yet, to approach the passage solely in that light might be equated to seeing only "the letter" of the revelation. Latter-day Saints might miss its "spirit" and therefore the spiritual implications of the calling if no effort is made to read beyond the obvious fact that with matrimony comes mutual obligations. In fact, the Saints might miss the intent of the revelation should they fail to understand why Christ dwells on what had better be a given in a marital relationship. Who can think that there was no comfort and no consoling words, no meekness or humility in Joseph and Emma's marital relationship? Did it take the opening of the heavens for them to know about those things? The answer to those questions is a definite no. Nothing in their relationship indicates that Emma, who had already been through a lot of persecutions and had just confirmed her fidelity through her baptism, had given Joseph and the Lord any reason to doubt that she was an affectionate wife. Yet, the Lord gave a revelation on the subject.

Beyond the obvious matrimonial considerations of the revelation then, readers should also engage with the text. A careful and informed reading can, for instance, call attention to the fact that instead of contractual terms like *duty* and *responsibility*, the Lord used the word *calling*. Latter-day Saints are very familiar with this word, which adds an extra layer of significance to matrimony: the term *calling* has profound spiritual and ecclesial, that is, institutional, implications within Christianity. For instance, after having surveyed Martin Luther's use of the word *calling* and its prevalence in Protestantism, sociologist Max Weber came to the conclusion that the word suggests "a God-given mission."[10] The notion of "vocation" is sometimes used in association with, or as a synonym for, *calling*. In a religious context, that "vocation," as used by Luther, becomes a charge that the believer "ought to accept as a divine decree," "the 'destiny' which he must embrace," or "*the* mission imposed by God."[11] This religious understanding of the term continued in Joseph and Emma's days and in the larger Protestant tradition in America.[12] Whether it was through a dream, a vision, a strong feeling, or a conviction after having listened to a sermon or read a biblical passage, being "called" was always understood to be a divine communication that had the potential to permanently alter the course of life.

In the case of Emma, however, it may be said that the call to comfort and console signaled the application of a divine seal on, and therefore a sacralization of, her matrimonial responsibilities. Indeed, in section 25, providing comfort and speaking words of consolation were no longer temporal or even part of normal intimate activities or signs of affections between husband and wife because Christ turned them into specific assignments within a larger religious project. In this sense, it may be said that by defining marriage and matrimonial duties in more than legal and contractual terms, Christ outlined the principles that would underpin eternal marriage in Doctrine and Covenants 132:7: temporal contracts become religiously efficacious only insofar as they are given divine imprimatur.

Emma's call further echoes countless scriptural stories where God brings to the fore a person of low social standing and empowers that person to fulfill his plan. This may be illustrated with examples from the Bible and from the Book of Mormon. In Alma 19, for instance, two women, Abish and the Lamanite queen, are empowered to "serve the role of Jesus" or to function as Jesus.[13] Abish, who is of the lowest standing as a slave, is identified as "one of the Lamanitish women" (Alma 19:16). But social standings and power structures are reversed in the story. Because of her previous conversion, Abish "knew that it was the power of God" that was working on King Lamoni and the queen, and she became instrumental in how the spiritual experience ended for everyone involved. Abish extends her hand to "raise [the queen] from the ground" (Alma 19:29), and the queen goes on to raise the king, and so forth.

The Old Testament story of the widow of Zarephath and Elijah the Tishbite also illustrates someone who is presumably of low social status becoming empowered. We learn in 1 Kings 17 that in spite of Elijah's immense power to control heaven and earth—including the power to end the drought so that the people, Elijah included, could find sustenance—God instead made Elijah rely on a vulnerable widow for that sustenance (see 1 Kings 17:9–16). In other words, the widow becomes as vital to the execution of Elijah's mission as the power he was entrusted with to bind heaven and earth.

Continuing with this line of reasoning, Emma's call to "be a comfort" can also be read as a disguised call for Joseph. It may indeed be argued that through Emma's call Christ also intended to teach Joseph about his own vulnerability and the need for him to rely on Emma. Christ's insistence on the phrase "my servant, [. . .] thy husband" (Doctrine and Covenants 25:5) can be read as supporting these arguments of the prophet's vulnerability and need to rely on Emma for assistance.

Of course, by 1830 Emma knew that Joseph was the Lord's "servant"—else why her baptism?—and that he was *her* husband. Hence the phrase "my servant, [. . .] thy husband" may seem like an unnecessary reminder. One way to make sense of it might be to begin with the form, the very structure of the statement. With the notions of vulnerability and reliance in mind, this structure seems to demonstrate the underlying message that Christ made Emma his human counterpart who—similar to Aaron and Hur's relationship to Moses, although in a different type of calling—helps steady the prophet (see Exodus 17:11–12). This means then that the callings of Emma and of Joseph were intertwined and interdependent: they were both called by Christ, and it almost seems like Joseph was incomplete, almost not a prophet, without Emma. In other words, they were bound through their respective callings—though not *sealed* yet—both in temporal, affectionate terms and as links in a chain that serve the purposes of God.[14]

If humility is required of Joseph to rely on Emma, it is a form of ascetism—a spirit of abnegation or self-denial—that was required of Emma to accept to serve God somewhat indirectly, through Joseph. But once again, reading the matrimonial aspect of the revelation in temporal terms is to stay on the surface, assuming that it continued the traditions in which it was given—that is, like most of her contemporaries, Emma was asked to take the back seat in order to facilitate the religious career of her husband.[15] But as will be demonstrated, such a reading is further countered by the calls to be an elect lady and a hymn compiler, calls through which Christ stepped up Emma's empowerment and inclusion in the pastoral life of his Church.

Emma as "Elect Lady" among Elect Ladies

Along with giving Emma the sacred matrimonial responsibility, Christ calls her "an elect lady" (Doctrine and Covenants 25:3). Emma and the other early Saints were well enough versed in biblical language to know that it was no ordinary thing to be named "elect lady." The title is used only once in the Bible in a passage that reads, "The elder unto the elect lady and her children" (2 John 1:1). The Prophet read this passage during the organization of the Relief Society in 1842 to further impress the significance of the title "elect lady" on the mind of the sisters, "to show that respect was then had to the same thing."[16]

Scholars debate whether the elect lady in the Johannine text refers to the Church, meaning the Church *of* Christ or the Church *chosen* by Christ;[17] one of the congregations of the Church of Christ; or to a real person. This last possibility is supported by the fact that John points to the existence of a second elect lady in verse 13, which reads, "the children of *thy elect sister* greet thee" (emphasis added), although this could also refer to the members of another congregation. This second reference occurs in spite of the use of the definite article *the* in "*the* elect lady" in 2 John 1:1. This article can either exclude the possibility of other elect ladies or signify that there is a *joint* or *co-* elect lady. In support of this idea of one elect lady among several, we may point to Christ's declaration to Emma in section 25: He refers to her as *an* elect lady, not as *the* elect lady.

Moreover, in the same revelation Christ expanded the title with the phrase "whom I have called" (Doctrine and Covenants 25:3), which means that an elect lady, in this specific context, is one who is called, chosen, or selected. Joseph further declared to the sisters of the society that the Lord had given Emma the title of "elect lady" because she was "elected to preside," implicitly over the Relief Society. Hence, tying the proposition of "one elect lady among several" to the prophet's explanation to the Relief Society, one may fairly conclude that by virtue of her selection, Emma had become the first among the sisters of the society, all of whom were "elect ladies" by virtue of their baptism and membership in Christ's Church.

Emma as Hymn Compiler and Organizer of Worship

Beyond Emma's role as president of the Relief Society, Rachel Cope has shown how the title of "elect lady" also applied in her assignment "to make a selection of sacred hymns [. . .] to be had in my church" (Doctrine and Covenants 25:11). Emma was "a unique exception" in religious America, Cope writes, because in that context hymn selection was a territory dominated by male preachers since immense practical and theological power came with it.[18] It is amply documented that hymns were so important and sought after by believers that "instead of hunting up a college or Biblical institute," itinerant preachers of the Methodist tradition—a group with which Latter-day Saints share a great deal[19]—relied on a most important library that consisted of three items: the Bible, a hymnbook, and a copy of the "Discipline," the Methodist "handbook of instructions."[20] Coming from the Methodist tradition, Emma surely understood the significance of hymn singing in worship. Michael Hicks proposes that "since choosing songs to be sung was often the duty of a congregational singing master, the revelation may have been designating Emma to lead the tunes."[21] This reading is irreconcilable with the clause "make a selection" that is used in the revelation.

Another possible reading is that through the call, Christ made Emma both conductor of church meetings and his officiator in a special ritual. As Christ's officiator, we can say that she symbolically welcomes and leads the ceremony for every Latter-day Saint who opens a hymnbook. The act of opening the hymnbook can then be compared to leaving behind a profane world and stepping into "a sacred space"[22] in which, through a ritual of prayer that takes the form of a "song of the heart," Latter-day Saint worshippers then and now present a righteous devotion that delights the very soul of God (see Doctrine and Covenants 25:12). As in all rituals, the validity of singing as a ritual rests on certain rules: the verse explicitly tells about the conditions worshippers have to be in (righteous) and how to sing (from the heart) so that their worship can delight the soul of the Lord. But these rules also imply that Christ placed a tremendous responsibility on Emma in calling her to compile hymns for the Church: successful performance of the ritual—and to a certain extent of the whole religious service—depended on her ability to choose songs that participants would embrace without reservations and would intone as though they were personal prayers that had originated in their hearts.

The novelty and uniqueness of a woman tasked with selecting hymns probably explains why John Whitmer—who is believed to have authored the introduction to the revelation in the 1833 Book of Commandments—specifically mentions "A Revelation to Emma [Smith] . . . giving her a command to select Hymns" and silences the remaining aspects of the revelation behind an "&c."[23] Indeed, this method of abbreviation is generally used in long book titles. Unfortunately, this summary, which emphasizes hymn compilation—though already a major move—has become the main aspect of elect lady that succeeding generations of Latter-day Saints retain. Because of that, the header may be said to have both oriented how the revelation is read and limited its scope.

Compiling hymns is, however, merely one of the many ways in which Christ empowers those who, on account of their gender and social standing, were precluded from greater involvement in religious life.

Emma as Exhorter to the Church

Christ did not make Emma a witness or endow her with apostolic authority. But as with hymnody, other passages in section 25 show that he elevated Emma in other areas of great social and religious import. This is evidenced in the call "to expound scriptures, and to exhort the church" (Doctrine and Covenants 25:7). The Prophet specified during the founding meeting of the Relief Society in 1842 that Emma was "ordained," meaning set apart, to "expound the scriptures to *all* and to teach the female part of [the] community."²⁴ The clause "to teach the female part of [the] community" suggests that even the Prophet may have missed the encompassing, churchwide nature of the call, and may even have set an unfortunate precedence for future readings of Doctrine and Covenants 25:7. There is evidence, as we will see, that this may also have been because he was not totally above the fray when it came to women's involvement in religions, even though he acted as the Lord's spokesperson in a revelation that empowered a woman.

Of course, the Relief Society was organized some twelve years after section 25 was revealed. It made sense in that context that the Prophet should specify that it was Emma's role, by virtue of her calling as elect lady, or president, to teach the sisters placed under her leadership. In spite of how the Prophet's specification would later be understood, it did not affect the call—from Christ —for Emma to "expound the scriptures" and to "exhort"²⁵ *all* in the Church. Through this call, Christ empowered Emma to help Church members—male and female—access the hidden meanings of holy writ. And that was no small thing.

Emma's Christic commission was one of ministerial function in the 1830 context of the revelation. At that time it was the role of preachers and exhorters, sometimes duly licensed,²⁶ to explicate scripture and exhort individuals to be better Christians. Such a call then was disruptive of the norms, as for the compilation of hymns, even though the presence of female preachers in the religious landscape was not totally unusual. Women like Joanna Bethune and Isabella Graham, her mother, had played "an especially active and determinative role"²⁷ in the rise of the American Sunday Schools between 1803 and 1824. We also know that during the period of "the hymnodic revolution that had swept through America" between 1780 and 1830²⁸ that "more than one hundred women crisscrossed the country as itinerant preachers."[29] Like their male counterparts, some female preachers were constantly on the road because they did not have a pulpit. However, Emma's call to expound scripture and to exhort the Church logically came with a pulpit because the call was obviously meant to strengthen the Church qualitatively from within and not quantitatively through missionary work.

The number of female preachers and teachers involved in the Sunday School movement does not mean that the context of Emma's call was one in which women were wholly accepted in religious life. The pulpit was still considered a "masculine space," as Catherine Brekus puts it,[30] a ground of bitter theological battles, even within the few denominations that tolerated female preaching. The mere idea of women praying in public horrified some of the greatest luminaries of the day. Peter Cartwright, a prominent revival preacher between 1803 and 1856, informs us that there were "fashionable objections to females praying in public" in the Methodist Episcopal Church to which he belonged.[31] In 1827 Asael Nettleton stood against such revivalist fathers as Charles Grandison Finney who was accused of having introduced in revivalism "the practice of females praying with males," among other "new measures," and of "rais[ing] an angry dispute," "a civil war in Zion—a domestic broil in the household of faith."[32] Lyman Beecher, Harriet Beecher Stowe's father, concurred with Nettleton. "There is no instance in the patriarchal age, of a woman offering sacrifice as an act of worship, and a symbol of prayer; and none in the tabernacle or temple service," he argued.[33] The suggestion made earlier that Joseph probably did not understand the encompassing nature of Emma's call to expound scripture and exhort the Church rests on the fact that he did share somewhat in those popular views expressed by Beecher.[34] In fact, female prayer for Beecher could eventually be tolerated only on the condition that even in matrimonial bonds, "it was the wife apart, and the husband apart"—they could not pray together.[35] Otherwise, he insisted, "no well educated female can put herself up, or be put up, to the point of public prayer, without the loss of some portion at least of that female delicacy . . . ;

and whoever has had an opportunity to observe the effect of female exhortation and prayer in public, will be compelled to remark the exchange of softness and delicacy for masculine courage, so desirable in man, so unlovely in woman."[36]

The last part of Beecher's argument refers to the highly demonstrative and physical aspect of exhortation in the context of revivalism. Overall, though, those who opposed the involvement of women in pastoral life, even in areas that did not require ordination or a degree in theology, were never without an excuse. As Beecher and Nettleton saw it, the involvement of women was the ruin of the churches; religious matters were deemed too sacred to be left to women because everything in them, from their tone to their physical appearance, made them a source of such distraction that rather than edifying, their presence at the pulpit was equated to its defilement.[37] Indeed, the view of the most adamant ministers was that women who dared to take the pulpit in the presence of men "were no better than prostitutes."[38]

Such strong language was certainly informed by two concepts: (1) the belief that with Eve—the archetypal woman—came sin and the demise of the Edenic world and (2) the Pauline injunction to "let your women keep silence in the churches" and to ask their husbands questions "at home: for it is a shame for women to speak in the church" (1 Corinthians 14:34–35).[39] In that context, even though the dynamics in the American religious landscape tended toward greater inclusion of women, as for hymnody, Emma's call to exhort and to expound the scriptures to everyone in the restored Church of Jesus Christ placed her in a position that was socially avant-gardist. That position arguably reveals more about Christ and his plan for women in his Church than is usually assumed. Through that revelation, Christ steers the Church back on a trajectory of greater inclusivity by suspending the injunction, which may have been unduly attributed to Paul, to bar women from speaking in churches and from holding institutional positions.[40]

Doctrine and Covenants 25 as Revelation for the Emmas of Christ's Church

As hinted at, I concur with Carol Cornwall Madsen's view that while "[the] specifics [of Doctrine and Covenants 25] are addressed to Emma, its principles are applicable to all" because of its canonization as scripture.[41] Joseph Smith, who acted as mediator between Christ and Emma, insisted on that universal dimension when he declared that "not [Emma] alone, but *others*, may attain to the same blessings" or privilege to expound scripture and exhort the Church.[42] Christ may have been pointing to that universal dimension in concluding the revelation with the phrase "this is my voice unto *all*" (emphasis added). Surely, there is ground to read "others" and "all" in the broad universal sense of "male and female." After all, the first verse of the revelation begins by indicating that "all those who receive my gospel are sons and daughters in my kingdom" (Doctrine and Covenants 25:1). When it comes to empowerment, however, "others" and "all" may generally be read more narrowly to refer to the women of Christ's Church.

With that understanding in mind, readers of the revelation logically come to see Emma as Christ may have viewed her: a type, and a model for *all*, especially for the female body of the Church. The revelation then stands as a reference point, the basis for a pattern of female participation and empowerment in Christ's Church. As mentioned previously, in that 1830 revelation, when Christ was laying the foundation of his Church once again on the earth, he frees Latter-day Saint women from the Pauline injunction not to speak in church. The revelation has a double significance in that it tacitly allows Latter-day Saint women to pray and speak on religious matters, and it explicitly mandates that they occupy the pulpit to explicate scripture and exhort the Church. This explicit mission recalls of course the responsibility entrusted to priesthood holders in a revelation given in the same organizational years "to teach, expound, exhort" the Church (Doctrine and Covenants 20:42, 46, 59). This similarity may have been part of what led Joseph to state that the Relief Society, meaning the sisters collectively, was "patterned after the priesthood."[43]

Another level of reading of the revelation may consist in seeing Emma as a type, a proxy for Christ.[44] Expounding and explaining to others the hidden and true meaning of scripture is one of the activities we see Christ doing throughout his earthly ministry. In Luke 24:27, for instance, we learn that "beginning at Moses and all the prophets," the resurrected Christ "expounded [. . .] in all the scriptures the things concerning himself" to the disciples he had joined on the road to Emmaus. Before his Crucifixion, we learn that after reading, for instance, from Isaiah 61, "the eyes of all them that were in the synagogue were fastened on him" (Luke 4:20), obviously eager to access the true meaning of the prophecy. With authority, Christ explained, "This day is this scripture fulfilled in your ears" (Luke 4:21). Interestingly, the scripture that was fulfilled indicates that Christ, anointed by the Spirit, had come "to preach the gospel to the poor; . . . to heal the brokenhearted, to preach deliverance to the captives, and recovering of sight to the blind, to set at liberty them that are bruised, to preach the acceptable year of the Lord" (Luke 4:18–19).

Assuming that after Christ's own eventful ministry "the acceptable year of the Lord" encompasses "the dispensation of the fulness of times" Christ speaks about in Doctrine and Covenants 112:30, we may argue that Relief Society presidents (who continue in Emma's stead)—and their sisters who are also elect ladies in the kingdom—act as proxy for Christ in that they are able to stand in the Church where he would have stood to "preach deliverance" to those who are spiritually "captives." Just like the sister's organization is "patterned after the priesthood," one may see in that a "pattern," a certain coherence with what Christ may have intended in calling Emma to exhort and expound: in these specific areas, at least, the Emmas of the Church are just like priesthood holders who represent Christ at the sacrament table and other rituals.

Like Christ in the Lukan passage, Emma may be said further to have received an anointing, when set apart by the proper authority, which entitles her to the Spirit of Christ (see Doctrine and Covenants 25:7), the Holy Ghost (Doctrine and Covenants 25:8), to "preach [that is, exhort and expound] the gospel" to Latter-day Saints who are "poor [in spirit]," who are "brokenhearted" or "bruised," to open the eyes of those who may be "blind" as to the true meaning of scripture, and to deliver those who are in a form of captivity.

Doctrine and Covenants 25 is addressed to Emma, but there is in the revelation an implicit reminder for Joseph and for the larger body of the Church, the males in particular, to acknowledge the Christic mandate and authority of their sisters in the area of teaching and exhortation. This is evidence in the modal "shalt" that precedes "be ordained," which further confers to the calling a sense of decree, something that must come to pass in Christ's Church. Modern prophets, seers, and revelators have made it clear that though not ordained to a specific priesthood office, a woman who is set apart to serve in the restored Church of Jesus Christ officiates under the same priesthood umbrella as do the ordained males of the Church. Like the men, those sisters are "given priesthood authority to perform a priesthood function," affirmed Elder Dallin H. Oaks in 2014 as a member of the Quorum of the Twelve Apostles.[45]

There is a twofold corollary to the clarification made by Elder Oaks. The first one is that Latter-day Saints who fail to acknowledge those sisters in their divinely appointed sacerdotal functions tacitly fail to see them and the Relief Society as Joseph Smith did, as an instrument of balance and perfection in the restoration process.[46] The second is that when Church members disregard women serving in their appointed positions, they disregard the priesthood, those who exercise the keys, and ultimately Christ, who provided for the calling of sisters.

Overall then, Doctrine and Covenants 25 shows a Christ who is consistent but who, in *restoring* his Church, literally repairs it and bridges loopholes in teachings that may have been brought into holy writ to marginalize women. Prior to Christ's Resurrection, we see him in the New Testament protecting women from ostracization,

forgiving and healing them physically and spiritually (see John 8:3–
11; Luke 7:36–50). This dynamic of inclusion and empowerment is
stepped up after the Resurrection: Christ "appeared first to Mary
Magdalene," we read in Mark 16:9. And, for the first time, Christ
gives a woman a major commission: he asks Mary to be his envoy,
to announce to "my brethren . . . I ascend unto my Father, and your
Father" (John 20:17). That in and of itself was remarkable, considering the low social recognition women had in Mary's culture. Like
Mary, Emma was the first in modern times to be given a commission that breaks away from established exclusionary practices. Mary's
calling to announce and Emma's calling to expound and exhort reveal
consistency in a dynamic of female inclusion and empowerment and
a Christ who does not change.

Conclusion

The objective in this paper has been to propose an interpretative
reading of Doctrine and Covenants 25 using a reading methodology
based on diachronic (historical) and synchronic (textual and intertextual) analyses. The question of *praxis* has not been developed much
because the intent was not to engage in any in-depth consideration
of that dimension. Yet it seems impossible not to hint at its significance, at least as an opening in lieu of a conclusion. The principle of
continuing revelation in the Church of Jesus Christ and the fact that
Latter-day Saints, like everyone else, learn as they go, plead for that
open-door approach when it comes to *praxis*.

By definition, *praxis* is the visible part of a principle or doctrine
upon which it is based. This definition, however, is true only insofar
as the doctrine is fully understood and adhered to. In a religious community, social factors—such as previous religious affiliation or non-
affiliation, the level of education of the adherents, and the broader
tradition in general—make it so that understanding and adhering to
doctrine can be easier said than done, the fruits (*praxis*) are not always
an exact manifestation of the tree (Christ and what he reveals). And

that is not necessarily because the members are recalcitrant toward a particular doctrine. The records do not hint that the early Saints had voiced any significant opposition to Emma's multiple divine callings at a time when female inclusion in religious life was the object of heated debates in the larger American religious landscape. Yet, there is a *hiatus*, a disconnect, between the revelation and its implementation in the history of the restored Church of Jesus Christ.

As noted by Marianne Holman Prescott, for a long time the early Saints followed "most other Christians in their day" and because of that, except in a few cases, they "reserved public preaching and leadership for men."[47] To that may be added the frustration created by the fact that women were not even invited to pray in the general conferences of the Church until April 2013. These restrictions have had ripple effects in and outside of the Church, fueling the sentiment that only the voice of "the brethren" matters in The Church of Jesus Christ of Latter-day Saints and that it was conceived and exists for modern patriarchs. But Holman Prescott also documents an evolution within the Church that consists in aligning more with the spirit of revelations that mandate the inclusion of women, a subject on which the apostolic voice of M. Russell Ballard, for instance, has been raised more than once and in multiple venues of the Church and its institutions.[48]

Aside from prayer and teaching and participation in the Church's temple rituals, women now sit as permanent members on several Church councils, most notably the Board of Trustees of the Church Educational System (the General President of the Primary and the General President of the Relief Society, who is also a member of the more reduced Executive Committee), on the Priesthood and Family Executive Council (General President of the Relief Society), Missionary Executive Council (General Young Women President), and the Temple and Family History Executive Council (General President of the Primary). In September 2018 the youth of the Church worldwide were presented with two well-trained and faithful historians—including a woman—to whom an apostle deferred by letting them address historical issues. About a year later, President Nelson announced a change in Church policy allowing women who carry a temple recommend to stand as witnesses for baptisms and temple sealings.[49] Interestingly, all of these forward-looking decisions actually bring the Church more in line with authorized precedents[50] and the spirit of empowerment that is found in Doctrine and Covenants 25. It is to be assumed that this trend will not only continue but that the leaders will further educate the membership of the Church so that their practice reflects even more what Christ has revealed for the equilibrium and full flourishing of his restored Church.

Notes

I take full responsibility for the "sins," though involuntary, that may appear in this paper. They would have been far more grievous were it not for colleagues like Kate Holbrook, Mark D. Ellison, Jason R. Combs, and my Sperry coeditors. They were generous with their time and provided very constructive feedback and references.

1. Of course, Church members are familiar with the injunction to "seek learning, even by study and also by faith" from "the best books" and in all sorts of disciplines so that they "may be prepared in all things" to worship and serve God (Doctrine and Covenants 88:80, 118; 109:7). But as President M. Russell Ballard reminded, the Saints should not exclude consulting those with expertise outside of the ecclesiastical structure because they can "be useful in answering *all* the questions we may have about scriptures, history, and the Church" (emphasis in original). M. Russell Ballard, "Questions and Answers," BYU Devotionals, 14 September 2017, https://speeches.byu.edu/talks/m-russell-ballard/questions-and-answers/.

2. Russell M. Nelson, "Spiritual Treasures," *Ensign*, November 2019, 77.

3. See Susan Easton Black, "The Sacred Role of Women," in *Doctrines of Exaltation* (Salt Lake City: Deseret Book, 1989), 1–14; Carol Cornwall Madsen, "The 'Elect Lady' Revelation (D&C 25): Its Historical and Doctrinal Context," in *The Doctrine and Covenants* (Provo, UT: Religious Studies Center, Brigham Young University; Salt Lake City: Deseret Book, 2004). A valuable reference beyond the Sperry volumes is Rachel Cope's

"A Sacred Space for Women: Hymnody in Emma Hale Smith's Theology," *Journal of Religious History* 42, no. 2 (June 2017): 243, 247.

4. As suggested in her title, Black's paper will be helpful for a perspective on womanhood and motherhood in section 25 and throughout the Doctrine and Covenants. The scope of Madsen's paper is a little broader, although the relevant context it provides focuses mostly on female converts who were around Emma.

5. See, for instance, William G. McLoughlin, *Revivals, Awakenings, and Reform: An Essay on Religion and Social Change in America* (Chicago: University of Chicago Press, 1978), 98–140; "The Upstart Sects Win America, 1776–1850," in *The Churching of America, 1776–2005*, ed. Roger Finke and Rodney Stark (New Brunswick, NJ: Rutgers University Press, 2005), 55–67; Ray B. West, *The Burned-Over District: The Social and Intellectual History of Enthusiastic Religion in Western New York, 1800–1850* (New York: Cornell University Press, 1950).

6. McLoughlin, *Revivals, Awakenings, and Reform*, 106.

7. See, for instance, the "Historical Introduction" page to Doctrine and Covenants 25 in "Revelation, July 1830–C [Doctrine and Covenants 25]," p. 34, The Joseph Smith Papers, https://josephsmithpapers.org/paper-summary/revelation-july-1830-c-dc-25/1.

8. For example, see Nicholas J. Frederick's paper, "Incarnation, Exaltation, and Christological Tension in Doctrine and Covenants 93:1–20," 11–41, in this volume.

9. Asael Nettleton and Lyman Beecher, two major actors of the religious scene, opposed "enthusiasm" or expressive forms of worship (which sometimes included extremes like rolling on the ground, speaking in tongues) so much that they "tested" their new converts and put them on probation for as long as six months before those converts could enjoy full fellowship. See McLoughlin, *Revivals, Awakenings, and Reform*, 122. For a Sperry reference, see J. Spencer Fluhman's "The Joseph Smith Revelations and the Crisis of Early American Spirituality," in *The Doctrine and Covenants: Revelations in Context* (Provo, UT: Religious Studies Center, Brigham Young University; Salt Lake City: Deseret Book, 2008), 71–85.

10. Max Weber, *L'Éthique protestante et l'Esprit du capitalisme*, trans. Isabelle Kalinowski, 2nd ed. (Paris: Flammarion, 1999), 126.

11. The quotations used here are based mostly on a French edition of Weber's *Protestant Ethic*, but there are several easily accessible English editions, with different translation nuances.

12. Zilpha Elaw, a black female preacher, traces the salvation of her soul and later ministry to an experience at the age of fourteen where "God [. . .] called me by an effectual call" through a dream and a vision of Jesus Christ. *Memoirs of the Life, Religious Experience, Ministerial Travels and Labours of Mrs. Zilpha Elaw, An American Female of Colour; Together with an Account of the Great Religious Revivals in America [Written by Herself]* (London, 1846), 3–7. Closer to Joseph and Emma's days was Charles Grandison Finney, whose experience and use of the word can be found in his *Memoirs of Rev. Charles G. Finney Written by Himself* (New York: A. S. Barnes, 1876), 265.

13. Nicholas J. Frederick, "Intertextuality in the Book of Mormon with Nick Frederick," Latter-day Saints Perspective Podcast, https://ldsperspectives.com/2018/08/22/intertextuality-book-mormon/. See also Nicholas J. Frederick and Joseph M. Spencer, "John 11 in the Book of Mormon," *Journal of the Bible and Its Reception* 5, no. 1 (2018): 81–106.

14. Steven Harper does not elaborate, but I concur that the linguistic "positioning of Joseph between the Lord and Emma" represents "perhaps the most compelling part of the revelation." See Steven C. Harper, *Making Sense of the Doctrine and Covenants: A Guided Tour through Modern Revelation* (Salt Lake City: Deseret Book, 2008), 108.

15. Likewise, viewed in purely temporal terms, the story in 1 Kings 17 is scandalous. It must have required great efforts on the part of the dying widow to risk shortening life expectancy for both herself and her son to execute the demand of a prophet who apparently was more comfortable being fed by others than finding bread "in the sweat of [his] face" until his death (Genesis 3:19).

16. "Nauvoo Relief Society Minute Book," p. 9, The Joseph Smith Papers, https://josephsmithpapers.org/paper-summary/nauvoo-relief-society-minute-book/6.

17. Latter-day Saint theologian Rosalynde Welch, for instance, opts for the definition that "elect lady" in the Johannine text refers to "a first-century Church of Christ and disciples" and postulates that by applying the title to Emma, Christ had made her both "figure" and "form" of his restored Church. See Rosalynde Welch, "Emma as Church, Emma as Christ: Kingdom and Salvation in Section 25," in *Latter-Day Saint Theology Seminar* (New York: Union Theological Seminary, 2019).

18. Cope, "Sacred Space for Women," 243, 247.

19. See, for instance, Christopher C. Jones's excellent thesis "We Latter-day Saints Are Methodists: The Influence of Methodism on Early Mormon Religiosity" (master's thesis, Brigham Young University, 2009), a title borrowed from a statement by Joseph Smith.

20. *Autobiography of Peter Cartwright, the Backwoods Preacher*, ed. William P. Strickland (New York: Carlton & Porter, 1857), 243.

21. Michael Hicks, *Mormonism and Music: A History* (Urbana: University of Illinois Press, 1989), 10.

22. Cope, "Sacred Space for Women," 242.

23. "Revelation Book 1," p. 34, The Joseph Smith Papers, https://josephsmith papers.org/paper-summary/revelation-book-1/18. The header to the 2013 edition of the Doctrine and Covenants takes a more generalist summarizing approach: "This revelation manifests the will of the Lord to Emma Smith, the Prophet's wife."

24. "Nauvoo Relief Society Minute Book," p. 8; emphasis added.

25. As can be noticed, the Prophet dropped this verb in his Relief Society remarks but left it standing in the original revelation.

26. Peter Cartwright, *Autobiography of Peter Cartwright*, 58, for instance, officially became an exhorter in the Methodist Episcopal Church at a conference when he received a license signed by his minister. See also Louis Billington, "'Female Laborers in the Church': Women Preachers in the Northeastern United States, 1790–1840," *Journal of American Studies* 3, no. 19 (1985): 380–81.

27. Edwin S. Gaustad and Leigh Schmidt, *The Religious History of America: The Heart of the American Story from Colonial Times to Today*, rev. ed. (San Francisco: HarperOne, 2004), 141.

28. Nathan O. Hatch, *The Democratization of American Christianity* (New Haven: Yale University Press, 1989), 146.

29. Catherine A. Brekus, "Female Preaching in Early Nineteenth-Century America," in *Women and the Church*, Christian Reflection (Waco, TX: The Center for Christian Ethics at Baylor University, 2009), 21.

30. Brekus, "Female Preaching," 21.

31. *Autobiography of Peter Cartwright*, 517.

32. Lyman Beecher and Asael Nettleton, *Letters of the Rev. Dr. Beecher and Rev. Mr. Nettleton, on the "New Measures" in Conducting Revivals of Religion* (New York: G. & C. Carvill, 1828), 10–11.

33. Beecher and Nettleton, *Letters*, 89.

34. Rising against Johanna Southcott, Jemimah Wilkinson, and other religious groups in which women had prophetic claims or played a significant role, Joseph declared on 1 April 1842, "Where do we read of a woman that was the founder of a Church in the word of God? Paul told the women in his day 'to keep silence in the Church, and that if they wished to know anything to ask their husbands at home;' he would not suffer a woman 'to rule or usurp authority in the Church;' but here we find a woman, the founder of a Church, the revelator and guide, the Alpha and Omega, contrary to all acknowledged rule, principle and order." See "History, 1838–1856, volume C-1 [2 November 1838–31 July 1842]," p. 1308, The Joseph Smith Papers, https://josephsmithpapers.org/paper-summary/history-1838-1856-volume-c-1-2-november-1838-31-july-1842/482); "History, 1838–1856, volume C-1 [2 November 1838–31 July 1842]," p. 1310, The Joseph Smith Papers, https://josephsmithpapers.org/paper-summary/history-1838-1856-volume-c-1-2-november-1838-31-july-1842/484). Black, "Sacred Role of Women," 12–15, uses similar references but does not raise the impropriety, even in the nineteenth century, of making the womanhood of rival prophets an argument rather than challenging their claims on other grounds. At any rate, a comparison between Joseph's statements and the revelation indicates that there was Joseph the man, who had his own views, and then there was Joseph the Prophet who, as mouthpiece for the Lord, declared revelations that went against the views of the man. The fact that Joseph used the question "Where do we read of a woman that was the

founder of a Church in the word of God?" suggests that in this instance, he relied on *an accepted cultural reading* of the text, not on revelation he had received from the Lord.

35. Beecher and Nettleton, *Letters*, 89.

36. Beecher and Nettleton, *Letters*, 91.

37. More specifically, Beecher saw the inclusion of women in religious life "as ultimately working ruin to our churches," as one way "churches were once laid to waste." Beecher and Nettleton, *Letters*, 15.

38. Brekus, "Female Preaching," 21.

39. Beecher quotes that passage in support of his argument and rejects 1 Corinthians 11:3–16, which indicates that women could pray and prophesy. Beecher and Nettleton, *Letters*, 90. In "Female Laborers in the Church," 381, Billington writes about how, in 1830, the Freewill Baptist Church also voted in conference that women were to remain silent in church matters.

40. The Pauline origin of the injunction is debatable. Biblical scholars generally agree that 1 Corinthians 14 was subjected to scribal tampering, which likely happened with 1 Timothy 2:11–12 and Titus 2:5. Harold W. Attridge, ed., *HarperCollins Study Bible* (New York: HarperCollins, 2006), 1952. Verses 34–35 in 1 Corinthians 14 actually interrupt the flow of Paul's argument, and it contradicts his earlier statements about women speaking in religious settings as found in 1 Corinthians 11:5, which suggests that women did pray and prophesy. See, for instance, Jason R. Combs, "Noncanonical Gospels," in *New Testament History, Culture, and Society: A Background to the Texts of the New Testament*, ed. Lincoln H. Blumell (Provo, UT: Religious Studies Center, Brigham Young University, 2019), 333; Karin B. Neutel, "Women's Silence and Jewish Influence: The Problematic Origins of the Conjectural Emendation on 1 Cor 14.33b–35," *New Testament Studies* 65, no. 4 (October 2019): 477–95. That the sacred text may have been tampered with is something Latter-day Saints have of course been warned about by the Prophet Joseph Smith. He stated in what has become the Church's eight article of faith: "We believe the Bible to be the word of God as far as it is translated correctly."

41. Madsen, "'Elect Lady' Revelation," 120.

42. "Nauvoo Relief Society Minute Book," p. 8, The Joseph Smith Papers, https://josephsmithpapers.org/paper-summary/nauvoo-relief-society-minute-book/5.

43. See the "Historical Introduction" to "Nauvoo Relief Society Minute Book," p. 10, The Joseph Smith Papers, https://josephsmithpapers.org/paper-summary/nauvoo-relief-society-minute-book/7.

44. Rosalynde Welch also comes to a similar conclusion in her presentation "Emma as Church, Emma as Christ" by putting the Doctrine and Covenants passage in dialogue with different profound and inspiring biblical passages such as Isaiah 42:1. Our readings differ however—or maybe support each other—in that the Christic figure she sees represented in Emma is that of a sacrificial lamb, "the suffering Christ" of the Atonement.

45. Dallin H. Oaks, "The Keys and Authority of the Priesthood," *Ensign*, May 2014, 51.

46. See the "Historical Introduction" to "Nauvoo Relief Society Minute Book," p. 10, The Joseph Smith Papers, https://josephsmithpapers.org/paper-summary/nauvoo-relief-society-minute-book/7. A clarification may be in order again. Joseph's rejection of the prophetic claims of women like Southcott and Wilkinson (see note 34), shows that there was, on the one hand, the Joseph who as a man of his time accepted and applied the *cultural reading* of the Pauline injunction; on the other hand, there was the Joseph who seems to have understood *from revelation* what the Lord wanted for the women of his Church—that they were to be organized "under and after the pattern of the priesthood." From this, one may infer that Joseph could not accept the claims of the women because they operated outside the order of priesthood God had revealed to him.

47. Marianne Holman Prescott, "Women's Voices Past and Present Impact General Conference and the Church for Good," *Church News*, 5 October 2018, https://churchofjesuschrist.org/church/news/womens-voices-past-and-present-impact-general-conference-and-the-church-for-good.

48. See, for instance, M. Russell Ballard, "Counseling with Our Councils," *Ensign*, May 1994; M. Russell Ballard, "Let Us Think Straight" (BYU devotional, 20 August 2013); and M. Russell Ballard, "Women of Dedication,

Faith, Determination, and Action" (BYU Women's Conference, 1 May 2015).

49. Sarah Jane Weaver, "Women Can Serve as Witnesses for Baptisms, Temple Sealings, First Presidency Announces," *Church News*, 2 October 2019, https://churchofjesuschrist.org/church/news/women-can-serve-as -witnesses-for-baptisms-temple-sealings-first-presidency-announces.

50. Joseph Smith approved the fact that Vienna Jacques, who is actually the other woman identified by name in the Doctrine and Covenants (90:28–29), stood as witness on 12 September 1840, as Jane Neyman was baptized by proxy for her son. See Alexander L. Baugh, "'For This Ordinance Belongeth to My House': The Practice of Baptism for the Dead Outside the Nauvoo Temple," *Mormon Historical Studies* 3, no. 1 (Spring 2002): 48; Alexander L. Baugh, "'For Their Salvation Is Necessary and Essential to Our Salvation': Joseph Smith and the Practice of Baptism and Confirmation for the Dead," in *An Eye of Faith: Essays in Honor of Richard O. Cowan* (Provo, UT: Religious Studies Center, Brigham Young University; Salt Lake City: Deseret Book, 2015), 115.

9

"A Revelation I Give unto You"
The Revelation of Jesus Christ to Emma Hale Smith

Joseph M. Spencer

Early in his Gospel, Mark reports that "many were gathered together" about Jesus in Capernaum, such that "there was no room to receive them" (Mark 2:2). Then, however, some came "bringing one sick of the palsy" (2:3), whom they lowered through the roof in order to bring him near to the thronged miracle worker from Nazareth. Mark reports, "When Jesus saw their faith, he said unto the sick of the palsy, Son, thy sins be forgiven thee" (2:5). Some eighteen hundred years later, according to a key text in the Doctrine and Covenants, the same Compassionate One looked on another suffering person, marveled at that person's faith, and announced the same joyful news: "Thy sins are forgiven thee" (Doctrine and Covenants 25:3). This time, however, he spoke not to one he called his son but to one he called his daughter (25:1). Christ's healing word came this time to Emma Hale Smith.

The revelation we know today as section 25 of the Doctrine and Covenants is remarkable for many reasons; in the following pages, however, we will focus on just a few of the many implications of this revelation. Summarily put, we will consider how the revelation's words find Jesus Christ revealing himself to Emma Smith. As in the Gospels, so in this revelation: Christ shows his awareness of the plight of women, their social suffering, and their consequent longing to participate more fully in God's work. This self-revelation provides us with an image of Christ, of the Christ who told the first generation of Nephites and Lamanites that he had "seen the sorrow, and heard the mourning of the daughters of [his] people in the land of Jerusalem, yea, and in all the lands of [his] people" (Jacob 2:31). I hope to trace this image of Christ through a careful reading of the revelation to Emma Smith. That image can only take shape slowly, emerging after careful analysis of the context and content of the revelation. By the end of this paper, however, it will be, I hope, perfectly clear.[1]

Historical Matters

On Monday, 28 June 1830, Emma Hale Smith was baptized by Oliver Cowdery. The ceremony took place in the morning while a crowd of fifty critics of the fledgling Church jeered. What began as a group of hecklers that morning, however, became a dangerous mob that night. The meeting during which Emma was supposed to receive the gift of the Holy Ghost was canceled when her husband was arrested and hauled away to face trial. Emma would not be confirmed a member of the Church of Christ for nearly two months. It was during the following weeks that the revelation we know as section 25 of the Doctrine and Covenants came to comfort Emma, whose "very heartstrings [had been] broken with grief."[2] It is difficult to know exactly what she felt or thought at the time. The fact that she waited so long to be confirmed, even though her husband was released from custody within days, led Fawn Brodie to a cynical interpretation: that Emma was "racked anew with doubt," in addition to being "frightened by the rancor that greeted her husband's preaching."[3] Brodie assumes too much, but she may be right in claiming that these events left Emma with questions.

An identifiable concern definitely bothered her. Just before the revelation to Emma came, her husband received a separate revelation explaining that members of the Church would support him, since he would "not have strength" in "temporal labors" (Doctrine and Covenants 24:3, 9). Brodie claims, without real evidence, that "the prospect of living off the dubious and intermittent charity of Joseph's followers was more than this proud girl could stomach. The Lord's command to leave their farm . . . filled her with fury."[4] Donna Hill more moderately suggests simply that "it would have been understandable if [Emma] had begun to question the value of what [her husband] was doing."[5] The revelation that subsequently came to Emma would thus address both her delayed confirmation and her concern about support, in addition to giving her specific assignments in the young Church.

The revelation, moreover, mentioned another key point of potential concern for Emma Smith. It acknowledged that there were things she had not seen that had been shown to others around her—perhaps especially the gold plates bearing the text of the Book of Mormon (Doctrine and Covenants 25:4).[6] Because this issue appears early in the revelation and is addressed so directly, commentators have often taken it to be the primary motivation for the revelation, using it as a reason to criticize Emma for her supposed faithlessness.[7] There is much to criticize in this traditional approach, but there is also something at least partially right about it, as we will see. There is no evidence that Emma was faithless or resentful, but it does in fact seem that verse 4 is the key to understanding the revelation.

We know a little about the revelation's aftermath. Emma Smith was indeed confirmed a member of the Church sometime after it was given, but she did not immediately take up the responsibilities it gave her. For instance, the revelation assigned her to assume Oliver

Cowdery's responsibilities as her husband's scribe, but due to a difficult pregnancy and then to Sidney Rigdon's baptism and arrival in New York, Emma never became an official scribe in the newly founded Church. Her well-known assignment to produce a collection of hymns was one she did not pursue for several years. And what may be the most interesting responsibility given her in the revelation—"to expound scriptures, and to exhort the church" (Doctrine and Covenants 25:7)—was not hers in the fullest sense until the organization of the Relief Society a decade later (although her work on the hymnbook gave her real opportunities to teach the Saints in important ways).[8] Only then would the revelation to Emma come out of its shell, as it were, serving almost as the foundational document for the organization.[9]

Despite gaps in the historical record (and therefore in our knowledge), the basic content of the revelation—its instructions and promises to Emma, its appointments and duties for her—is fully available in the published text. A brief outline of this content might therefore be useful. It is in fact relatively easy to divide section 25 into a few different parts:[10]

> Verses 1–3: Introductory address to Emma
> Verse 4: Identification of temptation to avoid
> Verses 5–6: First appointment—As scribe
> Verses 7–8: Second appointment—As teacher
> Verses 9–10: Aside addressing a concern
> Verses 11–12: Third appointment—As collector of hymns
> Verses 13–16: Concluding exhortation

It is immediately clear that Emma Smith's appointments make up the heart of the revelation. They are, moreover, all presented as tasks she was to throw herself into in fleeing the temptation to murmur. Everything else in the revelation works either to introduce those appointments or to provide general words of exhortation.

Straightforward as the text might seem, however, it was not at first as stable as one might guess from a quick reading of it. That is, the actual words of the revelation were in some cases changed between its original reception in 1830 and its first canonical publication in 1835 in the first edition of the Doctrine and Covenants (although the text has remained basically unchanged since 1835). These changes (or at least the most important of them) prove important to any close reading of the revelation, so they require at least a few words of introduction and summary—especially because it was the altered, canonical text of the revelation that shaped the founding of the Relief Society in 1842.[11]

The earliest existing manuscript of the revelation is not the original but a handwritten copy found in what is now called Revelation Book 1.[12] An equally early (perhaps earlier) copy—no longer extant—served as the prototype for a printing of the revelation in the critical work *Mormonism Unvailed*, published in 1834.[13] Some small changes were made to the revelation before it was printed by the Church for the first time in the never-exactly-completed Book of Commandments in 1833.[14] But most of the changes—and all the major ones—were made between the revelation's printing in 1833 and its publication in the first edition of the Doctrine and Covenants in 1835.[15]

The first two verses of what is now section 25 were altered most dramatically. They originally read as follows: "Emma, my daughter in Zion, a revelation I give unto you concerning my will."[16] This was changed for the canonized 1835 version to read as follows: "Hearken unto the voice of the Lord your God, while I speak unto you, Emma Smith, my daughter, for verily I say unto you, all those who receive my gospel are sons and daughters in my kingdom. A revelation I give unto you concerning my will, and if thou art faithful and walk in the paths of virtue before me, I will preserve thy life, and thou shalt receive an inheritance in Zion." It should be noted right away that the canonical version expands the earlier text more than it replaces it. The clause "a revelation I give unto you concerning my will" is unaltered, although it is recontextualized through additions to the text. From the original's "Emma, my daughter in Zion," the first part ("Emma, my daughter") is retained and appended to "Hearken unto the voice of the Lord your god, while I speak unto you."[17] And the prepositional phrase "in Zion" from the same prefatory clause is displaced to a position *after* "a revelation I give unto you concerning my will," where it comes to modify not *daughter* but *inheritance*: "and if thou art faithful and walk in the paths of virtue before me, I will preserve thy life, and thou shalt receive an inheritance in Zion."[18] There is the further addition in these opening verses of "for verily I say unto you, all those who receive my gospel are sons and daughters in my kingdom." This addition is also not without relation to the original revelation. The clause "verily I say unto you" anticipates and echoes the use of the same phrase in what is now verse 16 (which appeared as it stands now in the earliest version of the revelation also). That concluding verse for the revelation similarly points toward the general applicability of the revelation. Thus, verse 16's "this is my voice unto all" stands parallel to what is now verse 1's "all those who receive my gospel are sons and daughters in my kingdom."

The next passage to receive substantial editorial attention is what is now verse 6. Before 1835 it instructed Emma Smith to work with her husband as follows: "And thou shalt go with him at the time of his going, and be unto him for a scribe, that I may send Oliver whithersoever I will." As the text was altered in preparation for its 1835 canonical publication, it read thus: "And thou shalt go with him at the time of his going, and be unto him for a scribe, while there is no one to be a scribe for him, that I may send my servant Oliver Cowdery, whithersoever I will." One change here is particularly important: "while there is no one to be a scribe for him" has been introduced, apparently to clarify that Emma's appointment as scribe actually proved to be temporary rather than permanent. (Less remarkable is the fact that "my servant" has been inserted before "Oliver.") This change seems to indicate a process of displacing Emma from her original appointment as scribe in 1830.

The last significant change involves the alteration of a single word, yet it is the only revision to have received repeated attention from writers.[19] It comes in what is now verse 9. The clause "thy husband shall support thee *in* the church," as it has appeared in the revelation since the 1835 printing, appears in all earlier versions of the text as "thy husband shall support thee *from* the church." This is a slight change that makes a real difference. When the revelation is altered to say that Emma Smith's husband would support her *in* the Church (particularly following her appointment as a teacher), it gives the impression that Emma's fear mentioned in the same verse concerns her ability to perform her duties well. The text seems to assure her that she could overcome her anxieties through the support of her husband. When the revelation says instead, as in the earlier versions, that Emma's husband would support her *from* the Church, it gives the impression instead that her fear was about finances and living conditions.[20] The text then seems to assure her that her fears would not be realized because the Church would provide the necessary means for her family to survive.[21]

What might explain these several alterations made to the revelation in preparation for its 1835 publication? Some could see in each of them evidence for a systematic attempt to displace Emma Smith from positions of authority originally and divinely granted to her in 1830. She goes from being the Lord's daughter in Zion in the original text to being the Lord's daughter with just the *possibility* of an inheritance in Zion;[22] from being her husband's scribe to being a substitute scribe *only* when or as necessary; and from being a rightly worried woman with concerns about subsistence to being a potentially vacillating woman with doubts about her adequacy. Is this the right way to understand the several changes?

Revisions made in preparation for the 1835 publication of the Doctrine and Covenants often aligned the text of the revelations with what had taken place historically since their original reception.[23] Revelations that had been clarified or even altered by later revelations were edited to fit together. Some revelations were adjusted to reflect major changes in the Church's organization that had taken place with the loss of Jackson County in 1833.[24] In a few cases, revelations were revised to anticipate historical developments after a revelation was originally received. It seems that the changes to what is now verse 6 of Emma Smith's revelation are at least partially an example of this. Oliver Cowdery was indeed displaced from his position as scribe and expositor of scripture, but Sidney Rigdon joined the Church late in 1830 and soon took Cowdery's place. The adjustments to verse 6 make the revelation anticipate Rigdon's eventual centrality to the Church. Might this suggest, in fact, that the revisions to Emma's revelation served to displace her role in the Restoration? Is it not likely that Emma herself felt troubled by the changes to the text, which she would certainly have noticed? These are questions that require careful answers, and I will attempt to provide some as we look for the self-revelation of Christ in section 25.

Degendering a Revelation

With general historical matters out of the way, it is possible to turn directly to the text of section 25 to ask about the shape and bearing of the revelation of Jesus Christ to Emma Smith. What is the image of the Christ who reveals himself to this troubled daughter of God? What does he know of her suffering, and how does he respond to it? I will give my attention in the remainder of this paper to three distinct aspects of the revelation, all of which speak to these questions. First, I will look at the generalizing or universalizing gestures that appeared already in the original (1830) version of the revelation (in what is now verse 16) and that were worked into the later (1835) version of the revelation (in what is now verses 1 and 2). Second, I will reflect on the appointments given to Emma in verses 5–12, especially those that set her up to take over work that had been Oliver Cowdery's. Third and finally, I will consider in greater detail than above the relationship between these several appointments and the warning in verse 4 against murmuring.

As discussed above, the original version of Emma Smith's revelation concludes with a generalizing gesture: "And verily, verily, I say unto you, that this is my voice unto all."[25] This final, generalizing note of sorts perhaps sounds a bit strange since most everything else in the original version of the revelation is quite specific, addressed to a particular woman and her very particular circumstances. There are *some* other minimal gestures toward general concerns—most obviously in what is now verse 12, with its comment on "the song of the heart" being a prayer to the Lord. Nonetheless, at least as it was originally dictated, the revelation is largely local, particular, specific, and without (obvious) universal implications. One would have had to do a fair bit of "likening," as Latter-day Saints say, to draw more general implications. Is it right, then, that "this is my voice unto all" really meant to imply that the whole of Emma's revelation was of relevance to everyone—or even just to all women? Might it not in fact be important to insist that the revelation was intentionally and rightly directed originally just to this one woman in her rather particular circumstances?

It might in fact be wrong to understand the phrase "voice unto all" in verse 16 to have been an indication from the beginning that the whole revelation was intended to have universal implications. It may be better to see verse 16 as just explaining and expounding on a shift from *thou* to *you* at the end of the preceding verse: "And except thou [singular] do this, where I am you [plural] cannot come" (Doctrine and Covenants 25:15).[26] (This may be the best explanation, in fact, since the earliest extant manuscript of the revelation shows that there was some confusion about the pronouns in verse 15.)[27] There is thus reason to think, exegetically, that the "voice unto all" is not the one heard throughout the revelation, but the one heard specifically in verse 15: "Keep my commandments continually, and a crown of righteousness thou shalt receive. And except thou do this, where I am you cannot come."

Even if the original revelation had no strong gestures toward generalization, however, we have already seen that editorial work on the revelation between 1830 and 1835 produced several such gestures. As we have seen, what was originally simply "Emma, my daughter in Zion, a revelation I give unto you concerning my will" became eventually the whole of what is now verses 1 and 2. Those two verses in their final form include several generalizing traits. Such, for instance, is the expansion of "Emma, my daughter": "Emma Smith, my daughter; for verily I say unto you, all those who receive my gospel are sons and daughters in my kingdom" (Doctrine and Covenants 25:1). This revision marks a clear shift from the particular ("Emma, my daughter") to the general or the universal ("all those who receive my gospel are sons and daughters in my kingdom"). It is most significant that what had originally been exclusively gendered female ("my daughter") becomes either degendered or both-gendered ("sons and daughters in my kingdom").[28]

Another generalizing gesture deserves mentioning or at least revisiting briefly. The alteration to verse 9 ("support thee *from* the church" to "support thee *in* the church") also has a generalizing function. Only certain readers of this revelation can identify with Emma Smith's particular concerns about her and her husband's doomedness-to-poverty, but many or even all readers can identify with concerns about inadequacies in fulfilling divinely appointed responsibilities. With this particular editorial change, the revelation suggests that Emma had such a concern and so allows her to become a mirror in which readers can see themselves. The fact is that many people faced with serious responsibilities in the Church fear those responsibilities and hope for some sort of support. There may well have been unfortunate side effects of this change as already noted, but the gesture of generalization is of real practical significance, regardless of its other effects.

Why this emphasis on generalization or universalization? There is reason to think that this emphasis is due in large part to the aims of the 1835 publication in which the relevant changes first appeared. Earlier efforts at publishing the revelations (in Church-owned newspapers and in the Book of Commandments) involved little or no editing. The revelations were largely left as originally dictated, with a level of detail (and a tone of familiarity) that can make them feel irrelevant to a general readership. This was especially true in the 1833 never-quite-finished Book of Commandments in which Emma Smith's revelation first appeared in print. The revelations were there ordered chronologically, as if they could, without any historical narrative to frame them, chronicle on their own the Lord's interventions in the earliest history of the Church.[29] But when plans formed to produce the Doctrine and Covenants in 1835, the purpose behind publishing the revelations changed drastically. The Doctrine and Covenants was to be less a chronicle of the Lord's communications to the Saints and more what might be called a handbook for the Church. The revelations were dechronologized and arranged instead according to their relevance to the practical interests of the institution.[30] The editing to which many of the revelations were subjected was clearly aimed at fitting them into this institutional context. Revisions were often apparently aimed at introducing general applicability into revelations that were arguably too particular to be of general interest.

What is now section 25 was among those edited for inclusion in the first edition of the Doctrine and Covenants. Thus, that project's investment in making all revelations of general benefit and not just of historical interest seems to have motivated many of the changes to Emma's revelation. This, however, raises important questions. How are we to think about altering the historically accurate wording of a revelation in order to give it more universal appeal or applicability? And specifically in terms of the revelation to Emma, how are we to think about such an alteration when it degenders (or at least begins to degender) the only revelation addressed specifically to a woman in the whole Doctrine and Covenants? Do these changes amount to (the beginnings of) erasing women from the canonized revelations? And should we worry that the changes accompanied the institutionalization of the Church and the centralization of an exclusively male priesthood? Does that mean that the "general" being appealed to is more male than genderless?

Such questions perhaps focus especially on the alteration that introduces talk of sons into a revelation originally given to a daughter. Is it a productive or a positive thing to have men encroach on a revelation originally given to a woman? Is it a productive or a positive

thing even to have other women encroach on a revelation given originally to just one particular woman, Emma Smith? These are difficult
questions. However, although there are ways in which these changes
might or even should make us nervous, there is reason to explore a
possible *positive* response to such difficult questions. What if we were
to explore the possibility that the introduction of sons into a revelation given originally to a singular daughter gestures in the direction
of *her inclusion* in a much broader community? Might it be that the
changes, rather than erasing women or this woman from the revelation, help in some ways to emphasize women's or this woman's inclusion in the Restoration? This is worth exploring, but it requires looking at two other aspects of the revelation in some detail.

Serving as Scribe, Expounding Scripture

Section 25 details three responsibilities given to Emma Smith that
promised to bring her out of the margins of the early Church. It is
possible to give this series of appointments a very strong reading.[31]
We might argue (as we have already suggested several times) that
Emma was originally given to take the place of Oliver Cowdery in the
budding Restoration movement. To make this case and so to outline
the possibility of the revelation's pointing in the direction of Emma's
involvement—both originally and after revisions—it is necessary
to provide a little background about the role Cowdery played in the
early part of the Restoration.

Most Latter-day Saints are familiar with Cowdery's basic story.
He stumbled onto the Restoration when he boarded with Emma
Smith's in-laws in New York during the winter of 1828–29. The following April, he made his way to Pennsylvania to meet the Prophet
and immediately assumed the task of writing down the dictated text
of the Book of Mormon. From that point, Cowdery became a central
figure in the Restoration. Only a month after beginning to serve as
scribe, he joined the Prophet on the banks of the Susquehanna River
to receive the Aaronic Priesthood at the hands of John the Baptist.

Sometime later, he was present too when Peter, James, and John appeared to give the keys of the Melchizedek Priesthood. In connection with these events, Cowdery was divinely appointed to write what might be called the constitution of the Church—though what he drafted was replaced with a revealed document that is now section 20 of the Doctrine and Covenants.[32] Cowdery was also privileged to be among the three witnesses who themselves saw an angel bearing the gold plates.

Cowdery was thus the early recipient of a great deal of privilege. Matters became strained, however, between him and the Prophet in the months following the April 1830 organization of the Church. Cowdery fell in with Hiram Page and the famous revelations he claimed to receive through his own seer stone (see Doctrine and Covenants 28). He also wrote a high-handed letter criticizing the Prophet for his handling of the revelations that had been legitimately received.[33] The most egregious of these events (the Hiram Page episode) occurred after Emma Smith's revelation came, but even by the time the revelation was received, Cowdery's relationship to the Prophet—and to God—was in an increasingly precarious position. Several revelations from the summer of 1830 suggest that the Lord was beginning to ease Cowdery out of the central position he had held to that point—that of the "second elder" in the Church of Christ (Doctrine and Covenants 20:3)—thus freeing up the most privileged office in the Church next to seer, translator, prophet, apostle of Jesus Christ, and elder of the Church that Emma's husband was (see Doctrine and Covenants 21:1).[34] Finally, by the fall of 1830 Cowdery was sent away from the Church's eastern headquarters to serve a mission among "the Lamanites" in the West and was moved from the center to the margins of the Church (Doctrine and Covenants 32:2; see 30:5).[35]

Who was to assume Cowdery's central position when the Lord moved him from the center to the margins of the movement? According to the revelation to Emma Smith, it was straightforwardly to be Emma. This is clearly the implication of verse 6 in the original version of the revelation: "And thou [Emma] shalt go with him [Joseph] at the time of his going [to the churches in Fayette, Manchester, and Colesville], and be unto him for a scribe, that I may send Oliver whithersoever I will." Emma was to be her husband's new scribe. She was also to take over Cowdery's other responsibilities, according to verses 7 and 8: "And thou shalt be ordained under his [Joseph's] hand to expound scriptures, and to exhort the church, according as it shall be given thee by my Spirit. . . . And thy time shall be given to writing, and to learning much." All of these responsibilities had previously been Cowdery's.

It seems clear, then, that Emma Smith was not being granted a few token positions through the Lord's revelation to her. She was instead being given the most central position in the early movement next to that of prophet. The revelation appointed her to assume a role that had been outlined, according to the Book of Mormon, more than three thousand years before Emma's revelation was given. The Book of Mormon records a prophecy about a spokesman for the prophet of the Restoration, a spokesman interpreters routinely assume to have been Oliver Cowdery (or his eventual replacement, Sidney Rigdon): "And the Lord said unto me [Joseph of Egypt] also: I will raise up unto the fruit of thy loins; and I will make for him a spokesman. And I, behold, I will give unto him that he shall write the writing of the fruit of thy loins, unto the fruit of thy loins; and the spokesman of thy loins shall declare it" (2 Nephi 3:18).[36] It was this sort of scripturally mandated position into which Emma was being inserted in her revelation.

Unfortunately, as already mentioned, it seems that Emma did not actually assume the assigned responsibilities in 1830—at least not in any permanent fashion. This may be because she was, as she soon found out, in the beginnings of a difficult pregnancy with twins, who would eventually both die. Or it may be because Cowdery did not end up leaving to fulfill his missionary responsibilities for some time, giving him an opportunity to sort out some of the tensions between him and the Prophet. Or it may be because Sidney Rigdon arrived as a kind of celebrity convert that December and immediately took over Cowdery's responsibilities, largely leaving Emma still at the margins of the movement. Or perhaps the roles and responsibilities given to Emma in her revelation were more than most members of the Church could handle at first in their social context, and it was easy for those in privileged positions to put off figuring out how to work for their fulfillment. Whatever the reason, however, Emma did not really become her husband's permanent scribe, nor did she become his spokesperson. And one of the apparent consequences of this fact is that in the preparation of the 1835 Doctrine and Covenants, verse 6 of the revelation was edited to conform to history as it had actually happened. As already noted, Emma's appointment was downplayed with the addition of the phrase "while there is no one to be a scribe for him."[37]

From this history, it would seem that Emma Smith's revelation failed to have its intended effect. Rather than bringing her into the heart of the Church, it seems to have eventually given her a complicated position in an edited, canonical revelation—and little more. But then this sad history was, it seems, radically reversed—at least in important respects—in Nauvoo. On 17 March 1842 the Relief Society was organized, and section 25 of the Doctrine and Covenants served as its founding document. The minutes of that organizing event read as follows: "President Smith read the Revelation to Emma Smith, from the book of Doctrine and Covenants; and stated that she was ordain'd at the time, the Revelation was given, to expound the scriptures to all; and to teach the female part of community; and that not she alone, but others, may attain to the same blessings."[38] This is heartening, and one can find real comfort in this belated adoption of the revelation's value and force.[39]

It is clear, at any rate, from the minutes of the earliest meetings of the Relief Society that the organization was intended to be the female counterpart to the male priesthood and that Emma was its president as her husband was the president of the male parallel. She and her counselors were to "preside just as the [First] Presidency, preside over the church," approaching the Prophet only "if they need his instruction."[40] The Prophet in fact went so far as to say that "the Society should move according to the ancient Priesthood" in order "to make of this Society a kingdom of priests as in Enoch's day."[41] And still more famously, a little over a month after the organization of the Relief Society, Joseph "spoke of delivering the keys to this Society," announcing: "I now turn the key to you in the name of God and this Society shall rejoice and knowledge and intelligence shall flow down from this time."[42] At last Emma took a place like the one appointed to her more than a decade earlier.

Of course, the history of women in the Church after the beginnings of the Relief Society in Nauvoo is another complicated story. But if, as the Prophet told Emma Smith and her sisters in those early meetings of the Relief Society, the first serious fulfillments of Emma's revelation constituted "the beginning of better days,"[43] there is reason to think that there is something about this revelation in particular that heralds real possibilities for moving women from the margins to the center of the Restoration, beginning historically with Emma herself. Her several appointments first announced in 1830 promised her a place at the heart of the movement. Her responsibility to assemble a hymnbook—the best known of her appointments in the revelation— was itself, as Rachel Cope has shown, already a remarkable gesture toward overcoming assumptions about women's roles.[44] And we have seen that her other two appointments were ones that were held originally by Oliver Cowdery (and then later by Sidney Rigdon), but they came to be hers eventually through the Relief Society.

We might ask, though, whether overcoming assumptions is an intention native to the revelation itself. And with such a question, we might finally come to the questions raised at the outset of this investigation: Is there actually any reason to see in the self-revelation of Jesus Christ to this particular woman a real concern for a marginalized and emotionally suffering woman? Does the Christ of the New Testament's Gospels show himself in this revelation to Emma Smith in a substantial way? To show that the answer to these questions is positive, it is necessary to turn to one last feature of the revelation—the meaning of the warning to Emma not to murmur.

Moving Out of the Margins

We have already mentioned the unfortunate fact that a certain reading of verse 4 in section 25 has played a traditionally dominant role in the interpretation of the revelation to Emma Smith. Taking the Lord's injunction to Emma to "murmur not" as a clear indication that she *was* already murmuring, commentators have often taken this revelation as evidence that Emma expressed a wrongly inspired sense of entitlement as *the* wife of *the* prophet. Emma's biographers summarize this sad history of interpretation: "That single line urging Emma to 'murmur not' would later give rise to speculation that Emma had complained of not seeing the record. Future writers would use that phrase to condemn Emma, but nothing in the Elect Lady revelation approaches the chastisements Joseph occasionally received."[45] We might quote just one example of this interpretation: "The inference from this revelation is that Emma was a proud, fearful, murmuring woman, and later events corroborated this analysis to a large extent."[46]

Such interpretations read far too much into the text of the revelation. It is especially of concern when commentators go on to suggest that the Lord's revealed response to the temptation to murmur is basically to tell Emma Smith just to be "obedient to her husband."[47] All the same, there is *one* thing that proves ironically right about such approaches to the revelation. We will consider briefly the possibility that they rightly recognize that the injunction not to murmur in verse 4 is a key for interpreting the text, even if they incorrectly gauge the meaning of the injunction.

Emma Smith's biographers note the important point in the words quoted above about the tradition of interpreting verse 4. Every conclusion drawn that "Emma had complained of not seeing the record" is ultimately a "*speculation*."[48] The revelation does not say to Emma that she *had* murmured and had therefore done wrong.

Rather, it simply tells her not to murmur. All that is implied here, strictly speaking, is that Emma faced a real—and, frankly, obvious—*temptation*. She would unquestionably have been tempted to murmur. But the crucial question is this: *What* would have tempted her to murmur? The answer is clear from the text. She was tempted to murmur *because of her marginalized status*. The full injunction reads as follows: "Murmur not because of the things which thou hast not seen" (Doctrine and Covenants 25:4). Emma has, despite her unfailing support for her husband, been left out of many things in the early history of the Church—first and foremost of seeing the plates, but this is arguably representative of many other things she had not yet been privileged to participate in. What is remarkable is that *the Christ of this revelation explicitly recognizes this fact*. It is therefore crucial to see that verses 5–12, containing Emma's several appointments, immediately follow and appear to be in direct response to verse 4, containing the Lord's explicit recognition of her marginalized status. This revelation thus not only grants empowering appointments and responsibilities to Emma but also serves directly and explicitly as a conscious *call for Emma to move out of the margins* as she assumes her new responsibilities.

Verse 4 may thus indeed be the key to understanding the revelation, though not in the sense traditionally assumed. It does not suggest that Emma Smith was proud or prone to complaining. It implies, rather, that she faced a real—and perhaps unavoidable—temptation just to mope on the margins, maybe even to use her marginalization as an excuse not to take up any serious responsibilities. It is a real temptation for every marginalized person to remain at the margins, if only so as to wear one's marginalization as a badge—murmuring loudly to draw attention to one's being left out. The revelation, however, cautioned Emma against such self-congratulatory murmuring, inviting her instead to move out of the margins and into the beating heart of the Church, appointing her to a series of remarkable responsibilities in the young movement of the Restoration. The Christ who reveals himself in this remarkable text sees her marginalization—reveals himself as one who sees marginalization—and he works to overcome it. But as he does so, he calls on her to overcome her own self-marginalization. She must not covet her own having been left out or revel in the opportunity to complain.

Interestingly, this remarkable gesture is accompanied by a kind of *apology* in the same verse of the revelation. What Emma Smith had not seen (the gold plates, for instance) had been "withheld from [her] and from the world" specifically because it was "wisdom in [the Lord] in a time to come."[49] Here the Lord provides an explanation of his sometimes painful decision to withhold certain things from his daughter. But that the Lord felt *an* explanation was called for is remarkable. The Lord himself apparently felt it necessary to justify not having given Emma a position of central responsibility sooner. He nonetheless explains—and herein lies a mystery—that this was "wisdom . . . in a time to come." These words deserve the closest scrutiny, and there is reason to think they can bear delicious fruit for women who feel or simply are marginalized still in the forward motion of the Restoration. When is the time that was still "to come" when Emma's passing marginalization, imposed but then removed, would serve the Lord's wisest purposes? Might that time come again and again whenever a woman reads the revelation to Emma and sees in it the possibility of a divine call to participate directly and centrally in the work of building the kingdom of God? As the Lord taught Emma to embrace the summons to participate fully in the Restoration, this revelation teaches every marginalized soul—daughters and sons alike (see Doctrine and Covenants 25:1)—to embrace such a divine summons here and now.

Conclusion

It is often lamented that the Doctrine and Covenants contains only one revelation specifically addressed to a woman. And there is no doubt that we can find "great cause to mourn" in this fact (Helaman 15:2). As hard as it may be to hear it, however, there may be something salutary in this situation as well. The marginalized status of one particular woman in the early history of the Church—representative in a real way of all women in the early history of the Church—allowed the Lord to draw the attention of every reader of the Doctrine and Covenants to the whole problem of marginalization, the marginalization of women and of every other category of persons those with privilege tend to ignore. We have in section 25 an explicit recognition on the Lord's part of the sufferings that come with being left out of the work of the kingdom of God, and we have there too a recognition of the temptations that might accompany the same experience or status. The sad facts of historical sexism and misogyny are lamentable, to say the very least. But the God who speaks in the revelations of the Doctrine and Covenants knows how to consecrate very real afflictions for gain (see 2 Nephi 2:2). Without valorizing the bad, we can see in the Lord's way of addressing bad situations a reason to rejoice.

Jesus Christ revealed himself to Emma Smith in 1830, and he continues to reveal himself to every careful reader of the text that resulted from that experience. He revealed himself then, as he reveals himself now, to be a God of the marginalized and the overlooked. Those in power in nineteenth-century American culture might not have been attentive to the needs and hurts of so many surrounding them, but the Lord was aware, and he was doing something about it. The revelation to Emma really did mark the beginning of better days, better days for women and—if we read the revelation carefully and thoughtfully today—for everyone pushed to the margins of the Restoration in any way. We need not wait much longer for "a time to come" in which we embrace all those we tend to overlook. The revelation to Emma Hale Smith calls on us all to realize what we fail to see around us and to join with the Lord of revelation in calling absolutely everyone to be a part of the work of building the kingdom of God.

Notes

1. These reflections had their beginnings in 2011, when Nikki Hunter invited me to develop and to share my thoughts on the revelation to Emma Smith. Accordingly, I wrote a two-part blog post on the subject, published at the Latter-day Saint blog *Feminist Mormon Housewives*. The original posts can be read at https://feministmormonhousewives.org/2012/01/emma -my-daughter-in-zion-a-preliminary-study-of-dc-25-part-1/ and https:// feministmormonhousewives.org/2012/01/emma-my-daughter-in-zion -a-preliminary-study-of-dc-25-part-2/. I decided to return to these reflections and develop them, thanks to an invitation from Carter Charles, but also after and in connection with the 2019 project of the Latter-day Saint Theology Seminar, held at Union Theological Seminary in New York City. During that two-week seminar I had the opportunity to work with great care through the text of the revelation to Emma Smith alongside remarkable interlocutors, including Rachel Cope, Jenny Reeder, Robin Jensen, Katherine Payne, Hannah McLaughlin, and Timothy Farrant— along with Rosalynde Welch, who codirected the seminar with me and with James Faulconer, who joined us for the two weeks of discussion. This seminar culminated in a public symposium, "'Given Thee by My Spirit': Reading D&C 25," held on 29 June 2019 at Union Theoloical Seminary. The papers from that conference are now in preparation for publication as part of the Latter-day Saint Theology Seminar's published proceedings. I owe thanks to all these friends and colleagues, whose reflections on the text have sharpened my own reading greatly.

2. Linda King Newell and Valeen Tippetts Avery, *Mormon Enigma: Emma Hale Smith* (New York: Doubleday, 1984), 33. These are the words of John Reed, the lawyer who defended Emma's husband in the two trials mentioned and who, during the course of those trials, made a brief visit to Emma and subsequently commented on her emotional state.

3. Fawn M. Brodie, *No Man Knows My History: The Life of Joseph Smith, the Prophet* (New York: Vintage, 1971), 89.

4. Brodie, *No Man Knows My History*, 89.

5. Donna Hill, *Joseph Smith: The First Mormon* (Garden City, NY: Doubleday, 1977), 114.

6. The focus on the plates is present throughout the literature on the revelation. See, for instance, Stephen E. Robinson and H. Dean Garrett, *A Commentary on the Doctrine and Covenants*, vol. 1 (Salt Lake City: Deseret Book, 2000), 170; and Jill Mulvay Derr, Carol Cornwall Madsen, Kate Holbrook, and Matthew J. Grow, eds., *The First Fifty Years of Relief Society: Key Documents in Latter-day Saint Women's History* (Salt Lake City: Church Historian's Press, 2016), 20.

7. See, for instance, Joseph Fielding Smith, *Church History and Modern Revelation*, vol. 1 (Salt Lake City: Deseret Book, 1946), 117. See the general comments on this trend in Newell and Avery, *Mormon Enigma*, 33, a point to be discussed again in the last part of this essay. For a more recent handling of the passage, see Matthew J. Grow, "'Thou Art an Elect Lady': D&C 24, 25, 26, 27," in *Revelations in Context: The Stories behind the Sections of the Doctrine and Covenants*, ed. Matthew McBride and James Goldberg (Salt Lake City: The Church of Jesus Christ of Latter-day Saints, 2016), 33–39.

8. See Rachel Cope, "A Sacred Space for Women: Hymnody in Emma Hale Smith's Theology," *Journal of Religious History* 42, no. 2 (June 2018): 242–64, who makes the case that Emma Smith's work on the hymnbook was a partial fulfillment of her responsibility to teach the Saints.

9. See Carol Corwall Madsen, "The 'Elect Lady' Revelation (D&C 25): Its Historical and Doctrinal Context," in *Sperry Symposium Classics: The Doctrine and Covenants*, ed. Craig K. Manscill (Provo, UT: Religious Studies Center, Brigham Young University; Salt Lake City: Deseret Book, 2004), 117–33. See also the brief report on the use of the revelation at the foundation of the Relief Society in the official minutes of that founding meeting: Derr et al., *First Fifty Years of Relief Society*, 32.

10. It is striking that commentaries on the Doctrine and Covenants have not provided an analysis of the structure of the revelation to Emma Smith. The divisions in the revelation tracked here are relatively obvious, however.

11. See, again, Derr et al., *First Fifty Years of Relief Society*, 32.

12. See Robin Scott Jensen, Robert J. Woodford, and Steven C. Harper, eds., *Revelations and Translations, Volume 1: Manuscript Revelation Books,*

vol. 1 of the Revelations and Translations series of *The Joseph Smith Papers*, ed. Dean C. Jessee, Ronald K. Esplin, and Richard Lyman Bushman (Salt Lake City: Church Historian's Press, 2011), 38–41. The same document, with focused historical notes, can also be found in Michael Hubbard MacKay, Gerrit J. Dirkmaat, Grant Underwood, Robert J. Woodford, and William G. Hartley, eds., *Documents, Volume 1: July 1828–June 1831*, vol. 1 of the Documents series of *The Joseph Smith Papers*, ed. Dean C. Jessee, Ronald K. Esplin, Richard Lyman Bushman, and Matthew J. Grow (Salt Lake City: Church Historian's Press, 2013), 161–64; and in Derr et al., *First Fifty Years of Relief Society*, 17–21.

13. See E. D. Howe, *Mormonism Unvailed: Or, A Faithful Account of that Singular Imposition and Delusion, from Its Rise to the Present Time* (Painesville, OH: E. D. Howe, 1834), 101–2.

14. See Joseph Smith, *A Book of Commandments for the Government of the Church of Christ* (Independence, MO: W. W. Phelps, 1833), 58–59. This can be seen in Robin Scott Jensen, Richard E. Turley Jr., and Riley M. Lorimer, eds., *Revelations and Translations, Volume 2: Published Revelations*, vol. 2 of the Revelations and Translations series of *The Joseph Smith Papers*, ed. Dean C. Jessee, Ronald K. Esplin, and Richard Lyman Bushman (Salt Lake City: Church Historian's Press, 2011), 70–71.

15. See Joseph Smith, *Doctrine and Covenants of The Church of the Latter Day Saints* (Kirtland, OH: F. G. Williams, 1835), 178–79. This can be seen in *JSP*, R2:488–89.

16. In Revelation Book 1, the text was first copied as just "A Revelation I give unto you concerning my will." The words "Emma my daughter in Zion" were added, apparently as an editorial addition or perhaps as a correction at some subsequent point. The text as it stands in *Mormonism Unvailed* is "A commandment to Emma, my daughter in Zion, A. D., 1830.—A revelation I give unto you concerning my will." The two sources taken together suggest that the earliest text included both "Emma, my daughter in Zion" and "A revelation I give unto you concerning my will." The combination of both lines appears in the 1833 Book of Commandments version of the revelation's opening.

17. "Smith" is added to "Emma" as well.

18. Clearly, the notion of Zion drew much attention from the early Saints during 1830. Its role in Latter-day Saint thought also changed in significant ways between 1830 and 1835. For some context, see Kerry Muhlestein, "One Continuous Flow: Revelations Surrounding the 'New Translation,'" in *The Doctrine and Covenants: Revelations in Context*, ed. Andrew H. Hedges, J. Spencer Fluhman, and Alonzo L. Gaskill (Provo, UT: Religious Studies Center, Brigham Young University; Salt Lake City: Deseret Book, 2008), 40–65.

19. Fawn Brodie points to this change in a footnote; see Brodie, *No Man Knows My History*, 90. Even earlier, it was pointed out in Harry M. Beardsley, *Joseph Smith and His Mormon Empire* (Boston: Houghton Mifflin, 1931), 94. See also Richard P. Howard, *The Church through the Years: The Reorganization Comes of Age, 1860–1992* (Independence, MO: Herald Publishing House, 1993), 406.

20. See the comments in Steven C. Harper, *Making Sense of the Doctrine and Covenants: A Guided Tour through Modern Revelations* (Salt Lake City: Deseret Book, 2008), 86.

21. This last change might seem insignificant despite the different impressions the two versions of the passage give the reader. The implications for the flow and even the structure of the revelation are, however, somewhat larger than might seem at first. The revelation originally addressed Emma Smith's wholly legitimate worries about her husband's inability to provide substantially for the family. Verses 9 and 10 were in that context a reassuring aside appended to the words through which Emma received her first appointments in the Church (as laid out in the structure in the previous section of this paper). Emma was, like her husband, to forget temporal matters and take up the work of the kingdom of God, both as her husband's scribe and as a teacher in the Church. With the change of a single word, however, the revelation suggests that verses 9 and 10 were not an aside about Emma's temporal concerns but a direct comment on her relationship to her second appointment (and perhaps to her first appointment as well).

22. Throughout this paper, I use the title *Lord* instead of the more academically acceptable *God* (except where the latter seems more appropriate). I do

this because the revelation itself identifies the speaker as "the Lord" but also because the title *Lord* is less theologically fraught than *God* might be. It is traditionally—and I think rightly—understood that the Lord speaking in the revelations in the Doctrine and Covenants is, generally speaking, Jesus Christ rather than God the Father. The revelation to Emma Smith thus contains the self-revelation of Christ, in my view, more than the self-revelation of God the Father. This is important in trying to understand the Christ of the Doctrine and Covenants.

23. For a good survey of the publication history of the Doctrine and Covenants, see Richard E. Turley Jr. and William W. Slaughter, *How We Got the Doctrine and Covenants* (Salt Lake City: Deseret Book, 2015).

24. A good example of both of these categories of change is the revelation now canonized as section 42 of the Doctrine and Covenants. It contains two distinct revelations given a few weeks apart that were eventually stitched together as if they were a single revelation. The text also contains revisions that introduce into it references to institutions that did not exist—such as the high council—at the time of the revelations' original reception, but that were of great institutional importance by 1835. See, for extended analysis of this revelation in particular, Grant Underwood, "'The Laws of the Church of Christ' (D&C 42): A Textual and Historical Analysis," in *Doctrine and Covenants: Revelations in Context*, 108–41; and Joseph M. Spencer, *For Zion: A Mormon Theology of Hope* (Salt Lake City: Greg Kofford Books, 2014), 81–157.

25. This is certainly how this line has been interpreted. See, for instance, Jill Mulvay Derr, Janath Russell Cannon, and Maureen Ursenback Beecher, *Women of Covenant: The Story of Relief Society* (Salt Lake City: Deseret Book, 1992), 9; and Madsen, "'Elect Lady' Revelation," 120. The latter's comments are worth quoting at some length. After citing the phrase "this is my voice unto you," Madsen says, "Thus, in significant ways, [the revelation] transcends the merely personal, fitting the parameters of scripture and thereby acquiring permanence, authority, and universality. While its specifics are addressed to Emma, its principles are applicable to all." Against such interpretations, however, and for some helpful discussion of the problematic ramifications of introducing generalization into

a revelation like this one, see Rachel Cope, "Ungendering the Text: An Historical Re-reading of D&C 25," in *Given Thee by My Spirit: Reading D&C 25*, ed. Joseph M. Spencer and Rosalynde Welch (Proceedings of the Latter-day Saint Theology Seminar, forthcoming).

26. For some remarkable reflections on how this *thou* and this *you* are inter-connected, see Rosalynde Welch, "Emma as Church, Emma as Christ: Kingdom and Salvation in Section 25," in *Given Thee by My Spirit*.

27. As can be seen in that manuscript, the scribe, John Whitmer, originally wrote *thou* instead of *you* in "where I am you cannot come"—then wipe-erased it and wrote *ye* over the top of *thou*. Sidney Rigdon later crossed out *ye* and wrote *thou* above the line. After all this, what ended up in print in both the 1833 Book of Commandments and the 1835 Doctrine and Covenants was *you*. See *JSP*, R1:40–41.

28. It seems clear that these editorial alterations were made in part with an eye to the "voice unto all" from verse 16. Slipped in between "Emma Smith, my daughter" and "all those who receive my gospel are sons and daughters in my kingdom" is a phrase that appears also in the potentially generalizing verse 16: "Verily I say unto you" (this phrase introduces "this is my voice unto all" in verse 16).

29. This is exactly, according to the revealed preface to the Book of Commandments, what the revelations were meant to do when they were collected and published. See what is now Doctrine and Covenants 1:24–28.

30. Revelations concerning the priesthood and the establishment of the New Jerusalem were privileged, and nonrevelatory material like the Lectures on Faith and several official statements of belief were included in the volume.

31. For a similar reading of this portion of the revelation in many ways, see Carter Charles's own essay, "'Thou Shalt Be Ordained to Expound Scriptures and to Exhort the Church': How Christ Includes and Empowers Women in Doctrine and Covenants 25," 195–220, in this volume.

32. For helpful background on this assignment, see Scott H. Faulring, "An Examination of the 1829 'Articles of the Church of Christ' in Relation to Section 20 of the Doctrine and Covenants," *BYU Studies* 43, no. 4 (2004): 57–91.

33. For a brief review of these dissensions, see Richard Lyman Bushman, *Joseph Smith: Rough Stone Rolling* (New York: Alfred A. Knopf, 2005), 119–21.

34. The most important revelation raising questions about Cowdery's place in the Church at the time is Doctrine and Covenants 28, given in response to the Hiram Page incident. See also, however, Doctrine and Covenants 23:1–2; 24:10–12; and, of course, 25:6.

35. Cowdery was soon back in full favor, though there were other occasional tensions and a brief period of excommunication—favor enough, in fact, to take the lead in searching out and ordaining the members of the 1835 Quorum of Twelve Apostles, as well as to stand next to Joseph in 1836 when the next set of priesthood keys were granted in the newly dedicated Kirtland House of the Lord. Shortly thereafter, though, Cowdery reinvented his earlier struggles against Joseph's authority and found himself excommunicated by 1838; he was not rebaptized until after Joseph's death.

36. On the identification of this spokesman, see George Reynolds and Janne M. Sjodahl, *Commentary on the Book of Mormon*, 7 vols., ed. Philip C. Reynolds (Salt Lake City: Deseret Book, 1955), 1:256; Daniel H. Ludlow, *A Companion to Your Study of the Book of Mormon* (Salt Lake City: Deseret Book, 1976), 129; and Monte S. Nyman, *I Nephi Wrote This Record: Book of Mormon Commentary* (Orem, UT: Granite, 2004), 423.

37. It is interesting to note that Oliver Cowdery was himself among those making revisions to the revelations in preparation for the 1835 Doctrine and Covenants.

38. Derr et al., *First Fifty Years of Relief Society*, 32.

39. See especially, as before, Madsen, "'Elect Lady' Revelation." For a rather different appreciation of Emma Smith's later reflections on the revelation, see Harper, *Making Sense of the Doctrine and Covenants*, 88–89.

40. Derr et al., *First Fifty Years of Relief Society*, 31.

41. Derr et al., *First Fifty Years of Relief Society*, 43.

42. Derr et al., *First Fifty Years of Relief Society*, 56, 59.

43. Derr et al., *First Fifty Years of Relief Society*, 59.

44. See Cope, "Sacred Space for Women."

248 JOSEPH M. SPENCER

45. Newell and Avery, *Mormon Enigma*, 33.

46. Francis M. Gibbons, *Joseph Smith: Martyr, Prophet of God* (Salt Lake City: Deseret Book, 1977), 90.

47. Smith, *Church History and Modern Doctrine*, 1:117. Note, significantly, that the revelation never speaks of Emma needing to exhibit obedience to her husband; it speaks only of being "a comfort" for him, serving as his scribe, being ordained by him, being supported by him from the Church, and "delight[ing]" in him.

48. Newell and Avery, *Mormon Enigma*, 33; emphasis added.

49. For a heavily theological exploration of the phrase "a time to come" in this revelation, see my own "The Things of a Better," in *Given Thee by My Spirit*.

10

Zionic Nonviolence as Christian Worship and Praxis

Patrick Q. Mason

The twentieth and twenty-first centuries have seen nothing short of a revolution in the academic study of the New Testament and early Christianity. As the contours of the first decades and centuries of Christian history become clearer through scholarly research, Latter-day Saints must confront the question of what exactly it means to be participating in and bringing about the restoration of "primitive" Christianity. Since the time of Joseph Smith, the Restoration has commonly been understood to center on the reorganization of an ecclesiastical hierarchy that mirrors (or at least echoes) that found in the New Testament. Hence, the sixth article of faith of The Church of Jesus Christ of Latter-day Saints insists upon a reestablishment of "the same organization that existed in the Primitive Church."[1] Yet the Restoration has always sought to be more than the mechanical replication of a two-thousand-year-old organizational chart. Indeed, the Restoration also aspires to recapture the spirit, power, and authority of early Christianity—not simply its offices and forms. An 1842 editorial published in the Church's periodical *Times and Seasons* suggests that the first generation of Latter-day Saints understood God to be restoring "the gospel as [it] existed in the primitive days"—namely, "the pure principles of truth as taught by our Lord Jesus Christ, and taught and administered in by the Apostles."[2]

Among the "pure principles of truth" taught by Jesus, his apostles, and their successors known as the church fathers was a prohibition on killing. The early Christian community, which the modern Church seeks to emulate and restore, featured nonviolence as a central component of the disciple's life. Jesus's teaching from the Sermon on the Mount to "love your enemies, bless them that curse you, do good to them that hate you, and pray for them which despitefully use you, and persecute you" (Matthew 5:44) was, according to theologian Preston Sprinkle, the most frequently quoted verse during Christianity's first four centuries. "For early Christians," Sprinkle contends, "enemy-love was the hallmark of what it meant to believe in Jesus."[3] Historians agree that a serious commitment to nonviolence featured prominently in Christianity until the Roman emperor Constantine declared the religion legal early in the fourth century CE. Throughout the Christian movement's first three centuries, the church fathers forbade killing.[4] They rooted their position in explicit biblical teachings and in a more organic understanding of the Christian community as being defined by mercy, forgiveness, graciousness, peace, and most of all, love. As historian Roland Bainton further affirms, "The pacifism of the early church was derived not from a New Testament legalism, but from an effort to apply what was taken to be the mind of Christ. Christianity brought to social problems, not a detailed code of ethics or a new political theory, but a new scale of values."[5]

While some scholars have claimed that Christians were absolute pacifists until Constantine, recent research has revealed a more complex situation, especially around the question of whether Christians could rightly serve in the military. Both textual evidence and archaeological discoveries attest that particularly by the third century some Christians did serve as Roman soldiers; those who converted while in the army neither received church discipline nor were forced to abandon their profession. Nevertheless, the church fathers remained deeply skeptical about whether one could be a faithful Christian and serve in the Roman military for two primary reasons: first, soldiers (especially officers) were required to make sacrifices to the emperor, which Christians considered to be a form of idolatry; and second, a major component (or at least realistic possibility) of a soldier's duty was to kill other human beings, which the church regarded as a grievous sin.[6] After reviewing the complex historical record and scholarly debate, scholar Lisa Cahill concludes that "there is a well-substantiated theological and pastoral consensus in the centuries before Constantine that compassion, forgiveness, peace, and peacemaking are regulative Christian ideals, and that killing by Christians is never acceptable."[7]

The early Christians' reticence to defend the empire by violence did not go unnoticed. For instance, Celsus, a second-century pagan critic of Christianity, complained that "if all men were to do the same as you [Christians], there would be nothing to prevent the king from being left in utter solitude and desertion and the forces of the empire would fall into the hands of the wildest and most lawless barbarians."[8] Such critiques could draw on ample evidence from Jesus's life and teachings, the historical record, and writings of contemporaneous church leaders. Tertullian, a prominent leader and apologist in the late second- and early third-century Christian church in north Africa, acknowledged that those who pursued a military profession could sincerely accept Jesus. Nevertheless, he wrote that "in disarming Peter" in the Garden of Gethsemane, Jesus "unbelted every soldier."[9] The eastern church father Origen, writing shortly after Tertullian in the third century, acknowledged the legitimacy of governments but plainly articulated his skepticism toward Christians employing violence in the service of the state. He based his view on the claim that Christ forbade any form of homicide, even against "the greatest wrongdoer."[10] In sum, the testimony of Christians in the "primitive church" was clear: killing was forbidden for followers of Christ, who were called to be peacemakers and build a countercultural community founded on principles of love, forgiveness, and peace.

The Book of Mormon compounds this peace witness of the New Testament and early Christian church. To the surviving Nephites gathered at the temple at the time of his appearance, the resurrected Christ delivered a discourse very similar to the Sermon on the Mount recorded in Matthew. While the two addresses feature a few key differences, virtually identical are the Savior's so-called hard sayings, in which he commands his followers to turn the other cheek, love their enemies, and pray for their persecutors rather than retaliate against them (see Matthew 5:38–44; 3 Nephi 12:38–44). Just as the early Christians in the Old World embraced nonviolence, so too did the converted Lehites. In the wake of the people's transformational encounter with the resurrected Christ, the entire society had "no contentions and disputations," leading to "peace in the land" for nearly two hundred years. Because of "the love of God which did dwell in the hearts of the people," the society experienced no "strifes, nor tumults . . . nor murders" (4 Nephi 1:2–4, 15–16). Prior to the coming of Christ, war had featured prominently in the experience of God's covenant people in both the Bible and the Book of Mormon. This changed, however, after Christ delivered a higher law of love (see Matthew 5; 3 Nephi 12). The New Testament and Book of Mormon jointly attest that nonviolence became a central component of Christian discipleship for those blessed souls in both hemispheres who directly witnessed Jesus's ministry and Resurrection, as well as for the generations that immediately followed after them.

The question before us is whether a deep individual and collective commitment to Christian nonviolence is an essential feature of what the Restoration seeks to restore. After all, it is not a foregone conclusion that any particular aspect of a previous dispensation will be a featured component of the current one. Many Old Testament and Pauline teachings about women, for instance, have not had a determinative effect on Restoration theology or practice.[11] My contention here is that the revelations given to Joseph Smith and canonized in the Doctrine and Covenants emphatically affirm that nonviolence is a central feature of how to worship the Prince of Peace.[12] In other words, I argue that the nonviolence of the early Christian church in both the ancient Mediterranean world and the Book of Mormon's promised land was neither incidental nor a historical particularity. Nonviolence was and is an integral feature of Christian life and worship, organically emerging from core teachings and principles of the gospel. If the Restoration seeks to restore the power and spirit of early Christianity in addition to its forms, then a deep and countercultural commitment to nonviolence should be similarly integral to modern disciples' understanding and witness of Christ's redeeming work.

Divine guidance regarding how members of the restored Church should navigate a world of violence came first in the context of Joseph Smith's Zion revelations. The Restoration's Christian peace witness developed further in revelations that pointedly addressed violence in the context of persecution in Missouri beginning in 1833 and the subsequent formation of Zion's Camp. Generally speaking, Smith's revelations in the first two years after the organization of the Church featured an apocalyptic tone and perspective in which the political structures and events of this world were seen as virtually inconsequential in light of the impending return of Christ. Beginning in 1833 the revelations transitioned to a more accommodationist position, allowing for negotiation and even friendship with secular political structures.[13] However, the revelations remained consistent in counseling the Saints to eschew violence and raise the standard of peace, even toward aggressors. If violent conflict cannot be avoided, it is better that disciples of Christ suffer bloodshed than inflict it. The Saints are always free to choose the path of violence, but doing so is never the preferred option and will typically initiate (or continue) a cycle of destructive consequences with multigenerational implications. In short, if the Saints want to worship Christ and build Zion, they will have to learn to be peacebuilders.

Revealing a Nonviolent Zion

As early as January 1831, less than a year after the establishment of the Church of Christ, Joseph Smith's revelations recognized that the world inhabited by latter-day disciples of Jesus is a violent one. In addition to hearing of "wars in far countries," Church members in the United States could not assume that violence would always remain safely distant. "Ye know not the hearts of men in your own land," the Lord ominously warned (Doctrine and Covenants 38:29). No doubt this was unsettling to those who heard or read the revelation. Shortly thereafter, the Lord confirmed that in the last days peace would be "taken from the earth" (Doctrine and Covenants 1:35). What could the followers of Christ do in such a time of travail? The answer came loud and clear in a March 1831 revelation: build Zion.

The commandment to gather had been given just two months earlier (see Doctrine and Covenants 38). Now the purpose of that gathering became clearer. Church members were to consecrate their money so as to purchase land as an inheritance for themselves and future generations of Saints. This would be no ordinary communal society. This was to be the New Jerusalem built on the American continent according to ancient prophecies (see Ether 13:6–8). The New Jerusalem would be "a land of peace, a city of refuge, a place of safety for the saints of the Most High God" (Doctrine and Covenants 45:66). This city—like the city of Zion that Enoch and his people built (see Moses 7:16–20)—would be so full of the glory and terror of the Lord that the ungodly would not even approach it (see Doctrine and Covenants 45:67). Crucially, the Latter-day Saint Zion was not intended only for the Saints. Rather than an exclusivist or tribal utopia, Zion would be a cosmopolitan community of peace, a refuge for "every man that will not take his sword against his neighbor" (45:68). Lovers of peace, the revelation prophesies, would gather from "every nation under heaven" (45:69). Indeed, in an era of world-consuming violence, those gathered to Zion would be "the only people that shall not be at war one with another" (45:69). Although a purely spiritual reading of this revelation is possible, the text itself is insistent that what is at stake in building Zion in the last days is protection from real violence and actual war. Zion is an alternative political community that offers a prophetic counterpoint to a world both infected and infatuated with violence.[14]

As Joseph Smith and other early Church leaders prepared to build the city of Zion in western Missouri, further revelations instructed them that their settlement of the region should occur in an orderly and peaceable fashion. "Wherefore, it is wisdom," the Lord counseled in July 1831, "that the land should be purchased by the saints" (Doctrine and Covenants 57:4). Mutual exchange with existing settlers would allow Church members to secure the land of Zion as their "everlasting inheritance" without conflict or animosity (57:5). A month later, the Lord underscored his prior instructions. The Saints were understandably enthusiastic about the prospect of establishing Zion in anticipation of Christ's Second Coming. But it seems that some of them may have believed they could do so by any means necessary—that the end of building Zion justified any methods whereby it was accomplished. The Lord chastised them and rejected this consequentialist ethic. First, he reminded them that the land upon which they would build Zion was rightfully *his*, not *theirs*. The Saints' assembly upon the land should be deliberate, organized, and lawful. He reemphasized what he had commanded them a month earlier, namely that they should purchase the lands. This would have the advantage of establishing a rightful claim that could not be denied by others and would not stir up anger among their neighbors (see 63:24–27).

The Lord did acknowledge that there was another possibility, one that apparently lurked in some of the Saints' hearts: They could obtain the land of Zion "by blood" (Doctrine and Covenants 63:29–31). They could come as conquerors, as modern-day crusaders in pursuit of their holy land. They could arm themselves and forcefully push out the current inhabitants. Perhaps, given the sparse and largely disorganized population of settlers in western Missouri, they

might even succeed in the short term. Violence was a live option—
and one frequently taken by Americans as they moved west.[15] But
the Lord told them how that strategy would play out. The local settlers were already disposed to "anger against you [the Saints], and
to the shedding of blood" (63:28). If the Saints took up arms, they
would initiate a cycle of violence they would soon regret: "Lo, your
enemies are upon you, and ye shall be scourged from city to city, and
from synagogue to synagogue, and but few shall stand to receive an
inheritance" (63:31). True, as freewill actors the Saints could forsake
the path of peace and seek to establish themselves on the land by
force of arms. But the Lord said unequivocally, "You are forbidden
to shed blood" (63:31). The results for doing so would be disastrous,
even to the point of losing the Saints' inheritance. Wars were coming, the Lord prophesied, and "the saints also shall hardly escape"
(63:34). Their only real hope in a world of violence was to peacefully
establish Zion and gather there, to reject the temptation of shedding
other people's blood, and to declare the Christian gospel of peace (see
63:28–37; see also 87:8).

The principles outlined in these early revelations seem to have
sufficed for the first two years of settlement in Missouri. Even after he
left the church and turned critic, John Corrill testified of the Saints'
commitment to Christian nonviolence in the Restoration's earliest
years. Up until the summer of 1833, he asserted, "the Mormons had
not so much as lifted a finger, even in their own defence, so tenecious
were they for the precepts of the gospel—'turn the other cheek.'"[16]
That changed as the local settlers' antagonisms toward Church members escalated to the point of violent persecution in Jackson County,
with mobs destroying the Saints' printing press and newspaper
office and then tarring and feathering Bishop Edward Partridge and
Charles Allen. Under duress in late July Church leaders signed an
agreement to leave the county.[17]

More than eight hundred miles to the east, Joseph Smith was
only partially aware of what was happening in Missouri when he
received a revelation in early August 1833. The Lord expressed his

tender concern for the beleaguered Saints in Missouri, reiterating his earlier promises that he would protect Zion and her people, that he was "her high tower," and that the Saints could therefore rejoice until the time that he exacted his vengeance upon the wicked (see Doctrine and Covenants 97:20–21). "Zion shall escape if she observe to do all things whatsoever I have commanded her," the Lord assured (97:25). "But if she observe not to do whatsoever I have commanded her," then God's promise of protection was withdrawn, and Zion's inhabitants would be subject to "sore affliction, with pestilence, with plague, with sword, with vengeance, with devouring fire" (97:26). Would Zion trust God or trust in the arm of flesh?

Renounce War and Proclaim Peace

Four days later, on 6 August 1833, Joseph Smith received further divine instruction on how the Saints should respond to violence, not only in the immediate context of the Jackson County persecutions but as a more general rule. Canonized as section 98 in the Doctrine and Covenants, the revelation is a singular text in which the Lord provides in greater detail than anywhere else in scripture his law regarding retaliation. The revelation, presented as an "immutable covenant," opens by affirming that the Saints are justified in "befriending that law which is the constitutional law of the land," insofar as it supports freedom and maintains human rights and privileges (Doctrine and Covenants 98:3, 6). While a peaceable, well-ordered, and rights-respecting government led by "honest . . . good . . . and wise men" (and presumably women) is the ideal arrangement in the civil sphere, God recognizes that there will be times in which "the wicked rule [and] the people mourn" (98:9–10). It is precisely at the moment when the political order breaks down, or even takes on malicious forms, that the Saints will be tested in their willingness to abide by their covenant. God promised that the Saints need not be afraid of their enemies, at least not in the ultimate scheme of things. Significantly, however, his covenant with them did not entail a guarantee of temporal safety and security. To the contrary, he said that he would "prove [them] in all things," testing whether they were willing to "abide in [his] covenant, even unto death" (98:14). In the face of political evil, violence, and suffering, God offered straightforward guidance to his covenant people: "Renounce war and proclaim peace" (98:16).

"Renounce war and proclaim peace" sounds like a bumper sticker slogan. Far from being an empty platitude, however, God put teeth in his command by supplementing it with elaborate instructions about how the Saints should respond when confronted with violence—as individuals, members of families, and citizens of nations. Speaking first about violence against individuals and families, the Lord said that if the Saints were attacked by their enemies, they were to "bear it patiently and revile not against them, neither seek revenge" (Doctrine and Covenants 98:23). If they displayed forbearance in this way, they would be divinely rewarded. If they chose to fight back, however, then the violence they received in the first place would be counted as "being meted out as a just measure unto you" (98:24). In other words, it was not enough for the Saints to refrain from striking *first*—they were not to strike *back*. They were Christians, bound by the Savior's command to turn the other cheek, committed to follow Christ's example of suffering without seeking recrimination. If the Saints failed to live up to their Christian convictions and obligations, then the violence they received was just compensation for their choice to participate in rather than renounce violence. The revelation continued by saying that their blessings would increase exponentially if the Saints continued to forbear any additional acts of aggression, to the point of having their reward multiplied by a factor of eight hundred (see 98:23–26). My reading is that this is not meant to indicate a precise numerical measure of individuated blessings gained and counted but is rather a metaphoric expression of a substantial increase in divine favor and holiness for faithful covenant keepers.[18]

In short, the Lord's clearly preferred response to violence is forbearance and forgiveness. But is this the only way? What happens if the Saints (individually or collectively) simply can't take it anymore or give in to the very natural desire to violently defend their families and innocent victims from unjust and unchecked aggression? The Lord in his merciful understanding of human frailty makes provision for this—just as he did in providing the Mosaic law, Aaronic Priesthood, and law of tithing, all lesser laws designed to accommodate human inability to live a celestial standard. If your enemy attacks you once, the revelation states, you are commanded not to seek vengeance. If he attacks a second time, you are to warn him to cease his aggression. If he ignores your warning and attacks you or your family a third time, then the Christian response is still to "spare him" (Doctrine and Covenants 98:30; see 24–30). "Nevertheless," the Lord says, after this third unjust and unwarranted assault, if you cannot find it in yourself to once again turn a cheek that has already been bruised and bloodied from multiple attacks, "thine enemy is in thine hands; and if thou rewardest him according to his works thou art justified" (98:31).

The word *justified* is clearly intentional—it is repeated twice in the same verse and twice more (in different forms) in the ensuing verses (Doctrine and Covenants 98:36, 38). Unpacking that word is therefore essential to understanding how the Lord thinks about the Saints' potential use of retributive violence after being victimized multiple times. The theological definition of justification, informed primarily by the Pauline epistles, is to make righteous, or just, in the sight of God.[19] An attitude or action does not need to be justified if it is already just, or righteous. If an attitude or action is inherently holy or godly—pure love, for instance—it does not require justification. Only actions that are not godly in themselves, which depart in some way from a celestial standard of righteousness, need to be justified. The good news of the gospel is that God in his mercy and Christ in his love have provided a path of justification for those whose attitudes or actions are not always godly—that is, for all fallen humans. However, it is vitally important to recognize and appreciate the distinction between actions that are *justified*, or made right through the grace of God, versus those that are *sanctified*, or intrinsically holy. Sanctification may follow justification, but it does not inhere in it.

In short, for God to declare that he justifies a particular human attitude or action is also an implicit acknowledgment that the attitude or action is unholy in itself.

Applying this understanding to Doctrine and Covenants 98 reveals that even when God allows retributive violence, he does so under extremely strict and specific conditions. Even so, the violence committed by virtue of human frailty is still not inherently righteous but can nevertheless be justified, or made right, through his grace. Significantly, the Lord's preferred option of forbearance requires no justification (if done with pure motives), since it is the godly response to violence. Furthermore, the revelation underscores the fact that while we cannot always choose how others will treat us, how we respond is always an act of volition. Violence, even when thoroughly justified, is never the only option. Even in the most extreme circumstances, we can choose to "revile not" (Doctrine and Covenants 98:23). This was the path that Jesus took, and also what it means in a literal sense, when he commands each of his disciples to "take up their cross and follow me." The cross can be a metaphor for discipleship, but it was not a metaphor for Jesus. When he told his followers that in the moment of extremity they could opt to either "save their life" or to "lose their life for my sake," he was speaking both spiritually and literally (Matthew 16:24–25 New Revised Standard Version; hereafter NRSV). The same holds true for the Lord's covenant with his latter-day disciples as found in Doctrine and Covenants 98, in which God attests that he will try us "in all things, whether [we] will abide in [his] covenant, even unto death" (Doctrine and Covenants 98:14). Latter-day disciples of Jesus must be willing in the face of unjust violence to participate in "the sharing of his sufferings by becoming like him in his death" (Philippians 3:10 NRSV).

Christian nonviolence understands that how we choose to respond to violence will have multigenerational impacts. Indeed, this is another one of the trenchant insights of Doctrine and Covenants 98. The command to "renounce war and proclaim peace" is immediately and directly connected to a command to "seek diligently to turn the hearts of the children to their fathers, and the hearts of the fathers to the children" (98:16). Peacebuilders work not only for themselves and their neighbors but also for the sake of future generations. One of the great legacies we can leave our children—which will turn their hearts toward us—is peace. Over and over, the August 1833 revelation calls out the multigenerational nature of both conflict and reconciliation. If we choose to spare our enemies, it redounds not only to our credit but also to that of our children and descendants "unto the third and fourth generation" (98:30). But if our enemies persist in their aggression, then the negative effects of ongoing conflict will be visited upon their children and descendants also "unto the third and fourth generation" (98:46).

Both violence and nonviolence have a cyclical quality. Perhaps no text better attests this than the Book of Mormon, which repeatedly demonstrates the devastating effects of unresolved conflict on individuals, families, and nations. The sins and violence of the fathers become visited upon their children for generations, until someone— like the sons of Mosiah—interrupts the destructive cycle of violence and replaces it with a new cycle of reconciliation, forgiveness, peace, and love. The example of the Jaredites offers a sobering warning that if left to itself, violence has a metastasizing quality that will eventually consume everyone and everything in its path. But the Lord's promise in Doctrine and Covenants 98 is that even the most destructive cycle can be interrupted and transformed. If an aggressor's "children shall repent, or the children's children, and turn to the Lord their God, with all their hearts and with all their might, mind, and strength, and restore four-fold for all their trespasses wherewith they have trespassed, or wherewith their fathers have trespassed, or their fathers' fathers," then even a multigenerational conflict can be transformed, the cycle of vengeance can be arrested and reversed, and a new set of restored relationships can be nurtured to life (98:47). The message of the Lord to the Saints in 1833 and today is essentially twofold: Violence is an option that under certain restrictive conditions may be justified; but forbearance, sincere forgiveness, and reconciliation are always better, sanctifying options.

The Nonviolent Redemption of Zion

Two and a half months after Joseph Smith received the August 1833 revelation, Church leaders in Missouri decided to set aside their signed agreement that included the provision that the Saints would leave Jackson County. Instead they took up arms and announced that they would forcibly defend themselves, their families, their property, and their Zion. We should have nothing but sympathy for these bedraggled and victimized Saints. The depredations committed against them were real, and their impulse to protect life and property was natural and well-intentioned. They had received multiple offenses and had lifted the ensign of peace to their neighbors, and so according to the law revealed in the August revelation they were justified in defending themselves. It is therefore out of neither condemnation nor moral judgment but rather a sober assessment of the documentary evidence to observe that the Missouri Saints' self-defensive violence was a choice, but not the choice that God recommended to them as their primary or best option. To the contrary, as we have seen, God had repeatedly told them that he would defend Zion from its enemies, and that if they tried to secure it by blood they would "be scourged from city to city" and be met "with sword, [and] with vengeance" (Doctrine and Covenants 63:31; 97:26). The Lord's prophecies, alas, came true. Outgunned, the Saints' attempt at violent self-defense foundered. The Missourians overpowered them in a matter of only a few days. The original signed agreement—itself an injustice—had provided that half the Saints would leave by the end of the year and the other half in the early spring, thus allowing for an orderly migration. Now, however, the mob showed no mercy and drove thousands of Saints from their homes and farms with no additional time for preparation. Fortunately, the good citizens of Clay County welcomed the refugees and helped them through the winter.

As the Saints in Kirtland received reports of the persecution of their brothers and sisters in Missouri, they quite naturally wanted to do something in response. The matter weighed heavily on the mind and heart of Joseph Smith, who a few days before Christmas received a revelation with the Lord's instructions to the Church. The opening verses matter-of-factly addressed those who had been "afflicted, and persecuted, and cast out from the land of their inheritance" (Doctrine and Covenants 101:1). Rather than seeing them as innocent victims of a merciless mob, the Lord chastised them, saying that their afflictions had come "in consequence of their transgressions" (101:2). He pointed out their moral failures, speaking of "jarrings, and contentions, and envyings, and strifes, and lustful and covetous desires among them" (101:6). But he also suggested that they had failed to trust in his promise to protect them and lightly esteemed his previous counsel, including the obligation he gave them, as Christians, to receive suffering rather than inflict it (see 101:8). "For all those who will not endure chastening, but deny me, cannot be sanctified," the revelation sternly pronounced (101:5). The Saints had not denied Christ, certainly not in any formal sense, but by taking up arms they had rebuffed his words and his covenant. Perhaps their retributive actions were justified, but they were not sanctified and therefore were not worthy of Zion. Despite the Saints' lapses, however, God promised that he was full of compassion toward them, and they would be both remembered and redeemed (see 101:3, 9). Significantly, they had not lost Zion—they had simply forsaken its principles. "Zion shall not be moved out of her place," the Lord reassured the Saints, "notwithstanding her children are scattered" (101:17). Once they had prepared and purified themselves, "they and their children" would be eligible to return and reclaim the original promises (101:18). The Lord reiterated that the land of Zion could belong to the Saints, but only through legal purchase and lawful redress (see 101:70–71, 76–77).

Two months later, Joseph Smith once again sought the will of the Lord, this time after having heard firsthand of the Saints' sufferings from Parley P. Pratt and Lyman Wight, who had traveled from

Missouri to Kirtland to appeal for help. The Lord expressed sympathy and love for the beleaguered Missouri Saints and promised divine vengeance against their enemies. But, he repeated, as long as they failed "to observe all my words"—including presumably his previous counsel regarding Christian nonviolence—then "the kingdoms of the world shall prevail against them" (Doctrine and Covenants 103:8). The Saints had been called to be "a light unto the world, and to be the saviors of men," a reference to the Sermon on the Mount, where Jesus most famously outlined his higher law of nonviolent love (103:9; see also Matthew 5:14–16, 38–44). But they had failed to live up to that charge and thus had been "trodden under foot of men" (103:10). The revelation went on to speak of the redemption of Zion, which the Lord declared would come by power (see 103:15). This language may have excited those anxious to mount an armed campaign to reclaim Zion for the Saints. But the following verses should have deflated their militaristic expectations. The power that would redeem Zion was not that of armed violence. It was instead the same power that led Moses and the children out of Egypt—the power of God and of angels (see 103:16–19). What was required of the Saints was not their violent retribution for the wrongs they had suffered but an acceptance that loving and nonviolent suffering is a constituent aspect of Christian discipleship. "Let no man be afraid to lay down his life for my sake," the Lord counseled, for "whoso is not willing to lay down his life for my sake is not my disciple" (103:27–28). A violent conflict with their enemies would produce casualties. Significantly, however, the only potential loss of life mentioned by the Lord was that of the Saints. At no point in this or previous revelations did God give his blessing for the Saints to shed—let alone seek—the blood of their enemies.

What God did allow for was the formation of companies of up to five hundred Kirtland Saints to join Pratt and Wight on their return trip to Zion (see Doctrine and Covenants 103:30). When the Saints thought of redeeming Zion, they clearly had in mind the idea of reclaiming lost properties and perhaps exacting vengeance on their aggressors. God's mission statement for the company was rather different, however, and distinctly nonmilitaristic. Their task, under Joseph Smith's leadership, was to "organize my kingdom upon the consecrated land, and establish the children of Zion upon the laws and commandments which have been and which shall be given unto you" (103:35). If the group was to claim victory and glory, it would not be through force of arms, but rather a different kind of power: "your diligence, faithfulness, and prayers of faith" (103:36). The revelation initiating Zion's Camp, as the march from Ohio to Missouri came to be popularly known, was founded upon a call to faithfulness, not a call to arms. Nowhere did God declare Zion would be won back through violent means.

The Lord reasserted his will in a revelation that the Prophet received while in council with camp members on the banks of Fishing River on 22 June 1834. They had made the long, wearying march across the country and were nearing their destination of Jackson County. Governor Daniel Dunklin had just reneged on his earlier offer of sending the state militia to help the Saints reclaim their lands, and the sheriff of Clay County had communicated to Smith that the camp's march had raised considerable anxieties among the Saints' enemies that could lead to outright violence.[20] The outnumbered Saints were unsure of what to do when the Lord's instructions came. He chastised the Church once again for their failure to do all he had commanded them and insisted that "Zion cannot be built up unless it is by the principles of the law of the celestial kingdom" (Doctrine and Covenants 105:5). If the Saints insisted on living a lesser law, they would have to "wait for a little season for the redemption of Zion" until they had the occasion to be "taught more perfectly, and have experience, and know more perfectly concerning their duty" (105:9–10). In a statement that has often been interpreted as the Lord giving the camp members a release from their duty, in fact he was simply reiterating what he had taught them many times before: "For behold, I do not require at their hands to fight the battles of Zion; for,

as I said in a former commandment, even so will I fulfil—I will fight
your battles" (105:14).

Zion did not need a ragtag band of a couple hundred armed fron-
tiersmen to redeem it. The Lord could do his own work if and when
he so chose, as indicated by the violent storm that flooded Fishing
River and prevented the massing mobs from attacking the camp.[21]
In the meantime, God counseled the people to be "very faithful,
and prayerful, and humble" (Doctrine and Covenants 105:23) and
to gather their resources to purchase lands in Jackson County and
surrounding areas. "For it is my will that these lands should be purchased," the Lord reiterated (105:29). It was only through the purchase of the lands of Zion that the "armies of Israel" would be held
guiltless in "throwing down the towers" of their enemies (now located
on the lands the Saints held title to) and "scattering their watchmen"
(who no longer had legal right to the land) (105:30). At no point did
the Lord command the members of Zion's Camp to perpetrate violence against their enemies. So as to remove all doubt about the duty
of his disciples toward those who had persecuted them and spitefully
abused them, the Lord concluded the revelation by commanding that
the Saints "sue for peace, not only to the people that have smitten
you, but also to all people" (105:38). Followers of the Prince of Peace
should "lift up an ensign of peace, and make a proclamation of peace
unto the ends of the earth; and make proposals for peace unto those
who have smitten you" (105:39–40). As they transformed themselves
into emissaries of peace, the Lord promised the Saints that "all things
[would] work together for [their] good" (105:40).

The members of Zion's Camp had dramatically different responses to the Fishing River revelation. Nathan Baldwin, who had been
hesitant about bearing arms from the beginning of the expedition,
said that the revelation "was the most acceptable to me of anything I
had ever heard before, the gospel being the exception." Others could
hardly hide their distaste. According to William Cahoon, their negative feelings to some degree came from an understandable disappointment that they would not be "permitted at this time to restore our

Brethren & Sisters to their Homes and defend them." But others had been spoiling for a fight from the outset and now complained that they had marched across the country only to leave with their tails between their legs. George A. Smith recalled that several camp members "apostatized because they were not going to have the privilege of fighting." "They had rather die," Nathan Tanner remembered, "than to return without a fight."[22] This vengeful attitude stood in stark contrast to the express language of the revelation, which specifically said that the Saints had to be willing to lay down their lives if they were to be worthy of Zion (see Doctrine and Covenants 98:13–14). The failure of at least some in Zion's Camp to live up to the Lord's celestial law only punctuated the Lord's admonition that Zion would be theirs only when they had learned to abide by "the principles of the law of the celestial kingdom" (105:5).

Conclusion

Taken together, the revelations received by Joseph Smith during the eventful first four years of the restored Church's history pointed to a simple reality: Zion, the land of peace (see Doctrine and Covenants 45:66), would only become the Saints' inheritance once they learned to "renounce war and proclaim peace" (98:16) and to "make a proclamation of peace unto the ends of the earth" (105:39). The Restoration was never immune to the travails of a fallen world, and the Saints became personally acquainted with its violence all too soon. As Joseph Smith and his followers sought to restore the purity of early Christianity, the revelations counseled these latter-day disciples of Jesus to pursue the path of Christian nonviolence despite the violence they endured. They learned that true Christian worship and practice can never be divorced from the nonviolent example and character of Christ, who exemplified a redemptive willingness to suffer injustice rather than inflict it. An essential component of following the Prince of Peace and building Zion is embracing the nonviolence featured at the heart of the Christian gospel.

Notes

1. Articles of Faith 1:6.
2. "Letter from Tennessee," *Times and Seasons*, 15 June 1842, in Elizabeth A. Kuehn, Jordan T. Watkins, Matthew G. Godfrey, and Mason K. Allred, eds., *Documents, Volume 10: May–August 1842*, vol. 10 of the Documents series of *The Joseph Smith Papers*, ed. Matthew C. Godfrey, R. Eric Smith, Matthew J. Grow, and Ronald K. Esplin (Salt Lake City: Church Historian's Press, 2020), 154–55.
3. Preston Sprinkle, *Fight: A Christian Case for Nonviolence* (Colorado Springs, CO: David C. Cook, 2013), 142.
4. Roland H. Bainton, *Christian Attitudes toward War and Peace: A Historical Survey and Critical Reevaluation* (Nashville: Abingdon Press, 1960); Ronald J. Sider, *The Early Church on Killing: A Comprehensive Sourcebook on War, Abortion, and Capital Punishment* (Grand Rapids, MI: Baker Academic, 2012); Lisa Sowle Cahill, *Blessed Are the Peacemakers: Pacifism, Just War, and Peacebuilding* (Minneapolis: Fortress Press, 2019), chapter 3.
5. Bainton, *Christian Attitudes*, 53–54.
6. See Roland Bainton, *Early Christianity* (Princeton, NJ: D. Van Nostrand, 1960), 53; Diarmaid MacCulloch, *Christianity: The First Three Thousand Years* (New York: Penguin Books, 2009), 156; Justo L. Gonzalez, *The Story of Christianity, Vol. 1, The Early Church to the Reformation*, revised and updated (New York: HarperOne, 2010), 63.
7. Cahill, *Blessed Are the Peacemakers*, 74; see all of chapter 2.
8. Quoted in Bainton, *Christian Attitudes*, 68.
9. Quoted in Cahill, *Blessed Are the Peacemakers*, 77.
10. Quoted in Cahill, *Blessed Are the Peacemakers*, 87.
11. For examples, see Leviticus 15:19–33; 1 Corinthians 11:5–6, 14:34.
12. A note on method: This essay focuses primarily on Joseph Smith's canonized revelations as scripture that carry transhistorical authority and applicability for Latter-day Saints. I therefore quote from the modern Doctrine and Covenants rather than from the documentary sources as compiled and transcribed in the Joseph Smith Papers. In short, while my argument here is deeply informed by history, and I fully appreciate that all revelation

originates in historical particularity, my aims here are more exegetical and theological than historical.

13. See Mark Ashurst-McGee, "Zion Rising: Joseph Smith's Early Social and Political Thought" (PhD diss., Arizona State University, 2008); Richard Lyman Bushman, *Joseph Smith: Rough Stone Rolling* (New York: Alfred A. Knopf, 2005), 168. On early Latter-day Saint millennialism, see Grant Underwood, *The Millenarian World of Early Mormonism* (Urbana: University of Illinois Press, 1993).

14. See Mark Ashurst-McGee, "Zion as a Refuge from the Wars of the Nations," in *War and Peace in Our Times: Mormon Perspectives*, ed. Patrick Q. Mason, J. David Pulsipher, and Richard L. Bushman (Salt Lake City: Greg Kofford Books, 2012), 83–91; Patrick Q. Mason, "'The Wars and the Perplexities of the Nations': Reflections on Early Mormonism, Violence, and the State," *Journal of Mormon History* 38, no. 3 (Summer 2012): 72–89.

15. See Richard Maxwell Brown, *Strain of Violence: Historical Studies of American Violence and Vigilantism* (New York: Oxford University Press, 1975).

16. John Corrill, *A Brief History of the Church of Christ of Latter Day Saints (Commonly Called Mormons)* (St. Louis: printed by the author, 1839), 19; spelling as in original.

17. See Marvin S. Hill, *Quest for Refuge: The Mormon Flight from American Pluralism* (Salt Lake City: Signature Books, 1989), chapter 3.

18. In this respect I believe the enumeration of blessings functions something like Christ's command to forgive "seventy times seven" (Matthew 18:22; Doctrine and Covenants 98:40).

19. See Kenneth Appold, "Justification," in *The Cambridge Dictionary of Christian Theology*, ed. Ian A. McFarland et al. (New York: Cambridge University Press, 2011), 257–59.

20. See Matthew C. Godfrey, "'The Redemption of Zion Must Needs Come by Power': Insights into the Camp of Israel Expedition, 1834," *BYU Studies Quarterly* 53, no. 4 (2014): 125–46.

21. Matthew C. Godfrey, "'We Believe the Hand of the Lord Is in It': Memories of Divine Intervention in the Zion's Camp Expedition," *BYU Studies Quarterly* 56, no. 4 (2017): 125–28.

22. Baldwin, Cahoon, Smith, and Tanner, all quoted in historical introduction to Revelation, 22 June 1834 [D&C 105], The Joseph Smith Papers, https://josephsmithpapers.org/paper-summary/revelation-22-june-1834-dc-105/1#historical-intro; spelling modernized.

11

"The Kingdom of God and His Laws"

Joseph Smith's Revelations and Teachings on Christ's Kingdom and Church in the Council of Fifty

Gerrit Dirkmaat and Andrew C. Reed

During the months before Joseph Smith's death, he sought to establish God's kingdom on earth through a new organization that he called the Council of Fifty. This council was tasked with planning and preparing a constitution for this new government, a kingdom that would await the imminent return of Jesus Christ, who would then assume his rightful place at the head of that kingdom.[1] This doctrine of Christ's imminent return was familiar because of the New Testament's insistence upon the Lord's return but also because it was readily available in many of Joseph's canonized revelations. The closing passage from a late 1830 revelation instructed the Saints to "lift up your hearts and be glad, your redemption draweth nigh. Fear not, little flock, the kingdom is yours until I come. Behold, I come quickly" (Doctrine and Covenants 35:26–27).[2] In these council meetings, held during the last four months before his murder, Joseph delivered powerful teachings about what the government of God's kingdom should look like and how members of the Church should practice their religion. During this period, Joseph received his final revelations—revelations that captured the pinnacle of a prophetic career that had shaped thousands of Christian lives amid periods of deep hostility. These revelations and teachings "shed new light on the development of Latter-day Saint beliefs and on the history of Nauvoo and the Church during this critical era" and bring precision to the Saints' understanding of their role in God's kingdom. While these revelations were never included in the Doctrine and Covenants, they nevertheless reveal important insights into how Joseph Smith believed Latter-day Saints should live and act as they sought to do their part to prepare for the Second Coming of Jesus Christ.

For Joseph Smith and for the Council of Fifty, the expansion of the Restoration as a series of principles and practices that were comfortably cast in a religious framework provided the structure upon which the kingdom of God could be established. The incorporation of The Church of Jesus Christ of Latter-day Saints into God's broader designs for the millennial reign challenged the Council to see their relationship to Christ as expansive and dynamic. The Council of Fifty thought in concrete terms about the nature of Christ and his kingdom. As the council grappled with properly devising policy regarding the kingdom of God, its members learned to rely upon their hard-earned insights and collective genius as a medium to better comprehend and act upon prophetic counsel. In the end the council tested the decision-making mechanism as it endeavored to draft a constitution for the kingdom and prepared to live out its plan in the West. The Council of Fifty's implementation of principles developed and garnered through prophetic instruction demanded that the Saints continue to work both in practical and in theological ways toward the realization of the kingdom of God even after the death of the Prophet Joseph Smith.

The Council of Fifty produced a wealth of documentation about its deliberations on a variety of political matters as it looked for possible places of refuge from persecution and violence. At the same time, those debates and revelations were framed within theological and practical discussions about the ways that Nauvoo Saints could participate in the unfolding of the Second Coming of Christ. The anticipated Christ, as described by the members of the Council of Fifty, was characterized by his millennial reign and his full dominion of all the earth. Further, the immediacy of Christ became central to the Council members through their understanding that Joseph Smith was the temporary leader of that kingdom on earth who would usher in Christ's kingship.

Practical Context of the Council of Fifty

By early 1844 Joseph Smith had come to a conclusion that would have long-lasting implications for The Church of Jesus Christ of Latter-day Saints and its members. He had for years sought every means of political recourse to find someone, anyone, in the national government who would be willing to champion the Latter-day Saint cause. Joseph hoped someone would rebuke the murderous depredations of Missouri state troops and allied mobocratic forces and help the Saints finally recover lands that had been confiscated from them without remuneration. At the center of his interests and concern was the confiscated temple site of the New Jerusalem, placed by revelation in Jackson County (see Doctrine and Covenants 57). Assaults, thefts, house burnings, and even cold-blooded murders of children went unpunished following the so-called Mormon War in Missouri, and none of the murderers at Hawn's Mill or the violent assailants at De Witt or Far West had even been criminally charged. Between 1838 and 1844 Joseph's appeals for justice included a journey to Washington, D.C., and an interview with President Martin Van Buren, who famously refused to help on political grounds. Joseph desperately tried to get the Saint's story of persecution out to those who he believed could and would aid his community in righting the wrongs against them. In this case, Joseph's agenda was driven by the temporal safety of his people.

The matter of federal or state intervention on behalf of the Latter-day Saints was exacerbated by ongoing debates during the Jacksonian era about whether the government had the authority to intervene in matters of state jurisdiction.[3] The Latter-day Saint petition, as Patrick Mason has asserted, was destined to fail in halls of the federal government and presidency because it "barely registered on the national radar during the Joseph Smith era. Mormonism only became a national concern in the 1850s after the establishment of what outsiders saw as a Mormon theocracy in Utah territory and the Mormon's 1852 public announcement of plural marriage."[4] While this conclusion seems clear in hindsight, Joseph and the early Saints seemed to believe that their plight would gain favor if those in Washington could hear it from the Saints themselves.

In 1843, with another presidential election looming, Joseph had written to every rumored candidate of the upcoming 1844 presidential election, asking, "What will be your rule of action relative to us as a people?"[5] One by one, the candidates confirmed in writing what Joseph already knew from experience. With varying levels of pretense and sophistry, each presidential hopeful expressed some level of regret at the treatment of the Latter-day Saints but claimed to have neither the power nor the will to commit to render aid—or the force of law—to the beleaguered and persecuted religionists. Former secretary of war Lewis Cass, for instance, told Joseph that while he personally believed "the Mormonites [should] be treated as all other persons in this country are treated, . . . I do not see what power, the President of the United States can have over the matter, or how he can interfere in it."[6]

To make matters worse, antagonistic rhetoric in Illinois began to take on an alarming nature as it once had in Missouri, with one local newspaper declaring, "We see no use in attempting to disguise the fact that many in our midst contemplate a total extermination of that people: that the thousands of defenseless women, aged and infirm, who are congregated at Nauvoo, must be driven out, aye, driven, scattered like the leaves before the autumn blast!"[7]

Horrified by the implications of such sentiments and rebuffed by national politicians of both parties, Joseph Smith made the difficult decision for the Latter-day Saints to leave the United States entirely and set up their own kingdom with a just constitution and laws somewhere out in the West. By February 1844 he informed the Quorum of the Twelve Apostles of his plans "to send out a delegation & investigate the locations of California and Oregon to find a good location where we can remove after the Temple is completed & build a city in a day and have a government of our own—in a healthy climate."[8] The lack of helpful response from federal and state authorities, reminiscent of the Saints' experiences in Missouri, provided great urgency to the council's efforts to prepare to leave the country.

Plans to leave the United States proceeded more rapidly after March 1844 when Joseph organized the Council of Fifty. This group was tasked with seeking out a place where this new kingdom of God could be built outside the boundaries of the United States. Over the course of the next several months, its members considered multiple locations, including the independent Republic of Texas, Comanche or Cherokee lands, Oregon Territory (which was at the time jointly administered by Great Britain and the United States), and the vast expanses of Northern Mexico (which were essentially bereft of permanent white settlements and over which Mexico exercised no practical control).

Praxis and Prophetic Wisdom—Integral Parts of Modern Revelation

The revelatory nature and theological undergirding of the Council of Fifty gets lost when viewed through the lens of pragmatic immediacy. However, as we demonstrate, the ultimate aim of the council's efforts was to unite the Restoration project of prophetic authority, institutional church, and millennial reign through an aggressive political program. It is easy to focus on the overtly political nature of the Council of Fifty's work as it pushed for new lands and for increased

freedoms, security and protection. Much of the work of the council members focused on practical solutions to real-world problems
confronting the Saints in Nauvoo. The story of the Saints' desperate search for a new home outside the bounds of the United States
is a historically compelling narrative that is most easily understood
politically. But to overlook the deeply religious roots of the move—to
locate a space where theocracy and safety coalesced—is to misunder-
stand the motivation that prompted thousands to move west. As they
had previously in Ohio and Missouri, the Saints in 1844 sought to
relocate when the political and social circumstances became too hostile. In the process of deliberating on their options, they located the
impetus for migration in the revelations and the prophetic counsel
provided by Joseph and later by his successor, Brigham Young. In an
earlier revelation received during the hardships and disillusionment
that followed the revealed location of Zion to be in Jackson County,
Missouri, the Saints learned the necessity of physical suffering while
awaiting God's promised peace. By revelation, the Lord taught Joseph
and the Saints that "after much tribulation come the blessings" and
that they "shall be crowned with much glory; the hour is not yet, but
is nigh at hand" (Doctrine and Covenants 58:4). The tangibility of
revelation as both expedient and eternal within the Latter-day Saint
tradition is manifest in the revelations obtained by Joseph during the
Council of Fifty meetings. These two aspects of revelation were not
only parallel but also were intricately bound by the physicality of the
Christ the Saints hoped would soon return to the world.[9]

The Council believed that the events described in scripture would
be realized when their community and the individuals in it attained
an acceptable level of holiness. Those aspirations pointed toward yet
another phase of the Restoration project—the eventual fulfillment of
the promised return of the Savior to reign on the earth. The Saints'
efforts were cast within a broader understanding that the work of
God, the sonship of Jesus Christ, and the earthly existence of a people
seeking to be in direct communion with "the creator of the Universe
as their Priest, Lawgiver, King and Sovereign" were theologically

connected.[10] While the Saints awaited Christ's return, they were to be "anxiously engaged in a good cause, and do many things of their own free will, and bring to pass much righteousness; for the power is in them, wherein they are agents unto themselves" (Doctrine and Covenants 58:27–28). Revelatory teaching about Christ was often meant to illustrate an eschatological context within which Saints' immediate actions served as preparatory steps toward God's direct involvement in the world on their behalf. A revelation from 1833 makes this point clear. In Doctrine and Covenants 93, the most striking christological framing of Jesus Christ available in all of Latter-day Saint writing, Joseph learned, "I am the true light that lighteth every man that cometh into the world; and that I am in the Father, and the Father in me, and the Father and I are one—the Father because he gave me of his fulness, and the Son because I was in the world and made flesh my tabernacle, and dwelt among the sons of men" (Doctrine and Covenants 93:2–4). It is perhaps telling that in the very same christological revelation, the Saints learned that because of their knowledge of Christ and his nature, they were to "hasten to translate my scriptures, and to obtain a knowledge of history and of countries, and of kingdoms, of laws of God and man, and all this for the salvation of Zion" (Doctrine and Covenants 93:53). The practical commands of scripture were both immediate and connected to the broader purposes of God. Likewise, the Saints and the Council of Fifty understood their mission to build up the earthly kingdom of God and saw the detailed steps they took to do so as clear manifestation of their hopeful commitment to await the coming of the Lord that was "nigh at hand" (Doctrine and Covenants 58:4).

The Purpose of Counsel in the Council of Fifty

At one of the earliest council meetings, the select men gathered together and agreed that they should seek out a place to "go and establish a Theocracy either in Texas or Oregon or somewhere in California."[11] Passion ruled the meeting as the "brethren spoke very

warmly on the subject."[12] Joseph had encouraged the members of
the Council to "speak their minds on this subject and to say what
was in their hearts whether good or bad."[13] A council that simply accepted the first proposal in order to be agreeable defeated the entire
purpose of having a council. Joseph pressed that point, telling the
men that he "didn't want to be forever surrounded by a set of dough
heads and if they did not rise up and shake themselves and exercise
themselves in discussing these important matters he should consider
them nothing better than dough heads."[14] Thus, the purpose of the
Council of Fifty was to fully examine opinions, options, and revelations as a means of deciphering the way forward through reason and
prophetic instruction; such a process brought heated debate into the
room as council members spoke passionately about their views. For
Joseph and the Saints, the pattern of the heavenly council contained
in Joseph Smith's translation of the Bible, set out in Moses 4, made
clear that good and bad ideas needed to be heard in order to make
obvious to the council the proper order and logic of eventual decisions. The fact that God the Father had, according to scripture, provided a platform where diametrically opposed opinions in matters of
eternal consequence could be discussed openly may have suggested to
Joseph that his council, if predicated upon righteous principles, could
do the same. A few weeks later, as he further instructed the men on
the necessity of discussion and debate when a difference of opinion
arose, Joseph Smith taught that "the reason why men always failed to
establish important measures was, because in their organization they
never could agree to disagree long enough to select the pure gold from
the dross by the process of investigation."[15]

During the 11 March 1844 council meeting, Joseph Smith "gave
much instructions on many subjects and laid down the order of the
organization after the pattern of heaven."[16] If the Saints were going
to build the kingdom of God, the Council of Fifty would serve as
its model. This council, they believed, operated in accordance with
divine order, established long before the Restoration project ever
began (see Doctrine and Covenants 121:32). They endorsed the idea

of "forming a constitution which shall be according to the mind of God and erect it between the heavens and the earth where all nations might flow unto it." This new kingdom with its godly constitution would be a "standard to the people and an ensign to the nations."[17] Having determined to abandon the United States because of its flawed government and legal system, the men envisioned a kingdom with laws ordained by God. In essence, the work of the council could, if properly instituted and carried out, actually unite heaven and earth. Joseph and other members of the council hoped for and talked at length about such a kingdom, and while they used the language of hope and futurity, they also expected it to be realized in their council.

The council members sat in a semicircle, ordered from oldest to youngest. They voted audibly in this order, beginning with the eldest on each matter under consideration. Joseph Smith declared it "universally necessary before any resolution could become a law to have the vote of all the members of the council unless some of the members should be absent on business for the council." Thus the large council would have to unanimously agree on a decision or law for the proposed kingdom of God before it could be considered ratified. While the idea of unanimous consent of a political body sounds to the modern observer like a recipe for disaster (since one person could simply hold out against the other forty-nine), the reality was that those dissenting from the majority view had to have good reason for their position. Brigham Young later explained, "In the event of a negative vote being given on any subject, the member voting in the negative is called upon to give his reasons for thus voting. If his reasons are not good and based in righteous principles he will be called upon to suppress and waive them, and thus do away with his opposition. If this were not the case one brother through private pique alone could do manifest wrong and injury to men as good as himself, a principle which this kingdom cannot tolerate. If a member should persist in his opposition after it is proved to him that he is in the wrong, his opposition would sever him from the council."[18] In any case, while multiple views were expressed as Joseph directed, there is no record of such an obstinate holdout on any of the issues discussed in the council.

It was in one of the initial meetings—designed to organize the council and discuss its objectives—that Joseph received divine direction. As the gathered men began discussing what they should name the council, William Clayton recorded that "the Lord was pleased" to give Joseph Smith a revelation in response: "Verily thus saith the Lord, this is the name by which you shall be called, The Kingdom of God and his Laws, with the keys and power thereof, and judgement in the hands of his servants. Ahman Christ."[19] A few weeks later Joseph explained to the council the "meaning of the word 'Ahman' which signifies the first man or first God, and 'Ahman Christ' signifies the first mans son."[20] The name of the council was generally shortened in usage to simply "the Kingdom of God." Joseph would cap the size of the council at fifty, hence the more informal, and publicly palatable, designation—Council of Fifty. When Brigham Young took over as chair of the council following Joseph Smith's murder, he wrote in his journal that he "had a councel with the fifty righted up & organized." When William Clayton created the title page of the minutes of the organization, he wrote, "Record of the Council of Fifty or Kingdom of God."[21]

This revelation reflected Joseph's unique and radical theology and Christology, focused on the assertion that God not only had a body but that he was in fact a resurrected man who had progressed to godhood. Several years earlier Joseph had explained to a group of Saints that the Father and the Son "had a tabernacle," or body, in direct contravention of long-established Christian beliefs that held only Jesus had a resurrected body. In that sermon he explained, "The Great God has a name By wich he will be Called Which is Ahman."[22] Only a few weeks after receiving this revelation at the council meeting, Joseph greatly expanded upon this understanding of God the Father and Jesus in the address commonly referred to as the King Follett sermon. In Wilford Woodruff's account of that sermon, he recounted Joseph teaching that "I go back to the beginning to show what kind of being God, was, I will tell you & hear it O Earth! God who sits in yonder heavens is a man like yourselves[.] That god if you were to see him to day that holds the worlds you would see him like a man in form, like yourselves. . . . I want you to understand God and how he comes to be God. We suppose God was God from Eternity, I will refute that idea . . . It is the first principle to know that we may convers with him and that he once was a man like us, and the Father was once on an earth like us." Joseph declared not only that God was a man who had progressed to become God but that the righteous likewise would "enjoy the same rise exhaltation & glory untill you arive at the station of a God."[23]

Making Christ's Promise to Reign a Political Reality

The name of the council having been thus received by revelation, participants turned their attention to the constitution that would govern the new kingdom wherever they ended up settling. On the second day of council meetings, four prominent members—three of them apostles—were assigned to a committee with the daunting task of drafting a "constitution which should be perfect, and embrace those principles which the constitution of the United States lacked." John Taylor, Willard Richards, Parley P. Pratt, and W. W. Phelps spent several weeks poring over various founding documents as they felt their inadequacies in drafting such an important document.[24]

By April 4 the committee still had not delivered a draft of the constitution to the entire Council. After the committee described their difficulties, Hyrum Smith suggested that the document should be "as concise as possible to embrace all that was necessary for our guidance." As debate about the proposed constitution continued, Joseph Smith provided this guideline: "That it was right always to judge in favor of the innocent, and it was wrong always, to judge in favor of the guilty[.] He wanted to see a constitution that would compel a man to execute justice in favor of the innocent."[25] The brazenness with which Missouri state officials had disregarded the law and individual rights was no doubt on Joseph's mind. When this lawlessness was coupled with President Martin Van Buren's disregard for the Saints' plight, the move toward a declaration of political sovereignty became necessary. With these new instructions, the council resolved to have the committee present their draft constitution on the following day.

Accordingly, on April 5 John Taylor and Willard Richards tepidly gave their report of a draft constitution. Richards read what the committee had thus far composed and asked for more time to complete the draft. Taylor explained that one of the problems they encountered was the "lack of power and correct principles in the various governments on the earth." We do not know what was contained in this initial draft, but the records show that Hyrum Smith and Wilford Woodruff expressed their approval of the course taken thus far by the committee. As the discussion continued, Brigham Young expressed his thoughts on creating a constitution for the kingdom of God. Like the intention to create the New Jerusalem as a holy city, he "thought the law would be written in every mans heart, and there would be that perfection in our lives, nothing further would be needed." While the committee attempted to create a document by examining other forms of government, Young saw all of these governments as imperfect and corrupt. To Young, the Church and the kingdom of God were so distinct from the rest of the world that they could not be compared. Young asserted, "Revelations must govern. The voice of God, shall be the voice of the people. We want to build up the whole church, in all longsuffering." In the ensuing discussion, Joseph Smith shared another aspect he believed should be included in the new constitution: "We have a right to complain of the government untill they redress our wrongs."[26]

After another frustrating week with no progress on the draft constitution, committee member W. W. Phelps addressed the council. He recognized the gravity of the assignment given to the committee, citing the document they were creating as probably "the most important ever undertaken by any committee."²⁷ While he asked for more time, he also proffered a different solution to their impasse, telling the council "that inasmuch as we have a lawgiver appointed of heaven he was anxious that the committee could have his assistance to prepare the document."²⁸ Cornelius Lott immediately echoed his endorsement of bringing the Prophet onto the committee to draft the constitution because "no undertaking seems to go right without his assistance; . . . the shortest way is to have the president come to it first as last."²⁹

Surprisingly, when W. W. Phelps motioned that the Prophet be added to his committee, it was Joseph who objected. Joseph articulated that it was necessary for the committee to first "bring forth all the intelligence they could, and when their productions were presented to him [then] he could correct the errors and fill the interstices where it was lacking."³⁰ Perhaps sensing the surprise of the members of the committee, Joseph opined further on what exactly he thought the government of the kingdom of God should look like. He taught that while they were seeking to build a theocracy in their new home, he believed a "theocracy consisted in our exercising all the intelligence of the council, and bringing forth all the light which dwells in the breast of every man, and then let God approve of the document & receiving the snction of the council it becomes law. Theocracy as he understands it is, for the people to get the voice of God and then acknowledge it, and see it executed."³¹ Again, the pattern of council in Moses 4 provided the model. Within Latter-day Saint doctrine, there was a premortal life council during which Lucifer and Jehovah offered opposing plans. God the Father allowed all to hear both sides of the argument and then, as the head of that council, made a decision.

Joseph used the idea of vox populi vox Dei to show that the people both work for wisdom on their own but must be willing to draw upon prophetic counsel inasmuch as it clarifies, redirects, or corrects their own judgment. This meant the members of the council were to struggle to figure out the proper course of action themselves and then seek prophetic guidance when necessary. Joseph encouraged others to work on their own before he interjected opinion and guidance.

But why, given Joseph's prophetic role, would the committee need to present their best attempt at a constitution of the kingdom of God before he would help them? Joseph explained that if he were to simply receive the revelation for the document, council members might criticize the document, thinking to themselves that they could have produced a better product, or perhaps they might assail individual points. "There has always been some man," Joseph cautioned with an air of long and sad experience, "to put himself forward and say I am the great. . . . I want the council to exert all their wisdom in this thing, and when they see that they cannot get a perfect law themselves, and I can, then, they will see from whence wisdom flows. I know I can get the voice of God on the subject."[32] For Joseph, the council generally and the committee specifically needed to make every effort to create a constitution, and only then would they recognize that the best efforts of men's wisdom pale in comparison to the revelations of God.

Indeed, if the council simply relied on Joseph to tell them what to do, they would not increase their own abilities. Such idealization of human effort in connection with the process of revelation was not foreign to the Saints since they understood Joseph's desire to have them learn the pattern of revelation and then be able to apply it in their own lives. He wanted them to gain secular knowledge along with revealed knowledge. He explained, "I want every man to get knowledge, search the laws of nations and get all the information they can; . . . every man ought to study Geography, Governments and languages, so that he may be able to go forth to any nation and before any multitude with eloquence." In response to Joseph's teachings, W. W. Phelps arose and committed to following the Prophet's instruction, agreeing that, "If after all our labors we should not be able to get what we want we will then call upon our head."[33]

A week later Willard Richards, on behalf of the committee, sheepishly presented the more complete but still unfinished constitution, which included some of the direct teachings Joseph Smith had given in the council as well as the revelation he had received on the name of the council. The draft constitution highlighted key aspects: the supremacy of God the Father; the expansive nature of Christ's role as Savior, Redeemer, and King; the corrupt kingdoms established by human design; the role of the prophet and the fulfillment of prophecy; and the eternality of Christ's eventual reign upon the earth:

> We, the people of the Kingdom of God, knowing that all power emanates from God, that the earth is his possession, and he alone has the right to govern the nations and set in order the kingdoms of this world; that he only has a right to institute laws and establish decrees for the government of the human family; that he is our Father in heaven; and we, his legitimate children, inhabiting his footstool, and that no rule, law, government, dominion or power, unless instituted by him, can be productive of the greatest happiness, prosperity, exaltation and glory of his subjects:— And knowing also that none of the nations, kingdoms or governments of the earth do acknowledge the creator of the Universe as their Priest, Lawgiver, King and Sovereign, neither have they sought unto him for laws by which to govern themselves;—And knowing also, that there is not an original kingdom on the earth that holds the rightful authority from the king of Kings and Lord of Lords, to govern his subjects: but that all the nations have obtained their power, rule and authority by usurpation, rebellion, bloodshed, tyranny and fraud:—
>
> And knowing also, that no government, which has thus originated, has the disposition and power to grant that protection to the persons and rights of man, viz. life, liberty, possession of property, and pursuit of happiness, which was designed by their creator to all men; but that the cruelty, oppression, bondage, slavery, rapine, bloodshed, murder, carnage, desolation, and all the evils that blast the peace,

exaltation, and glory of the universe, exist in consequence
of unrighteous rule, and unlawful dominion, by which the
pure, the patriotic, the noble, the virtuous, the philanthropic,
. . . the righteous and wise servants of God have been persecuted, hunted, whipped, scourged, exiled, massacreed, sawn
asunder, crucified and slain in all ages of the world, under
all earthly authorities, and by every form of government,
from the days of murderous Cain, to the days of the exter-
minating [Lilburn W.] Boggs of Missouri; And that all the
pride, corruption, impurity, intrigue, spiritual wickedness in
high places, party spirit, faction, perplexity and distress of
nations, are the natural results of these illegitimate governments:— And knowing that God hath created all men free
and equal:— And having sought in vain among all the nations
of the earth, to find a government instituted by heaven; an
assylum for the opprest; a protector of the innocent, and a
shield for the defenceless:— an impenetrable Aegis for the
honorable of all nations; uncorrupted by the usurpations of
designing men, the contaminating influence of the love of
Gold, and the lawless intrigues of aspiring demagogues:—
unfettered by unrighteous legislation, and untrammelled by
the mandates of an unjust judiciary; not degraded by a super-
stitious or religious influence: A Realm where liberty spreads
undivided and operates unspent; and where truth and virtue
are the centre and circumference of the nation; are as enduring as the hills of eternity, and as omnipotent as the voice of
Jehovah:— To hasten the accomplishment of his purposes:
To fulfil the predictions of the prophets to establish a pure
government; to lift up an ensign to the nations, and establish
a standard for all people, that the strength, and the power,
and the glory, and the exaltation, and the kingdom, and the
dominion under the whole heavens, may become the kingdom
of our God and of his Christ, as has been predicted by all the
holy prophets since the world began, to be brought to pass on

the earth in the last days; where peace, union, harmony, fellowship, philanthropy, benevolence, virtue, and brotherly love shall reign triumphantly together in the bosom of every subject and where the elements, the light, the air, the water and the land shall be as free as the gift of their creator; where we can rest under the shadow of his wing, and where the supreme law of the land shall be the word of Jehovah:—

We have supplicated the great I am, that he would make known his will unto his servants, concerning this, his last kingdom, and the law, by which his people shall be governed: And the voice of the Lord unto us was,— Verily thus saith the Lord, this is the name by which you shall be called, the kingdom of God and his Laws, with the keys and power thereof, and Judgement in the hands of his servants, Ahman Christ,

Art. 1st. I Am, the Lord thy God, ruleing the armies of heaven above, and among the nations of the earth beneath; I have created all men of one blood; I set up one, and I put down another, and to me alone belongs the right, the power, the majesty, the glory, and the dominion; I alone am King of Kings, and Lord of Lords; I alone am the rightful lawgiver to man; I alone have a right to judge the inhabitants of the earth, which is my footstool; and I will acknowledge no other law, rule, power, Authority or dominion, than that which is instituted by me, the great I Am, And no other government, Kingdom, Dominion, authority, power, rule, or law, shall be acknowledged by my people.

Art. 2nd. I the Lord will do nothing but what I have revealed or shall reveal unto my servants the prophets and I have appointed one man, holding the keys and authority, pertaining to my holy priesthood, to whom I will reveal my laws, my statutes, my ordinances, my Judgements, my will and pleasure concerning my kingdom on the earth.

Art. 3rd. And my Servant and Prophet whom I have called and chosen shall have power to appoint Judges and

officers in my kingdom, And my people shall have the right
to choose or refuse those officers and judges, by common consent: And the judges who shall be approved by my people shall
condemn the guilty, and let the innocent go free! And shall
have power to execute, and shall execute, justice and judgement in righteousness, and punish transgressors throughout
all my kingdom on the earth; and if the judges or officers
transgress, they shall be punished according to my laws.—[34]

As Richards finished reading the draft constitution, fellow committee member John Taylor arose and apologized for the incomplete-
ness of what they had produced. Indeed, the committee felt that
trying to write a constitution for the kingdom of God was "tread-
ing on holy ground." After investigating the laws of other nations,
they concluded that they could not "refer to any constitution of the
world because they are corrupt." Furthermore, in their efforts they
had become convinced, as Joseph had predicted, that "there is no
constitution or law calculated for the universal good of the universal
world but those principles which emanate from God. If they can get
intelligence from God they can write correct principles, if not, they
cannot." Taylor went on to explain that "he was always convinced that
no power can guide us right but the wisdom of God." Because of his
conviction the committee felt they would need a revelation from God
to reveal the "first principles of the Kingdom of God." Taylor compared their first steps in creating the political kingdom of God on
earth to the first steps in the Restoration of the Gospel. "No one,"
Taylor explained, "knew how to baptize or lay on hands untill it was
revealed" through Joseph Smith. If direct revelation from God had
been necessary to bring religious truth to the earth, then the same
must be true for political truth, because "national affairs are equally
as far fallen and degenerate as religious matters."[35]

As discussion of the draft constitution continued, Erastus Snow
offered a mild critique on the phraseology that "God hath created all
men free and equal" because "millions of our fellow men are born in

bondage, they never enjoyed a breath of liberty."[36] This criticism of slavery echoed what Joseph Smith had set forth just a few months previous in his published presidential platform. Indeed, Joseph opened that document by discussing how troubled he was that while the Declaration of Independence declared all men are created equal and endowed with liberty but that "some two or three millions of people are held as slaves for life, because the spirit in them is covered with a darker skin than ours."[37] As the discussion on this point progressed in the council, Joseph reiterated that "all men were in the designs of God created equal, and inasmuch as some had greater capacities than others, it was required of them to possess the greater philanthropy."[38]

Remembering Joseph Smith's counsel to debate matters deeply and openly, Taylor welcomed this and any criticism of the document they had thus far produced, because they wanted to "find all the cracks they can and expose them" before it was given to President Smith. Perhaps himself musing about the preface to the Book of Commandments all those years ago, Joseph Smith told Taylor that "he did not intend to tear the thing to pieces, untill he had got the whole of it."[39]

At this point in the discussion, Brigham Young made a lengthy exposition of his thoughts. In an earlier meeting he had suggested that men should not need a written constitution because they should be guided by what they already knew was right and now he pressed that point. After the council had "done all we were capable to do, we could have the Lord speak and tell us what is right." While he was "willing to be ruled by the means which God will appoint," Brigham did not think a written constitution could stand the test of time. Why? Because when God gave revelation to humankind he did it "a little here and a little there" and he did not know "how much more there is in the bosom of the Almighty. When God sees that his people have enlarged upon what he has given us[,] he will give us more." To illustrate his point through exaggeration, Young asserted that he would "not be stumbled if the prophet should translate the bible forty thousand times over and yet it should be different in some places every time, because when God speaks, he always speaks according to the capacity of the people. . . . We may say we will have a constitution because it is fashionable, but [I] would rather have the revelations to form a constitution from . . . [I] would rather have the pure revelations of Jesus Christ as they now stand, to carry to the nations, than any thing else."[40]

As the debate over the constitution continued, Joseph Smith delivered some key instructions that were to inform their deliberations, especially in relation to what the expectation of the Lord was of those that were believers and participants in his forthcoming kingdom. "There is a distinction between the Church of God and kingdom of God," he began, "The laws of the kingdom are not designed to effect our salvation hereafter. It is an entire, distinct and separate government." Joseph continued to explain that the kingdom of God they intended to create, whether in Texas or in Mexico, would be a political entity. It would protect the members of the Church in their freedom to worship as they chose, but it would also protect those who wanted to worship God and Christ in their own way. "The church is a spiritual matter and a spiritual kingdom, but the kingdom which Daniel saw was not a spiritual kingdom; but was designed to be got up for the safety and salvation of the saints by protecting them in their religious rights and worship."[41]

Joseph Smith envisioned a kingdom that followed the revelations of the prophet with the consent of the people—"a Theodemocracy"— but that kingdom would also "tolerate man in the worship of his God" because the Church was "never designed to govern men in civil matters. The kingdom of God has nothing to do with giving commandments to damn a man spiritually. It only has power to make a man amenable to his fellow man." For Joseph, and for those in the council, the relationship between the Church of Christ and the kingdom of God was a matter of sincere and sustained discussion. As the Latter-day Saints anticipated the Second Coming of Christ, they expected the eventual reign of Jesus on earth. Article 1 in this draft of the constitution makes it clear that the expected outcome of the council's work would not be the rule of law but the rule of God upon the earth, which, for the council, was closely connected to Christ's work in very real ways. While some other Christians expected a rapturous and sudden entrance into the Millennium, the council sought to marry their theological understanding of God's sovereignty with their ability to bring real social and political change to the world they experienced in 1844. Some of the council members' thoughts on the relationship of church and kingdom are visible through an exchange among council members in the spring of 1844. During the 18 April 1844 meetings of the council, Elder Erastus Snow articulated one aspect of the project they were hoping to see materialize:

> The object is to ameliorate the condition of the human family. Get them so that you can preach the gospel to them, and get them to be baptized for the remission of sins; the influence of Gods kingdom is thereby exerted over them. They have been rebuked by this means; they acknowledge the government of Jehovah and submit to its laws, and yield obedience to its officers. He has been led to think that this work is not to be the work of a moment. After the Jews have come to Jerusalem &c then shall the heathen begin to learn of Jehovah, and the principles which have actuated us in the organization of this kingdom. When they have obeyed the first principles of the gospel they rise one step higher and then receive the order of the priesthood and go on from step to step.[42]

In response, Elder George Adams suggested that "the establishment of the Church of God was the stepping stone to the establishment of the kingdom of God and in its organization individuals had been called who were not members of the church, and he considered this a great argument in favor of the kingdom having influence over the nations of the earth."[43]

The end-of-time narrative, on which the Latter-day Saints so heavily focused through the ongoing revelations in the Doctrine and Covenants, could not be divorced from their understanding of the work of the council. The guidance to focus the Saints' work on specific tasks that lent themselves to the gradual building of the kingdom of God was always coupled with a dual purpose: pragmatic and eternal. Such instruction, given during the important meetings held for drafting the constitution of the kingdom, was in accordance with the message of the revelations recorded elsewhere in Restoration scripture (see, for example, Doctrine and Covenants 1:24, 38). Countless times, revelations received by Joseph reminded the Saints that only Christ was at the helm of the Restoration project, though all they received by way of the Church was administered by the chosen earthly head. The Articles and Covenants, established in connection with the foundation of the Church, make clear that the institution operates only by proper authority, delegated by Christ to do the work of the Father, to those who are appointed to administer the rites and privileges of membership in the Church. The model was established to accomplish the work necessary to bring about the Second Coming of Jesus Christ. By extension, the work of God was given a new, expansive scope through the work of the Council of Fifty.

Theodemocracy: A Praxis of Human Toleration and Divine Ascension

Though Joseph taught that the imminent Second Coming of the Savior was one purpose of setting up God's government and kingdom, he had taught several years earlier that when the Lord came again, the wicked or unbelievers "would Not all be Destroyed at the Coming of Christ . . . there will be wi[c]ked during" the Millennium."[44] Thus the work of the council was not only a practical step to provide space for the Saints to thrive but also an extension of the very theology upon which they built their community. Christ's impending earthly reign first needed human conditions to align with the broader purposes and designs of God. Zion was to be both a holy people and a holy place. The depth of the Restoration project spoke to both the practical concerns that would form a people qualified for heavenly help (see

Doctrine and Covenants 42, 45). At the same time, it connected the proper implementation of such pragmatic programs to the eschatological encounter with Jesus Christ. In fostering a protective government structure focused on religious freedom, the council found room for a broad program of social and governmental participation in the work of God. As such, this new government was calculated to protect the rights of Latter-day Saints and those of other faiths in a way that the United States government never had. Reflecting on the failure of the government to protect them from religious persecution, Joseph explained, "In relation to the constitution of the United States, there is but one difficulty, and that is, the constitution provides the things which we want but lacks the power to carry the laws into effect. We want to alter it so as to make it imperative on the officers to enforce the protection of all men in their rights."[45]

Joseph Smith, having long experienced intolerance at the hands of local, state, and federal officials, had deep conviction and passion for religious tolerance. Indeed, Nauvoo had passed an ordinance in 1841 declaring, "Catholics, Presbyterians, Methodists, Baptists, Latter-day Saints, Quakers, Episcopals, Universalists, Unitarians, Mohammedans [Muslims], and all other religious sects and denominations whatever, shall have free toleration, and equal privileges in this city." The law levied punishments for those who sought to disrupt this freedom of worship. Violators would face a considerable fine, and a possible prison term of six months could be the punishment for "any person be guilty of ridiculing, abusing, or otherwise depreciating another, in consequence of his religion, or of disturbing, or interrupting, any religious meeting."[46]

Now with the Saints facing new threats of eradication from their Nauvoo home and contemplating a desperate exodus out of the United States itself into some unknown and unsettled territory as a result of religious intolerance, Joseph Smith would not abide this kind of intolerance in the kingdom of God that Christ wanted them to establish.[47] In his lengthiest recorded discourse to the Council of Fifty, Joseph made a particular point to the men that there were members of the council and there would be members of the planned kingdom of God who were not members of the Church "nor profess any creed or religious sentiment whatever." The kingdom of God Joseph envisioned did not evaluate men on "their religious opinions or notions in any shape or form whatever" and upheld that "we act upon the broad and liberal principal that all men have equal rights, and ought to be respected, and that every man has a privilege in this organization of choosing for himself voluntarily his God, and what he pleases for his religion." Joseph believed that as people investigated the various religious truth claims, they would eventually "embrace the greatest light." At any rate, a compulsion in religious belief defeated the purpose of mortality because "God cannot save or damn a man [except] on the principle that every man acts, chooses and worships for himself."[48]

As Joseph continued this discourse, he raised the grim specter of the carnage associated with religious wars in world history. He declared to the men "the importance of thrusting from us every spirit of bigotry and intollerance toward a mans religious sentiments, that spirit which has drenched the earth with blood." Animated, perhaps, as he thought of the Saints' own suffering at the hands of the intolerant, Joseph made clear his feelings on religious bigotry to council members: "I will appeal to every man in this council beginning at the youngest that when he arrives to the years of Hoary age he will have to say that the principles of inollerance and bigotry never had a place in this kingdom, nor in my breast, and that he is even then ready to die rather than to yield to such things." Compulsion and persecution could not "reclaim the human mind from its ignorance, bigotry and superstition."[49]

Turning from the grand universal principle to a more personal reflection on it, Joseph Smith taught them that he did not choose his friends on the basis of their Church membership or lack thereof. Displaying the guiding aspect of mercy in his nature, Joseph poignantly taught, "We must not despise a man on account of infirmity. We ought to love a man more for his infirmity. . . . If I can know that a man susceptible of good feelings & integrity will stand by his friends, he is my friend." Then, perhaps with a premonition of his own impending death, Joseph added mournfully, "The only thing I am afraid of is that I will not live long enough to enjoy the society of these my friends." For Joseph, friendship was a divine principle, and Jesus Christ expected those relationships to extend beyond those that shared religious beliefs. To prove the point, he said, "When I have used every means in my power to exalt a mans mind, and have taught him righteous principles to no effect [and] he is still inclined in his darkness, yet the same principles of liberty and charity would ever be manifested by me as though he [had] embraced [the Gospel]." "Let us," he implored, "drive from us every species of intollerance."⁵⁰

William Clayton recorded that while Joseph passionately spoke, he had a ruler in his hand that he struck over and over again for effect until finally, near the end of his discourse, the ruler snapped in two. Without missing a beat, Brigham Young grabbed the imagery and declared, "So might every tyrannical government be broken before us."⁵¹

The revelation that W. W. Phelps had initially asked for, that John Taylor had subsequently sought, and that Brigham Young relied solely upon finally came on 25 April 1844 as the council met again to discuss the constitution for the kingdom of God. Joseph spoke the revelation in the voice of the Jesus Christ: "Verily thus saith the Lord, ye are my constitution and I am your God, and ye are my spokesmen. From henceforth do as I shall command you. Saith the Lord." The brief revelation was immediately and unanimously accepted as the government of the kingdom of God.⁵²

Brigham Young's sentiment that the new kingdom should be governed by simple obedience to the continuing revelations of God was validated in this second revelation to Joseph Smith received in the Council of Fifty. The lack of a written constitution necessitated that the group would have to continually rely on ongoing prophetic utterance and revelation, trusting that Jesus Christ would lead his Church and his kingdom "here a little and there a little" (2 Nephi 28:30) as circumstances dictated and Brigham had earlier opined.

Conclusion

Little did Brigham Young know that just two months later Joseph Smith would be dead, martyred before he could enjoy the society of his friends in the hoped-for kingdom of God. It fell to Brigham to carry out the imperatives of these two revelations from God and the teachings of Joseph Smith regarding the Saints' removal to a new land. When the grieving council members met again in early 1845, embittered by yet another failure of the United States and its boasted democracy in meting out retribution to the murderers of Joseph and Hyrum Smith, they took up the same measures that Joseph had been working on at the time of his death. As they prepared for an exploratory expedition, Brigham Young commented, "We know this was one of Josephs measures and my feelings are, if we cannot have the priviledge of carrying out Josephs measures I would rather lie down and have my head cut off at once. . . . While Joseph was living it seems as though he was hurried by the Lord all the time, and especially for the last year. It seemed he laid out work for this church which would last them twenty years to carry out. I used to wonder why it was that he used to be hurried so, not supposing he was going to die, but now I understand the reason."[53]

The task of putting into practice the teachings and revelations of Joseph Smith fell upon Brigham Young, and despite the difficulties that accompanied the monumental task, he always maintained Joseph's desires as his guiding star. He told the men of the council, "To carry out Josephs measures is sweeter to me than honey."[54] Although Brigham had not known it when Joseph was teaching the council, he would be the one waiting on the line-by-line revelation of the Lord as the Saints left the United States, moving to northern Mexico and into an unknown future.

Brigham Young's succession to the presidency solidified the practice that Latter-day Saints would receive both spiritual and temporal guidance from their prophet in ways that had been at least intended, if not modeled, in the Council of Fifty's plan to build the kingdom of God on earth. The Saints continued to look forward to a time when the long-prophesied city of Zion would be built and they would receive the associated blessings. While the immediate imperative of building the City of Zion and establishing a functioning theodemocracy ebbed with the tides of the next several decades, the final revelations and teachings of Joseph Smith left an indelible imprint on the men who formed the Council. The Lord's kingdom would be both a people and a place. Over the next three decades of his life, Brigham would fervently attempt put into practice what he believed were the intentions and teachings that Joseph had received from the Lord Jesus Christ himself.

Notes

1. Council of Fifty, "Record," 18 April 1844, Matthew J. Grow, Ronald K. Esplin, Mark Ashurst-McGee, Gerrit J. Dirkmaat, and Jeffrey D. Mahas, eds., *Council of Fifty, Minutes, March 1844–January 1846*, vol. 1 of the Administrative Records series of *The Joseph Smith Papers*, ed. Ronald K. Esplin, Matthew J. Grow, and Matthew C. Godfrey (Salt Lake City: Church Historian's Press, 2016), 124; hereafter cited as *JSP*, CFM.

2. Similar language connecting the temporary kingdom and the eternal kingdom occurs in Revelation 3:1, "Behold, I come quickly: hold that fast which thou hast, that no man take thy crown."

3. Antebellum politicians' avowal of state versus federal rights was often applied conveniently, depending on the issue at hand. As historian Matthew Karp has recently reiterated in his work, Southern slave-holding politicians like Calhoun and those that defended slavery in the Democratic Party generally invoked state's rights when it suited them but were really nationalists that often championed federal power "when the question involved the national government's direct relationship to slavery." Matthew Karp, *This Vast Southern Empire* (Cambridge: Harvard University Press, 2016), 5. Then men like Calhoun "eagerly embraced the proslavery clout of the federal government." Joseph Smith recognized this hypocrisy and responded to Calhoun's rejection by mockingly restating Calhoun's avowed

position vis-à-vis the Latter-day Saints, "[a state] can exile you at pleasure, mob you with impunity; confiscate your lands and property; have the legislature sanction it: yea, even murder you, as an edict of an Emperor, and it does no wrong, for the noble senator of South Carolina, says the power of the federal government is so limited and specific that is has no jurisdiction of the case. Joseph Smith to John C. Calhoun, 2 January 1844, Joseph Smith Collection, MS 155, box 2, folder 7, 4, Church History Library, The Church of Jesus Christ of Latter-day Saints, Salt Lake City, Utah; hereafter cited as CHL.

4.   Patrick Q. Mason, *The Mormon Menace: Violence and Anti-Mormonism in the Postbellum South* (Oxford: Oxford University Press, 2011), 7.

5.   Joseph Smith to John C. Calhoun, 4 November 1843, Joseph Smith Collection, MS 155, box 2, folder 6, 34, CHL.

6.   Senator Lewis Cass to General Joseph Smith, 9 December 1843, Joseph Smith Collection, MS 155, box 3, folder 4, 68–69, CHL.

7.   "Remarks on the Above," *Warsaw Message* (IL), 17 January 1844.

8.   Joseph Smith, Journal, 20 February 1844, Joseph Smith Collection, MS 155, box 1, folder 7, 276, CHL.

9.   Joseph's First Vision experience made clear for the Saints by 1844 that theirs was a heretical Christian movement when measured against the creedal definition of Jesus the Son and God the Father. The physical nature of Jesus mirrored the physical nature of the Father, and both natures were reflected in the physicality of human creation.

10. Council of Fifty, "Record," 18 April 1844, in *JSP*, CFM:111.

11. Council of Fifty, "Record," 11 March 1844, in *JSP*, CFM:40. It is important to note that in 1844 the entire area of Mexico encompassing modern-day Nevada, Utah, Colorado, and California was all designated "California" or "Upper California."

12. Council of Fifty, "Record," 11 March 1844, in *JSP*, CFM:42.

13. Council of Fifty, "Record," 10 March 1844, in *JSP*, CFM:39.

14. Council of Fifty, "Record," 10 March 1844, in *JSP*, CFM:39.

15. Council of Fifty, "Record," 11 April 1844, in *JSP*, CFM:79.

16. Council of Fifty, "Record," 11 March 1844, in *JSP*, CFM:43.

17. Council of Fifty, "Record," 11 March 1844, in *JSP*, CFM:42.

18. Council of Fifty, "Record," 10 March 1844, in *JSP*, CFM:44; and Minutes of Discussion, Council of Fifty, Papers, 1845–1883, CHL, as quoted therein.

19. Council of Fifty, "Record," 14 March 1844, in *JSP*, CFM:48.

20. Council of Fifty, "Record," 5 April 1844, in *JSP*, CFM:81.

21. Brigham Young, Journal, 4 February 1845, CFR 1234 1, CHL; JSP, CFM:20.

22. William P. McIntire, Notebook, CHL. There is no date for this entry, but context suggests it is 9 March 1841. Joseph had taught that Ahman was "the name of God in pure Language" in 1832. "Sample of Pure Language, between circa 4 and circa 20 March 1832," p. 144, The Joseph Smith Papers, https://josephsmithpapers.org/paper-summary/sample-of-pure-language-between-circa-4-and-circa-20-march-1832/1.

23. "Discourse, 7 April 1844, as Reported by Wilford Woodruff," p. [135], The Joseph Smith Papers, https://josephsmithpapers.org/paper-summary/discourse-7-april-1844-as-reported-by-wilford-woodruff/3.

24. Council of Fifty, "Record," 11 March 1844, in *JSP*, CFM:54.

25. Council of Fifty, "Record," 4 April 1844, in *JSP*, CFM:78–79.

26. Council of Fifty, "Record," 5 April 1844, in *JSP*, CFM:80–82, 84.

27. Council of Fifty, "Record," 11 April 1844, in *JSP*, CFM:91.

28. Council of Fifty, "Record," 11 April 1844, in *JSP*, CFM:91.

29. Council of Fifty, "Record," 11 April 1844, in *JSP*, CFM:91. Phelps possibly had in memory another time that a committee similarly struggled on a vastly important document. Just a year after the Church was founded, preparations were well underway to publish many of Joseph Smith's revelations in the Book of Commandments. Phelps was the printer heading up the effort, and William E. McLellin, Sidney Rigdon, and Oliver Cowdery had been appointed to write the preface of the sacred book. According to McLellin, when they "made their report" to a November 1831 Church conference, the assembled members "picked it all to pieces. The Conference then requested Joseph to enquire of the Lord about it, and he said that he would if the people would bow in prayer with him. This they did and Joseph prayed." Following the prayer, "Joseph dictated by the Spirit the preface found in the Book of Doctrine and Covenants" there in the same room with the conference attendees. In a rare broadly public display of the

reception of a revelation, Joseph Smith would "deliver a few sentences and Sydney would write them down, then read them aloud, and if correct, then Joseph would proceed and deliver more, and by this process the preface was given." Letter from W. H. Kelley, *The Saints' Herald*, 1 March 1882. Though the Book of Commandments' publication was stopped by violent mob attacks in 1833 and the pages strewn in the streets of Independence, the revelation Joseph Smith received as the preface to the book remained the first section of the subsequently published Doctrine and Covenants.

30. Council of Fifty, "Record," 11 April 1844, in *JSP*, CFM:91.

31. Council of Fifty, "Record," 11 April 1844, in *JSP*, CFM:91–92.

32. Council of Fifty, "Record," 11 April 1844, in *JSP*, CFM:92.

33. Council of Fifty, "Record," 11 April 1844, in *JSP*, CFM:93–94.

34. Council of Fifty, "Record," 18 April 1844, in *JSP*, CFM:110–14. The draft attempted to make sense of the future kingdom by seeing the component parts pulled together across vast expanses of time and space. For instance, the Constitution compared "the murderous Cain" to Gov. Lilburn W. Boggs, thus quickly closing the gap of a few thousand years. The draft constitution deliberately attempted to connect past and present dispensations of time.

35. Council of Fifty, "Record," 18 April 1844, in *JSP*, CFM:114.

36. Council of Fifty, "Record," 18 April 1844, in *JSP*, CFM:117.

37. *General Smith's Views of the Powers and Policy of the Government of the United State* (Nauvoo: Printed by John Taylor, 1844), CHL.

38. Council of Fifty, "Record," 18 April 1844, in *JSP*, CFM:118.

39. Council of Fifty, "Record," 18 April 1844, in *JSP*, CFM:118–19.

40. Council of Fifty, "Record," 18 April 1844, in *JSP*, CFM:120.

41. Council of Fifty, "Record," 18 April 1844, in *JSP*, CFM:128.

42. Council of Fifty, "Record," 18 April 1844, in *JSP*, CFM:124.

43. Council of Fifty, "Record," 18 April 1844, in *JSP*, CFM:125.

44. Discourse, 16 March 1841, Brent M. Rogers, Mason K. Allred, Gerrit J. Dirkmaat, and Brett D. Dowdle, eds., *Documents Volume 8: February–November 1841*, vol. 8 of the Documents series of *The Joseph Smith Papers*, ed. Ronald K. Esplin, Matthew J. Grow, Matthew C. Godfrey, and R. Eric Smith (Salt Lake City: Church Historian's Press, 2019), 75.

45. Council of Fifty, "Record," 18 April 1844, in *JSP*, CFM:128.

46. Minutes, 1 March 1841, in *JSP*, D8:52.

47. The sentiment against the Latter-day Saints was often so virulent that even after the majority of the Saints departed Nauvoo, one newspaper made clear that they wanted the nation completed cleansed from the Latter-day Saint stain: "We want to see a clean sweep made of Mormons and all their hangers on. Let every vestige and trace of the accursed system that has afflicted our county for years be eradicated; and not one living monument left to bring it again to remembrance." "All Mormons Must Leave," *The Janesville Gazette*, 24 January 1848.

48. Council of Fifty, "Record," 11 April 1844, in *JSP*, CFM:97.

49. Council of Fifty, "Record," 11 April 1844, in *JSP*, CFM:99–100.

50. Council of Fifty, "Record," 11 April 1844, in *JSP*, CFM:99–100.

51. Council of Fifty, "Record," 11 April 1844, in *JSP*, CFM:100.

52. Council of Fifty, "Record," 15 April 1844, in *JSP*, CFM:137.

53. Council of Fifty, "Record," 1 March 1845, in *JSP*, CFM:257.

54. Council of Fifty, "Record," 1 March 1845, in *JSP*, CFM:257.

12

Joseph Smith, Gethsemane, and the Crucifixion of Jesus Christ

John Hilton III

The Savior's Atonement is central to the theology of The Church of Jesus Christ of Latter-day Saints. The Prophet Joseph Smith wrote, "We believe that through the atonement of Christ all mankind may be saved by obedience to the laws and ordinances of the Gospel."[1] On another occasion, he revealed that those inheriting the celestial kingdom are "made perfect through Jesus the mediator of the new covenant, who wrought out this perfect atonement through the shedding of his own blood" (Doctrine and Covenants 76:69).

The specific phrase "perfect atonement through the shedding of his own blood" is unique to this revelation and perhaps ambiguous in its reference to a specific location or act in the Savior's atoning sacrifice. While some members of The Church of Jesus Christ of Latter-day Saints (herein referred to as the Church) might immediately locate such an event in Gethsemane, others would place it on the cross—and some might suggest both.

Curious to see which aspect of Christ's Atonement his students would emphasize, a BYU professor asked his students this question: "Where would you say the Atonement mostly took place? A. In the Garden of Gethsemane. B. On the Cross at Calvary." Approximately 750 students responded to this survey; 88 percent answered "In the Garden of Gethsemane," and 12 percent indicated "On the Cross at Calvary."[2] While certainly not a scientific study, these data suggest that many members of the Church believe Gethsemane is the most important location in the Savior's atoning sacrifice.

Perhaps this fact is not surprising given the powerful prose Elder James E. Talmage wrote regarding Gethsemane in *Jesus the Christ*[3] or Elder Bruce R. McConkie's memorable last conference talk, "The Purifying Power of Gethsemane."[4] While they both spoke of the importance of Christ's Crucifixion, their words regarding Gethsemane were particularly striking. The lack of Crucifixion imagery in chapels may also contribute to an emphasis on Gethsemane.[5] An additional reason for a focus on Gethsemane is that three prominent Church leaders—Joseph Fielding Smith, Marion G. Romney, and Bruce R. McConkie—occasionally gave preeminence to Gethsemane. For example, in a general conference talk delivered in 1953, Romney (then a member of the Quorum of the Twelve) said, "Jesus then went into the Garden of Gethsemane. There he suffered most. He suffered greatly on the cross, of course, but other men had died by crucifixion; in fact, a man hung on either side of him as he died on the cross."[6]

Such teachings were taken up in curriculum materials or publications such as the noncanonical but influential *Encyclopedia of Mormonism*, which states, "For Latter-day Saints, Gethsemane was the scene of Jesus' greatest agony, even surpassing that which he suffered on the cross."[7] Several scholars have noticed the Latter-day Saint emphasis on Gethsemane. Protestant theologian and scholar Douglas J. Davies argues that Church leaders have emphasized Gethsemane "to parallel and perhaps even to predominate over the crucifixion of Calvary as the prime scene of the act of atonement."[8] Davies writes elsewhere that "Mormonism *relocates* the centre of gravity of Christ's passion in Gethsemane rather than upon the cross and Calvary."[9] John G. Turner, another Protestant scholar of the Church, explains that for Latter-day Saints "the principal scene of Christ's suffering and, thus, his atonement, was at Gethsemane rather than on the cross."[10] These statements indicate that non–Latter-day Saint scholars see Gethsemane as having a distinctive theological place in our tradition.

Latter-day Saint scholars have made similar observations. For example, Robert Millet writes, "Because we had come to know, through the Book of Mormon and Doctrine and Covenants, concerning the purposes for the Master's pains in the Garden, we seem to have begun to place a greater stress upon Gethsemane than upon the cross."[11] Where does this greater stress on Gethsemane come from? The Bible? Restoration scripture? The collective voice of modern prophets?

While previous studies have clarified what the Bible, the Book of Mormon, and Church leaders after Joseph Smith have taught regarding Gethsemane and the Crucifixion,[12] to date there has been no specific examination of Joseph's revelations and teachings on Gethsemane and Calvary. The purpose of this study is to identify what the Prophet taught and revealed about these locations and whether his teachings focus on the soteriological value of one more than another.

After briefly reviewing previous studies regarding what the scriptures and Church leaders after Joseph Smith have taught regarding Gethsemane and Calvary, I will survey three sources from Joseph Smith's teachings and revelations: first, his revelations as given in the Doctrine and Covenants; second, inspired adjustments he made in his Bible translation; and third, his writings and sermons.

Teachings from the Bible, the Book of Mormon, and Church Leaders[13]

The New Testament emphasizes Calvary significantly more than Gethsemane. While the Synoptic Gospels provide a narrative account of Christ's prayers in Gethsemane, they make no explicit mention of any salvific importance related to this event, and John does not even mention Christ's suffering in Gethsemane. In contrast, the New Testament includes at least twenty-one passages that connect Christ's death with our salvation.[14] For example, Paul taught that Christ "died for us, that . . . we should live together with him" (1 Thessalonians 5:10).

The Book of Mormon likewise emphasizes the importance of the Crucifixion. Only one passage, Mosiah 3:7, makes a clear textual connection between our salvation and Gethsemane with its discussion of Christ bleeding from every pore because of his anguish for our sins. In contrast, eighteen Book of Mormon passages specifically describe the salvific power of the death of Christ.[15] For example, Nephi saw in vision Christ "lifted up upon the cross and *slain for the sins of the world*" (1 Nephi 11:33; emphasis added throughout). Abinadi proclaimed, "These are they whose sins he has borne; *these are they for whom he has died, to redeem them from their transgressions*" (Mosiah 15:12). Samuel the Lamanite declared, "[Christ] surely *must die, that salvation* may come; . . . this *death . . . redeemeth all mankind*" (Helaman 14:15–16). The Savior himself said at the temple in Bountiful, "Come forth . . . that ye may know that I . . . have been *slain for the sins of the world*" (3 Nephi 11:14).

Research has shown that modern Church leaders have mirrored this scriptural emphasis on Christ's Crucifixion: across a corpus of talks in the *Journal of Discourses* and published general conference reports from 1897 to 2018, for each reference by Church leaders to Christ suffering for our sins in Gethsemane, more than five speak of him dying for our sins.[16]

For example, in 1860 President Brigham Young taught, "Jesus was appointed, from the beginning, to die for our redemption, and he suffered an excruciating death on the cross."[17] President John Taylor taught that Christ was "crucified . . . to open up the way of life and salvation, that man might attain to exaltation,"[18] and President Wilford Woodruff said that the "Lord Jesus Christ . . . died as a ransom for the sins of the world."[19]

Recent Church leaders have continued this emphasis. President Gordon B. Hinckley stated that through "the offering of His life on Calvary's Hill, [Christ] expiated the sins of mankind, relieving us from the burden of sin if we will forsake evil and follow Him."[20] President Thomas S. Monson said that Jesus "died upon the cross to redeem all mankind."[21] President Russell M. Nelson exhorted, "Remember the Savior upon the cross suffering from the sins of the world."[22] Such quotations indicate a consistent focus by Church leaders on the atoning efficacy of Christ's death.

None of the foregoing is intended to diminish the importance of the Savior's salvific suffering in Gethsemane. Christ's suffering during his Crucifixion and in Gethsemane should not be held in competition. Rather, I am simply identifying emphases within the scriptures and the teachings of modern Church leaders. In the scriptures, as well as from Brigham Young to the present, leaders have more frequently placed emphasis on Christ's death than on Gethsemane when discussing our redemption from sin. I now turn to the topic of this study, which is to consider what Joseph Smith taught about these important subjects.

Methodology

As stated previously, to identify what Smith taught and revealed about Gethsemane and Christ's Crucifixion, I examined three corpora: (1) the revelations received by Smith and canonized in the Doctrine and Covenants, (2) the adjustments he made in his inspired translation of the Bible, and (3) Smith's teachings and writings.

In terms of the methodology used to identify relevant passages in the Doctrine and Covenants, I performed an electronic search looking specifically for words related to Christ's sufferings in Gethsemane as well as his death.[23] In addition to searching for explicit words such as *Gethsemane* or *Calvary*, I also searched related words such as *bleed* or *death*.[24] Some passages were ambiguous in their meaning. For example, in Doctrine and Covenants 38:4, Christ speaks of "the virtue of the blood which I have spilt." This could allude to suffering in Gethsemane that caused Christ to "bleed at every pore" (Doctrine and Covenants 19:18; see Mosiah 3:7; Luke 22:44) or to "the blood of his cross" (Colossians 1:20; see John 19:34; Hebrews 13:11–12; Alma 34:11–13; 3 Nephi 9:19). Although the scriptures indicate that the shedding of blood is a reference to death,[25] in order to avoid any bias toward the Crucifixion, I excluded passages about blood from this study if they were not explicit regarding location.[26]

To identify passages from the Joseph Smith Translation that might have bearing on Gethsemane or Calvary, I analyzed the New Testament verses identified in previous research as specifically relating to the salvific power of Gethsemane and the cross.[27] In addition, I examined the Joseph Smith Translation of narrative passages regarding the events of Gethsemane and Calvary.

To identify additional teachings from Joseph Smith regarding Gethsemane and Christ's Crucifixion I searched the Joseph Smith Papers website for a wide variety of relevant terms.[28] Statements that were clearly from Joseph Smith, authorized scribes, and unsigned editorials for publications of which Joseph Smith was the editor were all included in this study.[29]

The Doctrine and Covenants[30]

Revelations about Gethsemane

A revelation likely dictated in the summer of 1829 provides the clearest canonized description of Christ suffering for our sins in Gethsemane. In this revelation the Savior says, "I, God, have suffered these things for all, that they might not suffer if they would repent; but if they would not repent they must suffer even as I; which suffering caused myself, even God, the greatest of all, to tremble because of pain, and to bleed at every pore, and to suffer both body and spirit—and would that I might not drink the bitter cup, and shrink" (Doctrine and Covenants 19:16–18).

While this revelation does not use the word *Gethsemane*, the statement "bleed at every pore" echoes Luke 22:44 ("his sweat was as it were great drops of blood falling down to the ground"), and the statement "would that I might not drink the bitter cup" alludes to Matthew 26:39 ("if it be possible, let this cup pass from me"). These New Testament connections likely indicate that the revelation is connected to Christ's suffering in Gethsemane.[31] Although Joseph Smith did not refer to these verses in his later teachings or writings, one or more verses from Doctrine and Covenants 19:16–18 have been quoted in general conference more than 120 times, illustrating their significant impact.[32] Aside from Doctrine and Covenants 19:16–18, there are no other explicit references to Gethsemane in the Doctrine and Covenants, perhaps a surprising finding given the emphasis that many Church members place on Gethsemane.

Revelations about the Crucifixion

At least fifteen revelations given to Joseph Smith in the Doctrine and Covenants refer to Christ's death. In one instance, Joseph Smith received a revelation that mentions those who "denied the Only Begotten Son of the Father, having crucified him unto themselves" (Doctrine and Covenants 76:35). Four instances record the voice of Jesus Christ describing himself in a manner connected to his death, but not explicitly stating that he atoned for our sins in his Crucifixion. For example, on one occasion he said, "Behold the wounds which pierced my side, and also the prints of the nails in my hands and feet" (Doctrine and Covenants 6:37; see 45:4, 52). Christ's invitation to behold his wounds may remind us that he is our atoning Savior. On another occasion Jesus Christ appeared in a vision to Joseph Smith and Oliver Cowdery and identified himself, saying, "I am the first and the last; I am he who liveth, I am he who was slain; I am your advocate with the Father" (Doctrine and Covenants 110:4). Although this instance does not provide a direct statement about Christ atoning for our sins on the cross, it does provide a powerful connection between Christ's death and his role as our Savior and advocate.

Eight revelations received by Joseph Smith, which were later canonized in the Doctrine and Covenants, explicitly connect the death
of Jesus Christ with salvation from sin:

- "The Lord your Redeemer *suffered death in the flesh*;
  wherefore he suffered the pain of all men, *that all men
  might repent* and come unto him" (18:11).
- "He was *crucified, died*, and rose again the third day . . .
  that as many as would believe and be baptized in his holy
  name, and endure in faith to the end, *should be saved*"
  (20:23, 25).
- "Jesus was *crucified . . . for the sins of the world*, yea, for the
  remission of sins" (21:9).
- "I am Jesus Christ, the Son of God, who was *crucified for
  the sins of the world*" (35:2).
- "Jesus Christ . . . was *crucified for the sins of the world*"
  (46:13).
- "I, the Lord . . . was *crucified for the sins of the world*" (53:2).
- "Thus saith the Lord, . . . even he who was *crucified for the
  sins of the world*" (54:1).
- "Jesus [came] to be *crucified for the world, and to bear the
  sins of the world*" (76:41).

In addition, two revelations to Joseph Smith in the Doctrine and
Covenants focus on the connection between the death of Christ and
our resurrection, or being brought to Christ:

- "He hath risen again *from the dead*, that he might *bring
  all men unto him*, on conditions of repentance" (18:12).
- "For all the rest shall be *brought forth by the resurrection*
  of the dead, *through the* triumph and glory of the *Lamb,
  who was slain*" (76:39).

The revelations received by the Prophet Joseph Smith and published in the Doctrine and Covenants clearly emphasize the atoning
sacrifice of Jesus Christ. Only one passage describes his suffering in

the Garden of Gethsemane and at least fifteen passages discuss his death on the cross of Calvary.

The Joseph Smith Translation

The Garden of Gethsemane

The Joseph Smith Translation (JST) makes two interesting changes with respect to Christ's sufferings in Gethsemane, although neither impacts its saving significance. KJV Mark 14:33–34 states that Christ "taketh with him Peter and James and John, and began to be sore amazed, and to be very heavy; and saith unto them, My soul is exceeding sorrowful unto death: tarry ye here, and watch." The parallel Joseph Smith Translation states, "*The disciples* began to be sore amazed, and to be very heavy, *and to complain in their hearts, wondering if this be the Messiah. And Jesus knowing their hearts, said* to his disciples, Sit ye here, while I shall pray. And he taketh with him, Peter, and James, and John, *and rebuked them*, and said unto them, my soul is exceeding sorrowful, even unto death; tarry ye here and watch" (JST Mark 14:36–38). Thus, while in both versions Christ states that his soul is "exceeding sorrowful," the JST alters the phrases "sore amazed" and "very heavy" to describe the disciples. This change takes a Markan passage emphasizing Christ's mortality and shifts it to a high Christology passage in the JST by moving the human feelings of amazement and heaviness from Christ to his disciples.[33]

The other Gethsemane passage with a significant JST revision is Luke 22:44.[34] The KJV declares, "Being in an agony he prayed more earnestly: and his sweat was as it were great drops of blood falling down to the ground." The JST changes this slightly to be "*he* sweat as it were great drops of blood," perhaps shifting the emphasis from sweat to blood. Robert J. Matthews commented on this JST revision as follows: "This change tends to place the emphasis on the blood as such, instead of on the sweat that was 'as blood.'

In one instance sweat is the subject; in the other, it is the action brought about by the Savior's agony."[35] Even with the Joseph Smith Translation, the phrase "as it were" leaves it unclear whether Christ literally bled; however, restoration scripture and latter-day prophets have clarified this issue (for example, Doctrine and Covenants 19:16–18, as described above). These two JST revisions to Christ's recorded experience in Gethsemane are valuable but do not significantly influence our understanding of the atoning power of Gethsemane.

The Crucifixion

Within the narratives of Christ's Crucifixion, the JST revisions do not alter our view of Calvary's soteriological significance. In KJV Matthew 27:44, both thieves mock the Savior; however, in JST Matthew 27:47–48 only one thief does so, with the other crying to Jesus to be saved—similar to what takes place in Luke 23:42–43.[36] This request suggests that the thief believes not only that Christ will return as king but also that his Crucifixion has saving power.

Another interesting revision occurs regarding Christ's statement "Father, forgive them; for they know not what they do" (Luke 23:34).[37] JST Luke 23:35 adds a clarifying phrase—"meaning the soldiers who crucified him"—to make it clear who was the object of Christ's forgiveness, as well as the fact that they were being forgiven for the act of crucifying him.

A third revision of note occurs in the final statement Christ makes in Matthew's account. In the KJV, as Christ "yielded up the ghost," he "cried again with a loud voice" (Matthew 27:50), but no mention is made of what he said. The Joseph Smith Translation adds an additional statement made in the loud voice, stating, "Jesus, when he had cried again with a loud voice, *saying, Father it is finished, thy will is done,* yielded up the ghost" (JST Matthew 27:50).[38] The phrase "thy will is done," if connected to the Savior's cry in Gethsemane—"O my

Father, if this cup may not pass away from me, except I drink it, *thy will be done*" (Matthew 26:42)—could indicate that at least part of the cup the Savior referred to in Gethsemane was what would occur on the cross.

Throughout the remaining New Testament JST revisions, only minor changes are made to the references regarding Christ's Crucifixion, none of which have theological relevance to the event.[39] The most significant JST changes regarding Christ's Crucifixion occur not in the New Testament but in Joseph's translation of Genesis 1–8, later canonized in the Pearl of Great Price. In Moses 7:45, "[Enoch] cried unto the Lord, saying: . . . When shall *the blood of the Righteous be shed*, that all they that mourn *may be sanctified and have eternal life*?" In response to this question, the Lord showed Enoch "the day of the coming of the Son of Man, even in the flesh; and his soul rejoiced, saying: *The Righteous is lifted up*, and *the Lamb is slain*" (Moses 7:47). A few verses later, the Lord qualifies the phrases "the Righteous," "the Lamb," and "lifted up," showing to Enoch "the Son of Man *lifted up on the cross*, after the manner of men" (Moses 7:55). This removes any ambiguity as to the meaning of the phrases. These verses make it clear that the phrase "the blood of the Righteous be shed" equates with Christ's being "lifted up on the cross." In other words, Christ's Crucifixion is the answer to Enoch's earlier question "When shall the blood of the Righteous be shed, that all they that mourn may be sanctified and have eternal life?"

An additional (although not explicit) reference to the Crucifixion occurs in Moses 5:5, 7, in which Adam and Eve were commanded to "offer the firstlings of their flocks . . . [in] similitude of the *sacrifice of the Only Begotten of the Father*." The death of the animal typifies the death of Jesus Christ, the firstling of the Father's "flock" of children. As will be demonstrated later in this paper, Joseph Smith clearly viewed these earlier animal sacrifices as foreshadowings of Christ's death.

The Teachings and Writings of Joseph Smith

References to Gethsemane

Aside from the Doctrine and Covenants and Joseph Smith Translation, Joseph Smith did not make any specific references to Christ's suffering for our sins in the Garden of Gethsemane.[40] I have not been able to identify a time Joseph Smith used the word *Gethsemane*,[41] but he did use *garden* in reference to Gethsemane on one occasion. In a sermon given on 27 August 1843, Joseph Smith used Christ in Gethsemane as an example of not setting limits on our willingness to obey God's commandments. Smith said we should view "the son of God as saying it behooveth me to fulfil all righteousness also in the garden saying if it be possible let this cup pass from me. Nevertheless thy will be done."[42]

References to Christ's Crucifixion

Utilizing the methodology previously described, I located thirty-four statements by Joseph Smith regarding the Crucifixion of Jesus Christ.[43] In two instances, the word *crucified* was used as an adjective to describe the Savior when Joseph Smith said, "Preach Christ and him crucified," echoing the words of 1 Corinthians 2:2. For example, Joseph Smith once said, "Go in all meekness in sobriety and preach Jesus Christ & him crucified not to contend with others on the account of their faith or systems of religion but pursue a steady course."[44] On five occasions, Joseph Smith spoke of Christ's Crucifixion briefly or in passing. For example, on one occasion he paraphrased Acts 2:37 and 3:17, saying, "Several days after the people asked what shall we do, Peter says, I would ye had done it ignorantly speaking of crucifying the Lord."[45]

Five passages could not easily be categorized but were significant nevertheless. For example, Joseph Smith used Christ's Crucifixion to instruct the members of the Quorum of the Twelve in a letter written 4 August 1835. He wrote, "Remember that Christ was crucified, and you are sent out to be special witnesses of this thing."[46]

Another interesting reference occurs in the minutes of an 1842 Relief Society meeting when Joseph Smith talked about Christ's example of love while on the cross: "Nothing is so much calculated to lead people to forsake sin as to take them by the hand and watch over them with tenderness. . . . The nearer we get to our heavenly Father, the more are we disposed to look with compassion on perishing souls."[47] The minutes next record that Joseph Smith "then referred [those present] to the conduct of the Savior when he was taken and crucified."[48]

On 11 June 1843 Joseph Smith gave a sermon in which he expounded on "the sayings of Jesus (when on the cross) to the thief, saying this day shalt thou be with me in Paradise."[49] Joseph Smith, in discussing the meaning of the word *paradise*, said, "There is nothing in the original word in Greek from which this was taken, that signifies paradise, but it was this day thou shalt be *with me* in the world of Spirits, then *I* will teach you all about it, and answer your inquiries."[50] It is interesting to note that while Joseph Smith makes it clear that the penitent thief will not automatically be saved, he does rephrase the Savior's words to indicate that the Savior would personally attend to the thief in the spirit world. Such a gracious act, in the midst of the pain Christ was experiencing on the cross creates a powerful lesson of extending love and mercy to others even when we ourselves are hurting.

In addition to the previous quotations, two specific themes deserve discussion—the wickedness of those who crucified Christ and the fact that Christ was crucified for the sins of the world. There are also two specific statements regarding the shedding of blood and the fundamental principles of our religion that merit special attention. The following sections address those themes and statements.

The wickedness of those who crucified Christ

The most common theme surrounding Joseph Smith's discussion of Christ's Crucifixion was the wickedness of those who crucified Christ. There are eleven passages with this theme, most commonly in the context of how some people in Joseph Smith's day had the same spirit of hostility as Christ's persecutors had in his day. While not theologically relevant in terms of Christ's Atonement, it is nevertheless interesting to see how Joseph and early Saints used the term *crucifixion*. For example, in 1841 Joseph related an experience when "a number of men commenced abusing me in every way possible. They spit upon me, pointed their fingers at me saying 'Prophesy, prophesy' and thus did they follow the example of those who crucified our Savior not knowing what they did."[51] In 1844 he said that people in his day were as corrupt as those who crucified Christ and that if Christ "were here today and should preach the same doctrine he did then, why they would crucify him."[52] Similarly, he said later in the same year, "When a man begins to be an enemy, he hunts me. They seek to kill me; they thirst for my blood; they never cease. He has the same spirit that they had who crucified the Lord of Life: the same spirit that sins against the Holy Ghost."[53] While perhaps not theologically significant, they may indicate the personal connection Joseph felt with Christ.

The Crucifixion for the sins of the world

A key principle found in nine passages from Joseph Smith is that Jesus Christ was crucified for the sins of the world. One significant example of this statement comes as Joseph records the words of Jesus Christ in his 1832 account of the First Vision. Joseph wrote, "The Lord opened the heavens upon me and I saw the Lord. And he spake unto me, saying, 'Joseph, my son, thy sins are forgiven thee. Go thy way, walk in my statutes, and keep my commandments. Behold, I am the Lord of glory. I was crucified for the world, that all those who believe on my name may have eternal life.'"[54] Thus in his earliest written account of the First Vision, Joseph Smith shared the important detail that Christ introduced himself as one who offers redemption because of his Crucifixion. This is consistent with other introductions of the Savior in the Book of Mormon and Doctrine and Covenants (for example, 3 Nephi 11:14; Doctrine and Covenants 53:2).

Similar statements are found in blessings given by the prophet. When ordaining Oliver Cowdery to an office, Joseph said, "In the name of Jesus Christ who ~~died~~ was crucified for the sins of the world, I lay my hands upon thee, and ordain thee . . ."[55] This strikethrough of *died* appears in the original text. Its replacement with "was crucified" may not be significant, but it perhaps illustrates how in some cases at least "death" for Smith and other early Saints specifically meant "crucifixion."

In four separate instances Joseph referred to scriptures that describe Christ dying for the sins of humanity. One example comes from Romans 5:10, which states, "For if, when we were enemies, we were reconciled to God by the death of his Son, much more, being reconciled, we shall be saved by his life."

A second example provides Joseph's commentary on his inspired translation. In a letter written on 16 November 1835, he alludes to Moses 7:47 and writes, "God clearly manifested to Enoch, the redemption which he prepared, by offering the Messiah as a Lamb slain from before the foundation of the world: by virtue of the same, the glorious resurrection of the Savior, and the resurrection of all the human family."[56] In this instance, Joseph Smith connects redemption with the "Lamb slain," indicating that the death of Jesus Christ was the key component in Christ's Atonement.

On two separate occasions Joseph used or paraphrased Revelation 5:9. On one occasion he said, "The Lamb was worthy to take the book, and to open its seals; because he was slain, and had by his blood redeemed them out of every kindred and tongue, and people, and nation."[57] Another instance of his use of Revelation 5:9 will be discussed more fully below.

The shedding of blood

As explained above, references to the atoning blood of Christ were excluded from this study as it is unclear whether they referred to bleeding in Gethsemane or on the cross (or both). A specific example of this ambiguity, provided in the introduction, is the phrase "perfect atonement through the shedding of his own blood." In some instances, however, Joseph connected Christ's blood to his Crucifixion. As stated previously, Joseph pronounced a blessing on Oliver Cowdery in the name of "Jesus Christ of Nazareth, who was crucified for the sins of the world, that we through the virtue of his blood might come to the Father."[58] In at least two other instances, Joseph unmistakably equated the phrase "blood shed" with death.[59]

An unsigned letter from "The Elders of the church in Kirtland" (of whom Joseph Smith was one) to "Their brethren abroad" provides significant insight on the phrase "shedding of blood."[60] The letter states, "God . . . prepared a sacrifice in the gift of his own Son which should be sent in due time, in his own wisdom, to prepare a way, or open a door through which man might enter into his presence, from whence he had been cast for disobedience."[61] What is meant by this sacrifice? The letter next contrasts sacrifices offered by Abel and Cain:

> By faith in this atonement or plan of redemption, Abel offered to God a sacrifice that was accepted, which was the firstlings of the flock. Cain offered of the fruit of the ground, and was not accepted, because he could not do it in faith: he could have no faith, or could not exercise faith contrary to the plan of heaven. It must be the shedding of the blood of the Only Begotten to atone for man; for this was the plan of redemption; and without the shedding of blood was no remission; and as the sacrifice was instituted for a type, by which man was to discern the great Sacrifice which God had prepared; to offer a sacrifice contrary to that, no faith could be exercised, because redemption was not purchased in that way, nor the power of atonement instituted after that order.[62]

The connection between the phrase "shedding of the blood of the Only Begotten to atone for man" with Abel's sacrifice of the first animal to come from his flock indicates that in this passage, Christ's atoning blood is speaking of his death. The letter continues:

> Certainly, the shedding of the blood of a beast could be beneficial to no man, except it was done in imitation, or as a type, or explanation of what was to be offered through the gift of God himself; and this performance done with an eye looking forward in faith on the power of that great Sacrifice for a remission of sins. . . . The ordinance or institution of offering blood in sacrifice, was only designed to be performed till Christ was offered up and shed his blood.[63]

After clearly relating animal sacrifice (which involves the death of the animal) to the shedding of Christ's blood, the letter speaks about the Resurrection and how the ancients knew of the coming of Christ. Toward the end of the letter, Revelation 5:9 (briefly discussed above) is paraphrased: "The Lamb . . . was slain, and had by his blood redeemed them out of every kindred and tongue, and people, and nation." Consistently, this letter connects the shedding of Christ's blood with his death, and no other event. This, along with Joseph's other statements equating the shedding of blood with death may provide important interpretative insight into scriptural passages regarding the blood of Christ.

The fundamental principles

Joseph Smith declared, "The fundamental principles of our religion are the testimony of the Apostles and Prophets, concerning Jesus Christ, *that He died*, was buried, and rose again the third day, and ascended into heaven; and all other things which pertain to our religion are only appendages to it."[64] In this brief statement Joseph identified the *death* of Christ as being one of the "fundamental principles" of The Church of Jesus Christ of Latter-day Saints. This statement has been quoted in general conference more than a dozen times and used in many other church publications.[65] It is notable that it mentions Christ's death and Resurrection but omits any mention of Gethsemane.

Conclusion

In the Doctrine and Covenants, there is one reference to Gethsemane and fifteen references to Christ's Crucifixion. While the JST does not provide any doctrine-altering information about Gethsemane or the cross, it does provide two passages that clearly teach about the salvific nature of Christ's Crucifixion and none about the expiation of sins in Gethsemane. With respect to the teachings and writings of Joseph Smith there is one reference to the Savior in Gethsemane (although not about his atoning for our sins) and thirty-four references to Christ's Crucifixion, nine of which refer to its saving power.

The purpose of this research is not to undermine the importance or significance of Christ's experience in Gethsemane but rather to shed light on what Joseph Smith taught regarding Christ's sufferings in Gethsemane and his death on Calvary. In contrast with the statement from the *Encyclopedia of Mormonism* cited in the introduction, the teachings and revelations of Joseph Smith give Christ's death on the cross the primary locus of soteriological significance. Smith's teachings, combined with scriptural teachings and the words of later Church leaders make it clear that Christ's death on the cross was distinctly different from every other victim of crucifixion. Jesus "was *crucified for the sins of the world*" (Doctrine and Covenants 46:13). The teachings and revelations of the Prophet Joseph Smith clearly teach the centrality of the Crucifixion in the Atonement of Jesus Christ.

Notes

1. History, 1838–1856, volume C-1 [2 November 1838–31 July 1842]," p. 1285, The Joseph Smith Papers, https://josephsmithpapers.org/paper-summary/history-1838-1856-volume-c-1-2-november-1838-31-july-1842/459.
2. John Hilton III, "Teaching the Scriptural Emphasis on the Crucifixion," *Religious Educator* 20, no. 3 (2019): 133–53.

3. James E. Talmage wrote that in Gethsemane, "in some manner, actual and terribly real though to man incomprehensible, the Savior took upon Himself the burden of the sins of mankind from Adam to the end of the world." Talmage, *Jesus the Christ* (Salt Lake City: Deseret News, 1915), 613.

4. Bruce R. McConkie, "The Purifying Power of Gethsemane," *Ensign*, May 1985.

5. Terryl Givens, *People of Paradox: A History of Mormon Culture* (New York: Oxford University Press, 2007), 114, observes that Church members "shun virtually all representations of the cross . . . in both art and culture." It is important to note from a historical perspective that the dearth of the cross has not always existed among Latter-day Saints. Michael Reed points to a deemphasis of the cross in the mid-twentieth century, demonstrating that while in the early years of the Church there was some support for the use of the cross as a visual symbol, it became less acceptable over time. See Michael G. Reed, *Banishing the Cross: The Emergence of a Mormon Taboo* (Independence, MO: John Whitmer Books, 2012).

6. Marion G. Romney, in Conference Report, October 1953, 35. For eight similar statements made by General Authorities, see John Hilton III and Joshua P. Barringer, "The Use of *Gethsemane* by Church Leaders: 1859–2018," *BYU Studies Quarterly* 58, no. 4 (2019): 49–76.

7. S. Kent Brown, "Gethsemane," in *Encyclopedia of Mormonism*, ed. Daniel H. Ludlow (New York: Macmillan, 1992), 542.

8. Douglas J. Davies, *An Introduction to Mormonism* (New York: Cambridge University Press), 154.

9. Douglas J. Davies, *The Mormon Culture of Salvation* (Burlington, VT: Ashgate, 2000), 48; emphasis added.

10. John G. Turner, *The Mormon Jesus* (Cambridge, MA: Harvard University Press, 2016), 284.

11. Robert L. Millet, *What Happened to the Cross? Distinctive LDS Teachings* (Salt Lake City: Deseret Book, 2007).

12. See Hilton, "Teaching the Scriptural Emphasis"; Hilton and Barringer, "Use of *Gethsemane*"; and John Hilton III, Emily Hyde, and McKenna Trussel, "The Use of *Crucifixion* by Church Leaders: 1852–2018," *BYU Studies Quarterly* 59, no. 1 (2020): 49–80.

13. This section of the paper utilizes text and data taken from Hilton, "Teaching the Scriptural Emphasis"; Hilton and Barringer, "Use of *Gethsemane*"; and Hilton, Hyde, and Trussel, "Use of *Crucifixion*." Additional insights on the scriptural emphasis on Christ's Crucifixion are found in Gaye Strathearn, "The Crucifixion," in *New Testament History, Culture, and Society: A Background to the Texts of the New Testament*, ed. Lincoln Blumell (Provo, UT: Religious Studies Center, Brigham Young University; Salt Lake City: Deseret Book, 2019), 353–71; Millet, *What Happened to the Cross?*; and Eric D. Huntsman, "Preaching Jesus, and Him Crucified," in *His Majesty and Mission*, ed. Nicholas J. Frederick and Keith J. Wilson (Provo, UT: Religious Studies Center, Brigham Young University; Salt Lake City: Deseret Book, 2017), 55–76.

14. See John 3:14–15; 12:32; Romans 5:6, 8, 10; 1 Corinthians 5:7; 15:3; 2 Corinthians 5:15; Galatians 3:13; Ephesians 2:16; Colossians 1:20, 21–22; 2:14; 1 Thessalonians 5:10; Hebrews 9:15, 26; 10:10, 12; 1 Peter 2:24; 3:18; Revelation 5:8–9. Here, and throughout this paper, all Bible quotations come from the 2013 edition of the King James Version of the Bible with notes and supplementary material prepared by The Church of Jesus Christ of Latter-day Saints.

15. These verses are as follows: 1 Nephi 11:33; 2 Nephi 2:7–8; 9:5; 26:24; Mosiah 14:12; 15:7–9, 12; 18:2; Alma 21:9; 22:14; 30:26; 33:22; 34:15; Helaman 14:15–16; 3 Nephi 9:21–22; 11:14; 27:14; Ether 12:33. Note that some of these verses specify crucifixion or a cross, while others speak of Christ's death or being slain (which of course took place on the cross). For additional analysis, see Hilton, "Teaching the Scriptural Emphasis."

16. Hilton, Hyde, and Trussel, "Use of *Crucifixion*."

17. Brigham Young, in *Journal of Discourses*, 8:115 (8 July 1860).

18. John Taylor, in *Journal of Discourses*, 16:307 (16 November 1873).

19. Wilford Woodruff, in *Journal of Discourses*, 19:360 (30 June 1878).

20. Gordon B. Hinckley, "The Father, Son, and Holy Ghost," *Ensign*, November 1986, 50.

21. Thomas S. Monson, "Mrs. Patton—The Story Continues," *Ensign*, November 2007, 23.

22. Russell M. Nelson, "Our Sacred Duty to Honor Women," *Ensign*, May 1999, 39.

23. I used the program WordCruncher, available at http://wordcruncher .com. This corpus uses the 2013 edition of the Doctrine and Covenants.

24. The words searched were *bleed, blood, Calvary, crucified* (in all of its variant forms), *cross, cup, die, death, garden, Gethsemane, Golgotha, lifted up, sacrifice, slain,* and *sweat*. These words were selected based on their relevance to either the events of Gethsemane or Calvary.

25. See Genesis 37:20, 22; Deuteronomy 21:6–7; Matthew 23:35; Acts 22:20; 1 Nephi 4:10; Mosiah 17:10; Alma 1:13; 20:19; 39:5; Doctrine and Covenants 132:19, 26; 136:36; Moses 7:45, 47.

26. This follows the methodology of Hilton, "Teaching the Scriptural Emphasis."

27. See Hilton, "Teaching the Scriptural Emphasis."

28. The following terms were searched: *angel strengthening, body and* (*Christ, Jesus, Savior,* or *Lord*), *Calvary, cross, crucified, crucifixion, die, death, expiation, garden, Gethsemane, Golgotha, lifted up, pore, reconcile, reconciliation, sacrifice, sin, slain, thy will,* and *tree*. These searches were mostly completed by September 2019. I note the limitation that the material posted on the Joseph Smith Papers website is in flux; additional materials may be added, thus changing the overall results of this study.

29. Joseph Smith Translation revisions and revelations canonized in the Doctrine and Covenants were not considered in this section because they are treated elsewhere in the paper. References to relevant passages in the Book of Mormon were also not included. In addition, some writings and sermons from Joseph Smith were essentially identical but published in multiple places. For the purposes of this study, these were combined and only one reference was counted. For example, the statement "Darkness prevails, at this time as it was, at the time Jesus Christ was about to be crucified" appears in both "History, 1834–1836," p. [126], The Joseph Smith Papers, https://josephsmithpapers.org/paper-summary /history-1834-1836/130; and "Discourse, 12 November 1835," handwriting Warren Parrish, p. [31], The Joseph Smith Papers, https://josephsmith

papers.org/paper-summary/discourse-12-november-1835/2. Only the quotation from "History" was used in this study.

30. This section and the one that follows draw on Hilton, "Teaching the
Scriptural Emphasis."

31. The phrases "tremble because of pain" and "suffering both body and
spirit" could potentially also refer to the Crucifixion, although this is not
explicit in the text. Christ states that he "finished [his] preparations," perhaps indicating that Gethsemane was a completion of preparation that
would further culminate on the cross, resurrection, and Second Coming.
Mark E. Peterson used Doctrine and Covenants 19:18 specifically to discuss "blood shed on the cross." Peterson, "O America, America," *Ensign*,
October 1979. Similarly, Elder John Taylor (then of the Quorum of the
Twelve) connected Christ's sweating blood with his Crucifixion, stating,
"Jesus himself sweat great drops of blood, and in the agony of his suffer-
ing cried out, 'My God, my God, why hast thou forsaken me?'" Taylor, in
Journal of Discourses, 20:259.

32. Data taken from Stephen W. Liddle and Richard C. Galbraith, "LDS
Scripture Citation Index," http://scriptures.byu.edu.

33. See Dave LeFevre, "Christology in the Joseph Smith Translation of the
Gospels," in *Thou Art the Christ, the Son of the Living God: The Person and
Work of Jesus in the New Testament*, ed. Eric D. Huntsman, Lincoln H.
Blumell, and Tyler J. Griffin (Provo, UT: Religious Studies Center,
Brigham Young University, 2018), 367–68. Notwithstanding the JST,
some Church leaders have used the KJV Mark text to highlight Christ's
wonder at the pains of Gethsemane (perhaps alluded to in Doctrine and
Covenants 19:16–18). For example, Elder Neal A. Maxwell said, "Imagine,
Jehovah, the Creator of this and other worlds, 'astonished'! Jesus knew
cognitively what He must do, but not experientially. He had never per-
sonally known the exquisite and exacting process of an atonement before.
Thus, when the agony came in its fullness, it was so much, much worse
than even He with his unique intellect had ever imagined!" Maxwell,
"'Willing to Submit,'" *Ensign*, May 1985, 72–73.

34. This passage has a complicated textual history, and some people argue
that these verses are not part of the original text of Luke. For an in-depth

discussion of these verses, see Lincoln H. Blumell, "Luke 22:43–44: An Anti-Docetic Interpolation or an Apologetic Omission?," *TC: A Journal of Biblical Textual Criticism* 19 (2014): 1–35.

35. Robert J. Matthews, *A Plainer Translation: Joseph Smith's Translation of the Bible: A History and Commentary* (Provo, UT: Brigham Young University Press, 1975), 373.

36. In many instances throughout the JST, changes are made to harmonize differences between accounts in the four Gospels.

37. This passage has a complicated textual history. See Nathan Eubank, "A Disconcerting Prayer: On the Originality of Luke 23:34a," *Journal of Biblical Literature* 129, no. 3 (2010): 521–36.

38. Compare JST Matthew 27:50 with John 19:30.

39. Two such minor changes can be seen in the book of Hebrews. The JST changes the phrase "he is the mediator of the new testament . . . by means of death" (KJV Hebrews 9:15) to "he is the mediator of the new *covenant* . . . by means of death" (JST Hebrews 9:15; compare Jeremiah 31:31). KJV Hebrews 10:10 states, "We are sanctified through the offering of the body of Jesus Christ once for all," whereas the companion JST passage states, "We are sanctified through the offering *once* of the body of Jesus Christ."

40. On one occasion, speaking of the persecution early Saints had experienced in Missouri, an editorial in the *Times and Seasons* signed "Ed" said, "The cause of humanity cries aloud for help, while suffering Justice is *bleeding at every pore.*" While this statement bears a clear connection to Gethsemane, it does not directly reference Christ nor his suffering for our sins. See "Universal Liberty," *Times and Seasons*, 15 March 1842, 722, The Joseph Smith Papers, https://josephsmithpapers.org/paper-summary/times-and -seasons-15-march-1842/5.

41. Within the Joseph Smith Papers, the word *Gethsemane* appears one time, in a letter written from Orson Hyde. In 1842 Orson Hyde traveled to the Holy Land. Describing his experience of looking out at Jerusalem, he wrote, "The fact that I entered the garden and plucked a branch from an olive, and now have that branch to look upon, demonstrates that all was real. There, there is the place where the Son of the Virgin bore our sins and carried our sorrows." Context suggests Hyde may be referring to Gethsemane, but it

is also possible he is referring to the Savior's Crucifixion. See Orson Hyde, "A Sketch of the Travels and Ministry of Elder Orson Hyde," *Times and Seasons*, 15 July 1842, 851.

42. Joseph Smith, "Discourse, 27 August 1843, as Reported by James Burgess," p. [13], The Joseph Smith Papers, https://josephsmithpapers.org/paper-summary/discourse-27-august-1843-as-reported-by-james-burgess/4; spelling and punctuation modernized.

43. In two additional instances, Joseph used the word *crucify* but not directly in relation to Christ. For example, in a discourse given 16 June 1844, he used it as a way to show how people were opposed to his teachings: "Paul says there are Gods many and Lords . . . but if Joseph Smith says there is Gods many and Lords many, they cry 'away with him crucify him.'" "Discourse, 16 June 1844, as Reported by Thomas Bullock," p. [1], The Joseph Smith Papers, https://josephsmithpapers.org/paper-summary/discourse-16-june-1844-a-as-reported-by-thomas-bullock/1; spelling and punctuation modernized).

44. "Minutes, 30 March 1836," p. 188, The Joseph Smith Papers, https://josephsmithpapers.org/paper-summary/minutes-30-march-1836/2. See "Letter to Church Officers in Clay County, Missouri, 31 August 1835," p. 80, The Joseph Smith Papers, https://josephsmithpapers.org/paper-summary/letter-to-church-officers-in-clay-county-missouri-31-august-1835/4.

45. Joseph Smith, "Discourse, 10 March 1844, as Reported by Wilford Woodruff," p. [211], The Joseph Smith Papers, https://josephsmithpapers.org/paper-summary/discourse-10-march-1844-as-reported-by-wilford-woodruff/7; spelling and punctuation modernized.

46. Joseph Smith to the Quorum of the Twelve, "Letterbook 1," p. 92, The Joseph Smith Papers, https://josephsmithpapers.org/paper-summary/letterbook-1/104; spelling errors corrected. In context, Joseph appears to be exhorting missionaries not to worry excessively about their families. He said, "Your duty requires you to seek first the kingdom of Heaven and its righteousness, that is—attend to the first things first, and then all things will be added, and that complaint about your families will be less frequent—Don't preach yourselves crucified for your wives sake, but

remember that Christ was crucified, and you are sent out to be special witnesses of this thing."

47. "Nauvoo Relief Society Minute Book, June 9, 1842," p. 62, The Joseph Smith Papers, https://josephsmithpapers.org/paper-summary/nauvoo-relief-society-minute-book/59; spelling and punctuation modernized.

48. "Nauvoo Relief Society Minute Book, June 9, 1842," p. 62.

49. "History, 1838–1856, volume D-1 [1 August 1842–1 July 1843]," p. 1571, Joseph Smith, Discourse, 11 June 1843, The Joseph Smith Papers, https://josephsmithpapers.org/paper-summary/history-1838-1856-volume-d-1-1-august-1842-1-july-1843/216.

50. "History, 1838–1856, volume D-1 [1 August 1842–1 July 1843]," p. 1571; emphasis added.

51. "History, circa 1841, fair copy," p. 78, The Joseph Smith Papers, https://josephsmithpapers.org/paper-summary/history-circa-1841-fair-copy/78; spelling and punctuation modernized.

52. Joseph Smith, "Journal, December 1842–June 1844; Book 3, 15 July 1843–29 February 1844," p. [131], The Joseph Smith Papers, https://josephsmithpapers.org/paper-summary/journal-december-1842-june-1844-book-3-15-july-1843-29-february-1844/137; spelling errors corrected and punctuation modernized.

53. "Minutes and Discourses, 6–7 April 1844, as Published by *Times and Seasons*," p. 616, The Joseph Smith Papers, https://josephsmithpapers.org/paper-summary/minutes-and-discourses-6-7-april-1844-as-published-by-times-and-seasons/14.

54. "Joseph Smith, History, circa Summer 1832," p. [1], The Joseph Smith Papers, https://josephsmithpapers.org/articles/primary-accounts-of-first-vision.

55. Joseph Smith, "Journal, 1832–1834," p. [93], The Joseph Smith Papers, https://josephsmithpapers.org/paper-summary/journal-1832-1834/94. On another occasion, Smith blessed Cowdery, saying, "In the name of Jesus Christ of Nazareth, who was crucified for the sins of the world, that we through the virtue of his blood might come to the Father, I lay my hands upon thy head, and ordain thee . . ." "Account of Meetings, Revelation, and Blessing, 5–6 December 1834," p. [19], The Joseph Smith Papers, https://

josephsmithpapers.org/paper-summary/account-of-meetings-revelation
-and-blessing-5-6-december-1834/3.

56. "Letter to the Elders of the Church, 16 November 1835," p. 209, The Joseph
Smith Papers, https://josephsmithpapers.org/paper-summary/letter-to
-the-elders-of-the-church-16-november-1835/1.

57. "Letter to the Church, circa March 1834," p. [144], The Joseph Smith Papers,
https://josephsmithpapers.org/paper-summary/letter-to-the-church
-circa-march-1834/3 (note that this letter is designated as being from "The
Elders of the Church in Kirtland," of whom Joseph Smith was one, and
is unsigned); and "History, 1838–1856, volume D-1 [1 August 1842–1
July 1843]," p. 1523, The Joseph Smith Papers, https://josephsmithpapers
.org/paper-summary/history-1838-1856-volume-d-1-1-august-1842-1
-july-1843/166.

58. "Account of Meetings, Revelation, and blessing, 5–6 December 1834,"
p. [19].

59. In a letter written to Henry Clay on 13 May 1844, Joseph wrote, "A man
that accepts a challenge or fights a duel, is nothing more nor less than a
murderer, for holy writ declares that 'whoso sheds man's blood, by man
shall his blood be shed.'" "Letter to Henry Clay, 13 May 1844," The Joseph
Smith Papers, p. [2], https://josephsmithpapers.org/paper-summary
/letter-to-henry-clay-13-may-1844/1. While traveling with others in
Zion's Camp, Joseph recorded (for 16 May 1834), "I told them I felt much
depressed in Spirit, and lonesome, and that there has had been a great
deal of blood shed in that place, and whenever a man of God is in a place,
where many have been killed; he will feel lonesome and unpleasant."
"History, 1838–1856, volume A-1 [23 December 1805–30 August 1834],"
p. 7 [addenda], The Joseph Smith Papers, https://josephsmithpapers
.org/paper-summary/history-1838-1856-volume-a-1-23-december-1805-30
-august-1834/566.

60. The historical introduction to this document on the Joseph Smith Papers
websites states, "JS and other Church of Christ leaders in Kirtland prepared this installment for publication in the Church's newspaper, The
Evening and the Morning Star." "Letter to the Church, circa March 1834,"
p. [143].

61. "Letter to the Church, circa March 1834," p. [144.]

62. "Letter to the Church, circa March 1834," p. [143].

63. "Letter to the Church, circa March 1834," p. [143].

64. This comes from "Elders' Journal, July 1838," p. [44], The Joseph Smith Papers, https://josephsmithpapers.org/paper-summary/elders-journal-july-1838/12; emphasis added. A separate entry includes the statement on August 8, 1838: "I spent with Elder [Sidney] Rigdon in visiting Elder [Reynolds] Cahoon and the place he had selected for his residence, and in attending to some of our private personal affairs. Also in the afternoon I answered the questions which were frequently asked me while on my last Journey but one from Kirtland to Missouri, as printed in the Elders Journal." In Joseph Smith, "History, 1838–1856, volume B-1 [1 September 1834–2 November 1838]," p. 795, The Joseph Smith Papers, https://josephsmithpapers.org/paper-summary/history-1838-1856-volume-b-1-1-september-1834-2-november-1838/249.

65. A search of "testimonies of the apostles and prophets" on the Word-Cruncher corpus of General Conference talks (available at http://word cruncher.com) identifies seventeen separate instances of this quotation.

Index

"Son of Man," 125–27

soteriology

Christology as inseparable from, 63–64

implications of ontological framework of LDS doctrine for, 48–49

misunderstandings of LDS, 66n13

spirit adoptionism, 32n8

spirits

creation of, 47–48

degrees of, 69–70n27

discernment of, 135, 136

eternal nature of, 139

in premortal existence, 54–55, 83–84, 136

spiritual manifestations, 161, 214n9

spiritual progression. *See also* "grace to grace" / "grace for grace"

between humanity, Son, and Father, 46–47

of Jesus Christ, 21, 23, 28–31, 52–53

stages of, 46–47

temple and, 166–67

through suffering, 133–34

spirit world, 315. *See also* premortal existence

Sprinkle, Preston, 250

stars, 111

states' rights, 273–74, 297–98n3

Stavropoulos, Cristoforos, 78–79

Strauss, David, 36n27

study, connection between faith and, vii–viii

suffering. *See also* Atonement

blessings of, 276

Christ's wonder at, 72n36, 324n33

and equality with Christ, 131, 146–47

of Jesus Christ, 51–52, 60–62, 71n35, 72n41

and nonviolence, 258, 260, 263, 264

spiritual progression through, 133–34

Sunday School movement, 205–6

symbols, 175–77

T

Talmage, James E., 321n3

Tanner, Nathan, 267

Taylor, Charles, 100

Taylor, John, 38n36, 281, 282, 288, 306

temple

changes to, ceremonies, 192n77

comprehension of true light through, 115

origins of, rituals, 191n66

pedagogy and salvific ordinances in, 172–80

and spiritual progression, 166–67

teaching about, in home, 180

temptation

of Jesus Christ, 53, 60–62

of Moses, 125–26

Tertullian, 251

theocracy, 283

theodemocracy, 290, 292–95

theophany, 158–59, 167–68. *See also* First Vision

theosis. *See* deification

Trinitarianism, 15–16

True Light, 99–103, 115–18

   and Christ as Word, 102–3

   and degrees of glory, 106–8

   and oath and covenant of the
     priesthood, 108–9

   and Olive Leaf revelation,
     109–12

   and Second Comforter, 114–15

   and True Light revelation,
     112–13

   understanding of, in Restoration
     theology, 101–3

Turner, John G., 38–39n36, 148n2,
   305

Turner, Orsamus, 184n15

U

Unitarianism, 17, 18

United States

   appeals for redress to, 273–74

   constitution of, 293

   Saints' departure from, 275, 276,
     277–79, 296

Universalism, 160, 163–64, 172

universe, laws governing, 110–11

V

Van Buren, Martin, 273

violence, cyclical quality of, 261–62.
   See also nonviolence

vision(s). *See also* First Vision;
   theophany

   canonized as D&C 76, 106–8

   given to Joseph Smith and Sidney Rigdon, 127–28

   given to Phineas Young, 161–62,
     185n24

   Methodist views on, 161–62

W

Ware, Henry, 16

Ware, Kallistos, 77

washings and anointings, 176–77

weakness and Christ's human
   nature, 52

Weber, Max, 199

Welch, Rosalynde, 216n17, 219n44

Wesley, John, 39–40n43, 162–63

Whitmer, John, 204, 246n27

Whitney, Newel K., 20–21

wickedness, of those who crucified
   Christ, 315–16

Willsky-Ciollo, Lydia, 35n14

women

   D&C 25 as applicable to all,
     208–11

   inclusion and religious empowerment of, 196–97

   Jesus's awareness of plight of, 222

   priesthood authority of, 210

   and public religious worship,
     205–7, 212–13, 215n12,
     217–18n34, 218n37, 218n40,
     219n46, 220n50

Woodruff, Wilford, 123, 135,
   280–81, 282, 306

Word, Jesus Christ as, 25–26,
   39n37, 56, 102–3

works, salvation through, 161